COLD WAR
Building for Nuclear Confrontation 1946–1989

COLD WAR

Building for Nuclear Confrontation 1946–1989

Wayne D Cocroft and Roger J C Thomas
Edited by P S Barnwell

 Historic England

Published by Historic England, The Engine House, Fire Fly Avenue, Swindon SN2 2EH
www.HistoricEngland.org.uk

Historic England is a Government service championing England's heritage and giving expert, constructive advice, and the English Heritage Trust is a charity caring for the National Heritage Collection of more than 400 historic properties and their collections.

First published by English Heritage 2003
Reprinted by English Heritage, paperback edition with corrections 2004
Reprinted by English Heritage 2007, 2009, 2011, 2012
Reprinted by Historic England 2016

ISBN 978-1-873592-81-6

British Library Cataloguing in Publication data
A CIP catalogue record for this book is available from the British Library.

Historic England holds an unparalleled archive of 12 million photographs, drawings, reports and publications on England's places. It is one of the largest archives in the UK, the biggest dedicated to the historic environment, and a priceless resource for anyone interested in England's buildings, archaeology, landscape and social history. Viewed collectively, its photographic collections document the changing face of England from the 1850s to the present day. It is a treasure trove that helps us understand and interpret the past, informs the present and assists with future management and appreciation of the historic environment.

For more information about images from the Archive, contact Archives Services Team, Historic England, The Engine House, Fire Fly Avenue, Swindon SN2 2EH; telephone (01793) 414600.

Brought to publication by Adele Campbell, Andrew McLaren and Robin Taylor
Typeset in 9.5pt Charter
Edited by Janet Hadley
Indexed by Susan Vaughan
Page layout by Simon Borrough, revisions by Pauline Hull
Printed in Belgium by Graphius.

Front cover
RAF Upper Heyford, Oxfordshire. Hardened aircraft shelter
[GCN 306660-5]

Back cover
Barnham, Suffolk. Inner patrol path and watch tower, surrounding the former atomic bomb stores
[AA98/07801]

Contents

Foreword

The Cold War period touched the lives of a large proportion of the people of England, especially those of my own generation. For many the possibility of nuclear confrontation moved from being a matter of deep but largely unspoken apprehension to a cause for powerful and vocal protest, in a way that mirrored profound changes in contemporary society. The Cold War gave new significance and wide currency to some unfamiliar, and other more commonplace, names and phrases – 'the bomb', '4-minute warning', 'Bay of Pigs', and 'Gary Powers'. Attitudes and fears, from the alarmed or apocalyptic to the stoical and even the farcical, found expression in art and literature: ranging from Stanley Kubrick's film *Dr Strangelove* to the oratorio *Or shall we die?* by Ian McEwan and Michael Berkeley; from the barman in *The Hitchhiker's Guide to the Galaxy* who 'thought we were supposed to lie down and put a paper bag over our heads' to Jim Hacker in television's *Yes, Prime Minister,* who was wooed by 'the weapons system that Harrods would sell'.

These and many other cultural aspects of the Cold War have been much studied, yet the physical manifestations of the Cold War in England – its buildings and structures – have remained largely unknown. To the great landscape historian WG Hoskins, writing in the mid-1950s, they were profoundly alien and negative: 'England of the Nissen hut, the "pre-fab", and the electric fence, of the high barbed wire around some unmentionable devilment ... Barbaric England of the scientists, the military men, and the politicians.' Now these survivals from the Cold War are, in their turn, disappearing fast, like medieval monasteries and bastioned forts before them – only with more limited scope for regeneration and reuse. In such circumstances, it is clearly part of the remit of English Heritage to understand and record the scope and diversity of this body of material, to assess its cultural value, and to make the results of our work widely known. The task is the more necessary because the sense of urgency that this 'war' should end following the fall of the Berlin Wall in 1989 has meant that many of these structures have already been swept away. A lead from English Heritage is appropriate because of the pioneering nature of the investigation and the international dimension of the subject, and it is hoped that it will give confidence to those still looking after these sites.

Hence this study, initiated by the former Royal Commission on the Historical Monuments of England (RCHME) and brought to completion by English Heritage. It is founded primarily on archaeological and architectural fieldwork – understanding the field remains themselves – allied with the examination of historical plans and photographs. It has not sought to tap fully into the mass of documentary records that exist for these sites and their context before 1970, but rather it provides something complementary. For much of the period after 1970 it gives a conspectus of the physical remains, which is valuable both in its own right and also because it precedes the release of 'official' documentary records.

The work presented here formed the foundation of an assessment, undertaken through English Heritage's Monuments Protection Programme, of the conservation options for the most important, typical and representative survivals of Cold War monuments. The results were issued as a consultative document in 2001. In relation to that process, this book will help planners, local authority archaeologists, conservation officers and others working in the field – including the military authorities – to place the buildings and sites in a local, national and international context, and to find appropriate conservation solutions.

Concrete, based on sand and gravel aggregates, is the defining construction material of the Cold War age. From it were created miles of runways and dispersal bays, observer posts and bunkers, hardened shelters, missile launch pads and test stands. And much else besides. These concrete structures are now viewed as potentially recyclable, which could lead to the further loss of some of the most striking and characteristic physical remains of the era – as has already happened with the runways at Greenham Common. It is a pleasure, therefore, to acknowledge a grant from the Aggregates Levy Sustainability Fund towards the production of this book.

Perhaps more than any other aspect of the historic environment that English Heritage has addressed so far, these Cold War monuments had a place in networks that were far wider than England or Great Britain alone. The sites and structures described in this book therefore are of interest on the international stage, across Europe and beyond. Our care in promoting recording and prompting curation, though necessarily focusing on England, sets a pattern and fulfils obligations to those who were our allies and adversaries.

We are confident that this book will offer many readers their first authoritative insight into the built fabric of the Cold War in England. It will stimulate interest in this aspect of Britain's defence heritage: a national defence effort to which huge resources of state revenue and manpower were devoted. Many of the structures created were highly specialised in function and many were bizarre and almost totemic in appearance, adding a sometimes startling visual dimension to this unique project.

Sir Neil Cossons
CHAIRMAN, ENGLISH HERITAGE

Acknowledgements

The book originated in a recording project initiated by the Royal Commission on the Historical Monuments of England prior to its merger with English Heritage in 1999. English Heritage gratefully acknowledges the assistance of the many organisations, their representatives, and individuals who have granted access to sites for recording. Many of the sites illustrated in the book are owned, or have recently been relinquished, by the Ministry of Defence and we thank Richard Coombes and Antony Whitehead of Defence Estates, who facilitated access to many of them. We are also grateful to the commanding officers and staff of the active bases we have recorded for hosting our visits.

We would like to thank the following individuals for granting or arranging access: Flight Lieutenant Dean Atchison, Douglas Robb, and Roy Bullers (Air Defence, Command and Control Museum, RAF Neatishead); Lieutenant Colonel (retired) Brynolf (Swynnerton Training Camp); Keith Eldred (Gorse Industrial Estate, Barnham); Master Sergeant Bill Harris (retired), USAF (RAF Lakenheath); Mick Hickin, Estates Services Manager (Nottingham District Land Registry); Ian Hudson (Alconbury Developments Limited); Grant Lahoar and Angus Wainwright (National Trust Ordfordness); Flying Officer Millington (RAF Coningsby); Steven Potter (Dalkia Estate Management, Cambridge); Nicholas Rowe, Emergency Planning Officer (Kent County Council); Philip Slocombe, Emergency Planning Officer (Cheshire County Council); and Don Todd and Keith Watson (North Oxfordshire Consortium Limited, Upper Heyford).

We would also like to thank the keepers and owners of a number of Cold War bunkers that are now maintained as museums, for permitting photographic recording and access to original archive material: Dr James Fox, Mistley, Essex; Michael Parrish, Kelvedon Hatch, Essex; Rodney Siebert, Hack Green, Cheshire; and Victor Smith, Gravesend, Kent.

Most of the background research for this book was carried out at the Public Record Office, Kew, but also drew on the knowledge and archives of other libraries and institutions and their specialist staff. These included: Carlisle Aircraft Museum; RAF Museum, Hendon; Imperial War Museum (Frank Crosby, Stephen Woolford and Dr Neil Young); and the Royal Commission on the Ancient and Historical Monuments of Wales (Medwyn Parry).

The book has also benefited from the enthusiasm and information generated by the Airfield Research Group, in particular Aldon Ferguson and Paul Francis. The Research Study Group of Subterranea Britannica has been at the forefront of seeking out and recording Cold War bunkers, and making its information available through the internet. Its members Mark Bennett, Nick Catford, Andrew Emmerson, and Keith Ward have provided valuable information and references throughout the project. David Clark, John Guy, John Harwood, and Bernard Lowry of the Fortress Study Group, have also contributed much useful information. We also appreciate the help provided by Paul Barker, Roy Dommett CBE, David Hawkings, Air Vice Marshal (retired) Sandy Hunter, Barry Jackson, Brian Kervell, Christopher Leicester, and Michael Shackel. Dr Rebecca H Cameron (Air Force History Office, Bolling AFB) and Dr William G Johnson and Dr Colleen M Beck (Desert Research Institute, Las Vegas) have kept us informed us of recording initiatives in the United States. We are also grateful to those who contributed amendments to this edition, in particular Mike Barton, John Deal and Roy Dommett.

Many members of English Heritage staff have contributed to this book. The drawn illustrations were prepared by Allan Adams and the distribution maps were produced by Philip Sinton. Ground photographs were taken by Sid Barker, Keith Buck, Alun Bull, Steven Cole, Michael Hesketh-Roberts, Patricia Payne, Bob Skingle, and Roger JC Thomas; aerial photographs by Roger Featherstone, Damian Grady, and Peter Horne. Graham Brown, Tony Calladine, Kathryn Morrison, and Joanna Smith provided useful information from their fieldwork and research. Throughout its course the project has also profited from discussions with Dr John Schofield of the Monuments Protection Programme and Jeremy Lake of the Thematic Listing Programme, and from research carried out by Michael Anderton. The publication has also benefited from the work undertaken by Dr Colin Dobinson for the Council for British Archaeology's Twentieth Century Fortifications in England project, funded by English Heritage, to locate and analyse defence records preserved at the Public Record Office, Kew.

The project was managed by Dr Paul Barnwell, who also edited the draft manuscript; Paul Everson, Colum Giles and Dr Martin Cherry provided helpful comments on earlier versions of the text. Dr Colin Dobinson (as a consultant) read the manuscript and Dr Clifford Cole read it for the Ministry of Defence. Editorial support was provided by Adele Campbell and Dr Robin Taylor, copy editing was carried out by Janet Hadley and the design and layout by Simon Borrough. The index was prepared by Susan Vaughan. The French and German summaries were produced by Annie Pritchard and Norman Behrend.

Wayne D Cocroft and Roger J C Thomas

Summary

The Cold War was one of the defining phenomena of the late 20th century, but the defence installations built in Britain between 1946 and 1989 to carry out nuclear war have remained little known because of the secrecy that surrounded them. This is the first overview of the impact of the Cold War on the built environment of the United Kingdom.

The book begins with a brief account of the military and political events of the Cold War. There follow discussions of the sites most readily associated with the central themes of the Cold War – the deployment of nuclear weapons and the presence of large United States air bases. The credibility of the nuclear deterrent was dependent on a complex infrastructure of surveillance and early warning systems so that, if an attack did come, defences were ready to counter it. Any strike by nuclear weapons would have resulted in widespread devastation, and the Government set up a network of protected bunkers, which are discussed along with other civil defence structures. All these post-Second World War defence efforts required increasingly complex technological products, and their development was underpinned by specialised scientific research establishments and factories, which are also described. The book ends with a discussion of international initiatives to record and preserve key Cold War monuments. There is a list of key sources for readers who wish to pursue the topics in greater depth.

The book is based on original field investigation and research. It is heavily illustrated with photographs of the sites as they survive today, archive photographs (many not published before), modern and historic air photographs, site and building plans, and specially commissioned interpretative drawings.

Research carried out for the project has directly contributed to the assessment of Cold War structures for statutory protection in England, supporting that work by presenting a national context for the sites and structures selected for preservation. It also provides the basis for international comparisons.

Résumé

La guerre froide fut un des phénomènes déterminants de la fin du XXe siècle, mais les installations défensives construites entre 1946 et 1989, dans le but de mener à bien une guerre nucléaire, sont restées méconnues en raison du secret qui les entourait. Cet ouvrage constitue la première vision d'ensemble de l'impact de la guerre froide sur l'environnement bâti du Royaume-Uni.

Ce livre commence par un bref compte-rendu des événements militaires et politiques de la guerre froide. Suivent des discussions des sites les plus couramment liés aux thèmes centraux de la guerre froide – le déploiement des armes nucléaires et la présence de grandes bases aériennes américaines. La crédibilité de la dissuasion nucléaire reposait sur une infrastructure complexe de surveillance et sur des réseaux d'alerte avancée, si bien que, si une attaque devait se produire, les défenses seraient prêtes à la contrer. Toute frappe provenant d'armes nucléaires aurait eu pour résultat une dévastation à grande échelle, et le gouvernement avait mis en place un réseau de bunkers protégés qui sont étudiés en parallèle avec d'autres structures défensives civiles. Tous ces efforts défensifs postérieurs à la sec-onde guerre mondiale ont nécessité des produits technologiques d'une complexité grandissante et leur développement était assuré par des centres de recherche scientifique et des usines spécialisés qui sont également décrits ici. Le livre se termine par une discussion des initiatives prises au niveau international afin de répertorier les monuments clés de la guerre froide. Les lecteurs désireux d'approfondir leurs connaissances dans ce domaine trouveront une liste des sources clés.

Ce livre s'appuie sur une prospection de terrain et des recherches originales. Il est richement illustré de photographies des sites tels qu'ils ont survécu jusqu'à ce jour, de photographies d'archives (dont un grand nombre était jusqu'alors inédit), de photographies aériennes modernes et historiques, de plans des sites et des constructions, et de croquis interprétatifs éxécutés sur commission.

Les recherches menées dans le cadre de cette mission ont directement contribué à l'évaluation des structures de la guerre froide dans un but de protection officielle en Angleterre, elles ont soutenu ce travail en replaçant dans un contexte national les sites et les structures retenus pour être préservés. Elles fournissent également une base pour des comparaisons au niveau international.

Zusammenfassung

Der Kalte Krieg war eines der entscheidensten Phänomene des späten 20. Jahrhunderts, jedoch verbleiben die meisten, der zwischen 1946 und 1989 für die Durchführung eines Atomkrieges gebauten Verteidigungsinstallationen, durch die Geheimhaltung mit der sie umgeben waren, wenig bekannt. Dieses Buch ist der erste Überblick über den Einfluss des Kalten Krieges an dem bebauten Umfeld im Vereinigten Königreich.

Das Buch beginnt mit einer bündigen Wiedergabe der militärischen und politischen Ereignisse des Kalten Krieges. Danach folgen Debatierungen der Einrichtungen, die am meisten mit dem zentralen Inhalt des Kalten Krieges verbunden werden – die Aufstellung von nuklearen Waffen und die Gegenwart von grossen US-amerikanischen Luftbasen. Die Kredibiltät einer nuklearen Abschreckung hing zum grossen Teil von einer komplexen Infrastuktur mit Überwachungs- und Frühwarnsystemen ab, welche im Fall eines Angriffs die ständige Verteidigungsbereitschaft ermöglichten. Jeder Angriff mit Atomwaffen hätte in weitheerenden Zerstörungen resultiert und dieses veranlasste die Regierungen ein Netzwerk von Schutzbunkern zu bauen. Diese werden neben den anderen Zivilverteidigungsanlagen diskutiert. Alle dieser nach dem zweiten Weltkrieg durchgeführten Verteidigungsmassnahmen verlangten eine ständig höheres Mass an technolgischen Produkten, deren Entwicklung durch die Einrichtung von Spezialfabriken und – laboren gestützt wurden, welche auch hier beschrieben werden. Das Buch endet mit einer Diskussion der internationalen Initiativen zur Erhaltung und Auflistung der wichtigsten dieser Einrichtungen des Kalten Krieges. Eine Verzeichnis der Hauptquellen wird dem Leser die tiefere Verfolgung der verschiedenen Themen erleichtern.

Das Buch basiert auf originalen örtlichen Investigationen und Nachforschungen. Es ist sehr stark mit Fotografien der untersuchten Anlagen, wie sie zum heutigen Tage bestehen, illustriert. Daneben werden noch mehr archivierte Fotografien (viele niemals zuvor veröffentlicht), moderne sowie historische Luftaufnahmen, Anlagen- und Bauplänen und speziell in Auftrag gegebene erläuternden Zeichnungen verwendet.

Nachforschungen, welche für dieses Projekt durchgeführt wurden, haben direkt zu der Berurteilung von Strukturen des Kalten Krieges für gesetzliche Beschützung in England beigetragen und unterstützen diese Arbeit durch die Präsentation eines nationalen Kontext für die zur Erhaltung ausgesuchten Anlagen und Einrichtungen. Daneben erlaubt es gleichzeitig viele internationale Vergleichsmöglichkeiten.

Cold War timeline

Events in Britain	Global events
1945 *July* Labour government elected, under Clement Attlee	*8 May* Surrender of Germany – end of the war in Europe *26 June* United Nations charter signed *16 July* First US atomic bomb tested *17 July–2 August* Potsdam Conference *6 August* Atomic bomb dropped on Hiroshima, Japan *9 August* Atomic bomb dropped on Nagasaki, Japan *15 August* Surrender of Japan – end of the war in the Far East
1946 National Health Service Act passed Bank of England and coal industry nationalised *November* Military National Service introduced	*5 March* Churchill delivers 'Iron Curtain' speech at Fulton, Missouri, USA *1 August* US McMahon Act halts co-operation between US and UK in development of atomic weapons and information exchange
1947 Britain's railways, road services and electricity industry nationalised *January* Royal Observer Corps re-formed *January* UK decides to develop the atomic bomb *March* Treaty of Dunkirk signed with France	*5 June* US announces Economic Recovery Programme for Europe – the 'Marshall Plan' *21 August* India and Pakistan gain independence from Britain
1948 Gas industry nationalised *17 March* Britain signs Western Union Treaty (Brussels Treaty) – five-power collective security treaty *December* Civil Defence Act passed	*25 February* Communist coup in Czechoslovakia *31 March* Partial blockade of Berlin begins *20 June* Deutschmark introduced in western sectors of Germany *24 June* Surface routes to Berlin closed *25 June* Berlin airlift begins
1949 Air Ministry agrees Rotor plan to refurbish Britain's radar defences Iron and steel industry nationalised	*4 April* North Atlantic Treaty signed, NATO formed *May* State of Israel declared *12 May* Berlin blockade lifted *29 August* USSR explodes its first atomic bomb *21 September* Federal Republic of Germany (FRG – West Germany) founded *October* People's Republic of China founded *7 October* German Democratic Republic (GDR – East Germany) founded
1950 *July* Truman approves stockpiling of non-nuclear components of atomic bombs in UK *12 September* Britain announces £3,600 million rearmament programme	*March* US National Security Council document 68 recommends massive US rearmament *25 June* Korean War begins
1951 Construction of war rooms for regional commissioners begins Construction of anti-aircraft operations rooms begins *20 March* USAF Strategic Air Command (SAC) 7th Div HQ established at South Ruislip, West London *25 May* First British jet bomber, the Canberra, in RAF service *27 October* Conservative government elected, under Winston Churchill	
1952 *6 February* Queen Elizabeth II ascends to the throne *3 October* First British atomic bomb exploded at Monte Bello, NW Australia	*1 November* US explodes its first hydrogen bomb *4 November* Dwight D Eisenhower elected as US President

1953 *November* First RAF atomic bomb, 'Blue Danube', enters service	*5 March* Soviet leader Joseph Stalin dies, succeeded by Nikita Krushchev *17 June* Demonstrations in East Berlin and other East German cities *23 July* Korean War armistice signed *12 August* USSR explodes its first hydrogen bomb
1955 Army relinquishes responsibility for air defence *February* First V-bomber, the Valiant, enters service	*9 May* West Germany becomes an official member of NATO *14 May* Warsaw Pact formed
1956 Coastal defence is stood down *May* AVRO Vulcan V-bomber enters RAF service	West Germany is rearmed; its army, the *Bundeswehr* is formed *October* Hungarian uprising suppressed *November* Suez Crisis
1957 *April* Defence White Paper *Outline of Future Policy* *November* Victor V-bomber enters RAF service *8 November* Britain claims to have exploded her first hydrogen bomb, 'Grapple X'	*26 August* First Soviet inter-continental ballistic missile (ICBM) launched *4 October* First Soviet Sputnik satellite launched
1958 Royal Observer Corps assumes nuclear reporting role New plan to upgrade RAF early warning radar proposed Thunderbird surface-to-air missile enters service with British Army *January* Campaign for Nuclear Disarmament formed *July* Bloodhound Mk I surface-to-surface missile enters RAF service *October* First RAF air-to-air missile, Firestreak, enters service	
1959 Thor missiles deployed in Britain	*8 July* France refuses to allow stockpiling of US nuclear weapons unless under French control. 200 US tactical nuclear aircraft redeployed to West Germany and UK
1960 Military national service ends *13 April* Intermediate-range ballistic missile, 'Blue Streak', cancelled *June* First RAF supersonic fighter, the Lightning, enters service	*13 February* First French atomic bomb test *1 May* US pilot Gary Powers' U2 spy plane shot down over USSR *20 July* First successful launch of US Polaris submarine
1961 V-force reaches peak of 180 aircraft	*7 November* John F Kennedy elected as US President *12 April* Soviet cosmonaut Yuri Gagarin is the first man in space *17 April* Attempted US-backed invasion of Cuba at the Bay of Pigs *13 August* The Berlin Wall is erected
1962 *1 March* First 'Blue Steel' training rounds issued to RAF *August* British surface-to-surface missile, 'Blue Water', cancelled	*October* Cuban missile crisis *December* US Skybolt programme cancelled
1963 *30 January* Britain announces it is to build 5 nuclear-powered ballistic missile submarines (SSBN) and to purchase US Polaris missiles *February* 'Blue Steel' enters service *August* UK, USA and USSR sign Limited Test Ban Treaty *15 August* Phase out of Thor missiles is complete *17 September* Ballistic missile early warning system (BMEWS) at RAF Fylingdales operational Bloodhound Mk II introduced	Numbers in US ICBM force assumes primary deterrent role over SAC bomber alert force *22 November* John F Kennedy assassinated

1964	*1 April* Unified Ministry of Defence is created *October* Labour government elected, under Harold Wilson	*15 October* Nikita Krushchev ousted from power; Leonid Brezhnez appointed first secretary *16 October* China detonates its first nuclear weapon
1965	*6 April* New Tactical Strike Reconnaissance aircraft (TSR) 2, cancelled	*March* US Marines deployed in Vietnam
1966	*15 September* SSBN HMS Resolution launched	*7 March* France announces its withdrawal from NATO
1967		*5 June* Arab-Israeli Six-Day War begins *24 August* France explodes hydrogen bomb at Mururoa Atoll
1968	Substantial reduction in the size of the Royal Observer Corps *April* Stand down of Civil Defence *June* First Polaris submarine, HMS *Resolution*, in service	Political and social reform in Czechoslovakia – 'Prague Spring' *January* NATO adopts strategy of flexible response *30 January* Tet Offensive launched in Vietnam *20 August* Warsaw Pact forces move in to suppress Czechoslovakian dissent
1969	*30 June* 'Strategic quick reaction' passes from RAF to Royal Navy Polaris submarines *August* Troops sent to Northern Ireland to maintain order	*20 July* Apollo 11 lands on the moon *10 October* Willy Brandt elected as Chancellor of West Germany
1970		Strategic Arms Limitation Talks (SALT) I begin in Vienna
1972		*26 May* SALT I agreement signed
1973	*1 January* Britain joins European Union	*27 January* Vietnam peace treaty signed *October* Yom Kippur War and oil crisis *25 October* US forces on Stage 3 nuclear alert
1974	*14 March* First flight of Tornado prototype	
1975		*30 April* US pulls out of Vietnam *August* Signing of Helsinki Accords
1976		*8 September* Chinese Chairman Mao Tse-Tung dies *November* Jimmy Carter elected as US President
1977		Soviet SS-20 missiles deployed in Europe
1978		*17 April* Pro-Soviet coup in Afghanistan
1979	*May* Conservative government elected, under Margaret Thatcher	*June* SALT II signed, but not ratified *December* NATO decides to deploy 572 Pershing II and ground launched cruise missiles (GLCMs) *29 December* USSR invades Afghanistan
1980	*August* Results of Home Defence Review announced *July* Government announces its intention to purchase the US Trident missile system	*14 August* Strikes and riots in Gdansk, Poland *4 November* Ronald Reagan elected as US President
1981		*19 December* Military takeover in Poland
1982	*2 April–14 June* Falklands War against Argentina *June* Tornado enters service with RAF	*29 June* Strategic Arms Reduction Talks (START) begin in Geneva *10 November* Soviet President Leonid Brezhnev dies, succeeded by Yuri Andropov
1983	*June* Thatcher's Conservative government re-elected *15 November* First cruise missiles arrive at RAF Greenham Common	*23 March* President Reagan announces Strategic Defense Initiative: 'Star Wars' *1 September* Korean airliner KAL-007 shot down by USSR
1984		*9 February* Andropov dies, succeeded by Konstantin Chernenko *6 November* Reagan elected for second term as US President
1985		*March* START resumes *10 March* Chernenko dies, succeeded by Mikhail Gorbachev *19–20 November* Superpower summit meeting between Gorbachev and Reagan

1986 *June* Civil Protection Act passed, giving local authorities powers to use civil defence resources in situations other than war	*15 April* Operation 'Eldorado Canyon' – US attack on suspected terrorist targets in Libya
1987 *June* Conservative government re-elected	*8 December* US and USSR sign Intermediate Nuclear Forces Treaty – NATO Pershing II, GLCMs and Warsaw Pact SS-20s to be withdrawn from Europe
1988 *30 April* Last Lightning withdrawn from RAF service	*8 November* George Bush elected as US President
1989	*February* Last Soviet troops withdrawn from Afghanistan *2 May* Hungary opens its border with Austria *August* Non-communist government elected in Poland *9 November* Berlin Wall and other East German border posts opened *10 November* Bulgarian communist President Todor Zhikov resigns *December* Non-communist government assumes power in Czechoslovakia *December* Romanian leader Nicolae Ceausescu overthrown
1990	*2 August* Iraq invades Kuwait, Operation 'Desert Shield' begins, in which US and Britain defend Saudi Arabia and aim to force Iraq out of Kuwait *3 October* Germany reunified *10 November* Conventional Armed Forces in Europe (CFE) Treaty is signed
1991 *31 May* GLCM wing at RAF Greenham Common deactivated *September* Royal Observer Corps disbanded	*17 January* The Gulf War, Operation 'Desert Storm', begins *28 February* Gulf War ends *13 March* Last Pershing II missile leaves Germany *July* Dissolution of the Warsaw Pact *31 July* START I treaty signed *26 December* USSR dissolved

1
Introduction

For more than forty years the global split between the political ideologies of capitalism and Soviet bloc communism and the ensuing military stand-off, known as the Cold War, shaped the history of the late 20th century. Throughout this period the Cold War formed the backdrop to many spheres of national life – political, economic, scientific and cultural – rising to the fore in times of high tension between the superpowers. The most obvious physical evidence of this era are the remains of defence sites. To most people these places were secret and closed worlds, but the end of the Cold War has made it possible to gain access to previously restricted sites, many of which are revealed here for the first time.

We have taken the opening of the Berlin Wall, on 9 November 1989, as the symbolic end of the Cold War. The Wall represented the most potent expression of the ideological divide between East and West, and its fall was an archaeologically recognisable event. In its wake, the Soviet Union's (Union of Soviet Socialist Republics – USSR) grip on eastern Europe rapidly fell away and the West was able to reassess its defence needs, with the result that across western Europe there was a massive reduction both in military spending and in the area of land occupied by the armed forces (Fig 1.1). The Ministry of Defence under its 'Options for Change' policy had, by the mid-1990s, identified more than 100 major sites in England as surplus to its needs.

The sites were very varied, ranging from naval dockyards to 19th-century barracks, former munitions factories, and airfields modernised as recently as the 1980s. At the same time, the Home Office was able to re-examine its infrastructure for emergency government. It disposed of its network of bunkers and food and equipment stores and disbanded the Royal Observer Corps. Local councils were relieved of their responsibilities for organising emergency government in the

Figure 1.1
Ludgershall, Wiltshire, 1995. Surplus war reserve tanks, once stored to meet the expected war of attrition against the Warsaw Pact's 'shock armies', await decommissioning and disposal. Depots such as Ludgershall dealt with the routine maintenance and storage of vehicles. Rail access enabled rapid transport to embarkation ports. [BB95/08792]

Figure 1.2
Tunbridge Wells, Kent,
1997. Despite their air of
permanence, many Cold
War structures are now as
endangered as any earlier
remains. This 1950s war
room was demolished to
make way for an office
development.
[AA96/03020]

event of nuclear attack and the public utilities relinquished their 'hardened' standby control centres, which had been specially constructed or reinforced to withstand the effects of nuclear explosion.

The end of the Cold War also coincided with the fiftieth anniversaries of many major events of the Second World War and these helped to stimulate a wider interest in, and appreciation of, the historical importance of recent military remains. Many were on sites that had been 'closed' or secret, and there was little knowledge in the public domain about the range of structures that survived or what had taken place within them. The historic importance of some, such as the Royal Arsenal, Woolwich (London), the former Royal Gunpowder Factory, Waltham Abbey (Essex), and the Royal Naval College, Greenwich (London), was clearly recognised, and reports on them have been published elsewhere.

Other sites, or buildings on them, were recorded as part of a continuing commitment to document important structures threatened by change or demolition – such as the war room at Tunbridge Wells, Kent (Fig 1.2). We have paid special attention to monuments of the Cold War because it is the first time that many of them have been available for study. They are not well known or understood, and they are poorly represented

in the National Monuments Record. The primary source for this study was the sites themselves; their historical and technological context was provided by the sources listed at the end of the book.

'Monuments' of the Cold War we define as structures built, or adapted, to carry out nuclear war between the end of the Second World War and 1989. As such, they formed a significant but relatively small part of the post-1945 defence estate, many older sites having continued to meet the needs of the armed services; providing, for example, communal accommodation segregated according to rank, or training establishments steeped in military tradition. A distinctive feature of the Cold War was the permanent stationing, by the superpowers, of large numbers of their armed forces in the countries of allied nations. The different ways in which cultural expectations of US personnel – military and personal – expressed themselves through the physical fabric of their bases is explored in Chapter 4.

The architecture of the new buildings of the Cold War is severely functional. It is largely of concrete, steel and earth, and is an extreme example of the dictum that function dictates form. Some structures have strikingly innovative forms: the massive Rotor bunkers erected in the early 1950s, for example, represent a new type of architecture in the United Kingdom, and look as if their lineage starts in German wartime design. More often, however, centralised planning and the deployment of standardised weapons systems resulted in nearly identical site and structural types across the country, although minor variations may be found, created by local landscape or building materials. Prefabricated structures, widely employed during the Second World War, continued to be used, and many minor buildings were erected using prefabricated concrete or plywood panels, or were clad in asbestos sheets or aluminium sheeting – a post-war innovation. In contrast to the 1920s and 1930s neo-Georgian style which was favoured for the more prestigious government buildings, the few prominent structures erected after 1945 generally followed contemporary functional and utilitarian designs.

Many Cold War structures are as significant for the technological innovations they housed as for their new architecture and military function. The Cold War arms race was perhaps the chief driving force behind technological advance in the late 20th century, and new systems replaced old in a bewildering sequence. Information technology dominated all areas of military planning, and within the divided world of the Cold War the seeds of the modern global information age were sown, with many now common components and systems (including the transistor, modem and internet) resulting from military projects. The introduction of the germanium transistor also influenced the design of buildings, as computers could be made smaller and the ventilation equipment required to cool perhaps hundreds of valves was no longer needed.

In contrast to the two world wars, the Cold War was seen by many as a series of distant events played out on the frontiers of Europe or remote flashpoints. Closer to home the activities within military bases, surrounded by wire mesh fences and constantly lit up at night by floodlights, were a closely guarded secret. But while the confrontation did not intrinsically require mass participation, planning for nuclear war reached down to every home in the country as this study shows. Over the period, a sizeable proportion of the population had been drawn into the conflict as service personnel, through civil defence, or as people working in the defence industry. When a confrontation lasts for four decades different generations will have varying memories of it, ranging from the late 1950s Aldermaston marches, through the Cuban missile crisis, to the deployment of cruise missiles and the peace protests of the early 1980s. On the other hand, many people have lived through the period oblivious to the threat posed to them. What emerges is a very confused and partial collective memory of the Cold War, based on experience ranging from service within a narrow field, to being a peace campaigner looking at a site through a perimeter fence.

Every country's experience of the Cold War was unique. A nation's political alignment, along with its standing within its alliance bloc, its national aspirations and its economy, determined its access to technology. Geography was important in defining the role different countries played and how they experienced the decades of tension, while the legacy of existing defence structures and military doctrines influenced the types of facility constructed. Only when equivalent studies from abroad become available will the distinctiveness or otherwise of post-war British military installations become apparent.

Most of the sites in this book are in England. Defence planning, however, considered the United Kingdom as a whole, and this is acknowledged through national distribution maps and discussion of relevant sites in Scotland and Wales. Most popular studies of weapons systems have confined themselves to describing the more 'glamorous' components, such as aircraft or missiles – a trend reinforced by museums through their collecting and display policies. This book aims to redress the balance by describing the physical infrastructure needed to support the weapons systems. The chapters are organised thematically, each describing the organisation, function and operation of sites associated with a particular aspect of the Cold War, as well as their field remains.

There can be no doubt that the Cold War was one of the defining events of the late 20th century. This book presents one aspect of the British experience of the Cold War – its physical remains. We hope it will lead to a wider appreciation of the monuments and to more analytical recording, both here and abroad, as well as to the conservation of representative sites and structures. The importance of the physical legacy is particularly striking since many official documents from the period are lost or remain classified, and the memories (themselves often surrounded by security considerations) of those who worked on the sites are beginning to fade.

2
The Cold War: military and political background

This chapter sets out a broad overview of the political and military history of the Cold War, with a bias towards events in Europe – the main theatre of operations to which military bases in the United Kingdom were linked. It also provides a backdrop for the more detailed discussion of British Cold War defence technology and the physical reminders it has left behind.

Origins

In February 1945, before the war in Europe was over, Winston Churchill, the British Prime Minister, Franklin Roosevelt, President of the United States of America, and Joseph Stalin, leader of the Soviet Union, met at Yalta on the Black Sea, to draw afresh the borders of Europe and its nations. The decisions they took were confirmed in July by the Potsdam Conference in Berlin. Some in the West naively expected that the countries of eastern Europe which had been liberated by the armies of the Soviet Union would be allowed to determine their own destinies, but the communist parties in those countries subverted any emerging democratic government, and the eastern states were brought under Soviet domination.

As the division between the western democratic and capitalist countries and the communist states of the east widened, a new political vocabulary began to emerge. In March 1946 Churchill, suspicious of Soviet intentions even during the war, announced in a lecture at Fulton, Missouri, that an 'Iron Curtain had descended across Europe', using for the first time in public a phrase he had used in a private telegram to US President Harry Truman on 12 May 1945. Walter Lippman, an American journalist, is generally credited with coining the name 'The Cold War' in a series of articles published in 1947, and the term was quickly adopted by western politicians and journalists.

At the heart of post-war stability was the 'German question', or rather 'German questions' – Germany being divided into four occupation zones each controlled by one of the former wartime Allies: Britain, the United States, the Soviet Union and France. Although the capital, Berlin, lay within the Soviet zone, it was also divided among the four Allies, access to the western zones being along controlled road, rail and air corridors.

The immediate concern of all the Allies was to demilitarise Germany to prevent it again posing a threat. Among the western powers this priority was soon replaced by the pressure for economic reconstruction across Europe, which could only be achieved with German industry. The war-ravaged countries were too weak to recover unaided, especially after the severe winter of 1946–7, and in June 1947 the United States launched the European Recovery Programme (the Marshall Plan), to rebuild the economy in Europe and, it hoped, destroy the conditions in which communism might appeal to people.

Without military security, however, it was unlikely that there would be sufficient confidence for economic recovery. Accordingly, in the post-war years the focus of Britain's defence policy shifted from its empire to Europe. Britain concluded mutual defence pacts with France (Treaty of Dunkirk, 1947) and with the Benelux countries (Treaty of Brussels, 1949), agreeing to come to their aid if they were invaded and to keep British troops in Germany for fifty years.

From 1947 the United States of America committed herself to the containment of communist expansion, through what became known as the Truman Doctrine. This was soon tested when the western powers announced they were going to reform Germany's currency by introducing the Deutschmark in their zones, including Berlin: a clear demonstration of their intention to back the economic recovery of Germany's western sector and build an independent state there. In reaction to this, the Soviet Union closed the land routes into the city on 24 June 1948 in the hope of forcing out its former allies. Rather than breaking the blockade by forcing a land route into the city, which might have led to the outbreak of war, the three western nations began to airlift supplies into it, in an operation that lasted for eleven months and delivered 2,300,000 tons (2,336,800 tonnes) of materials. In order to deter the Soviet Union from contemplating further encroachments on the West, the United States Air Force deployed more aircraft to Britain. Amongst these were B-29s which were stationed on East Anglian airfields; they were known as the 'atomic bombers', though we now know they were armed only with conventional weapons.

Western resolve to counter the expansion of communism was further demonstrated on 4 April 1949, when the Washington or North Atlantic Treaty was signed, creating the North Atlantic Treaty Organisation (NATO), which committed the United States to the defence of Europe. A major conceptual turning point in post-war United States defence policy was *National Security Council document 68* (*NSC 68*), which argued that to contain the threat of communism the country needed to increase both its peacetime conventional and atomic capabilities. Truman, at first reluctant to raise defence spending, soon had his hand forced by external events.

The surprise invasion of South Korea by communist North Korea on 25 June 1950 diverted attention from Europe to the Far East. The United Nations Security Council condemned the attack and, on 27 June, called on its members to aid South Korea in repulsing it: following the Truman Doctrine, the United States committed its forces the same day. The British Government, led by Prime Minister Clement Attlee, was fearful both of Soviet expansionism and of any potential return by the United States to pre-war isolationism. Accordingly, a month later Britain demonstrated solidarity with the United States by announcing both the dispatch of a brigade to Korea and additional expenditure of £3,600 million (later increased to £4,700 million) on rearmament over the following three years. Between 1950 and 1952 the US military budget rose by 340 per cent. This marked a significant escalation of the arms race, manifested in Britain by renewed expenditure on military infrastructure and by an increased US presence.

The Korean War also raised the question of rearming West Germany to relieve the United States and Britain of some of the burden of defending western Europe. France, three times invaded within a century, was initially opposed to West German rearmament, as were Britain and the West German politicians who were trying to rebuild the country. French fears were gradually overcome, partly by Britain and the United States committing troops to the country, and partly as it became apparent that it was the Soviet Union which posed the greater threat. In 1955, West Germany (the Federal Republic of Germany) became a sovereign state and, with its armed forces rebuilt, was admitted to NATO. The Soviet Union protested against this action, despite the fact that military-style East German 'police' units had been in existence for some time, and formed the Warsaw Treaty Organisation (Warsaw Pact) to counter what it saw as the threat of NATO aggression.

The Soviet Union's grip on eastern Europe did not go unchallenged. After 1945, partisans waged a (still largely undocumented) struggle against the Red Army in many of the Soviet republics. In 1953, there were disturbances in Berlin and other cities in East Germany (the German Democratic Republic) against increased work quotas, order only being restored when Soviet tanks appeared on the streets. In 1956 a far more serious uprising took place in the Hungarian capital, Budapest, encouraged by the western Radio Free Europe: again Russian tanks suppressed the insurrection, and, short of provoking all-out war, the West could do nothing.

The attention of the West was also diverted in 1956 by the nationalisation of the Suez Canal by Egypt, which threatened both Britain's strategic interests in the area and British and French investments. The British and French jointly drew up a plan to seize the canal by force and, after an agreement with Israel to invade Sinai, Anglo-French forces invaded Egypt, provoking almost universal condemnation by the United Nations. Financial pressure on Britain by the United States, driven by the need for oil, forced it to reconsider, and the invasion forces were withdrawn in less than two months. A bout of empty sabre-rattling directed at Britain, France and Israel by Soviet premier Nikita Kruschev also made it possible for the Soviet Union to claim credit among its allies for bringing about the withdrawal.

The Royal Navy and the British Army during the Cold War

In the past the main military threat to Britain had been invasion. Now Britain and the rest of western Europe faced the threat of an attack with nuclear weapons causing devastation that might leave millions dead. Traditionally the Royal Navy had safeguarded the mainland from attack, while most of the regular army was committed to protecting Britain's overseas interests. A nuclear attack, however, would most likely be delivered by manned bombers or unstoppable missiles and it was these threats that most Cold War defences were designed to counter.

Post-war Britain remained an important, although declining, naval power. The post-war Royal Navy had inherited dockyards and facilities with many buildings dating back to the 18th century. With a declining fleet there was some rationalisation within the dockyards, but this was partly offset by the closure of overseas bases, which directed work

Figure 2.1
Devonport Dockyard, Devon. Interior of the frigate complex
[G30605/4]

back to the British yards. New types of vessels, in particular nuclear-powered submarines, did make new demands on the naval dockyards and in 1980 a new submarine refit complex was opened at Devonport, Devon. This joined other new complexes there which had been added during the 1970s, including the fleet maintenance base and the frigate complex (Fig 2.1).

In addition to protecting Britain's established overseas interests, the Royal Navy fulfilled the vital tasks of anti-submarine warfare and guarding the Atlantic Ocean, across which important reinforcements would travel to Europe in the event of war. The most important role given to the Royal Navy during the Cold War was in 1969 when the British nuclear deterrent passed from the RAF's V-force to missile-carrying Resolution class nuclear-powered submarines, whose home port was Faslane in Strathclyde, Scotland. Stores for the Polaris missiles were built nearby at Coulport, the design of the facility being based on the United States missile store at Bangor, Washington.

Throughout the Cold War a large proportion of the British Army, together with its heavy equipment, was committed to the defence of the inner German frontier: the British Army on the Rhine (BAOR), which consisted of four armoured and mechanised divisions and their supporting corps. In the late 1950s it accounted for 77,000 troops, though this was later reduced to around 56,000 – a figure which represented about one-third of the regular personnel of the army. As part of Britain's obligations to NATO, units of the BAOR were trained to operate nuclear weapons such as the American Corporal, Honest John and Lance missiles, the 8-inch atomic howitzer, and atomic demolition munitions: all were held in Germany and had no facilities in Britain. Structures built in Germany by the BAOR and the RAF fall outside the scope of this study, but installations (such as hardened aircraft shelters or those for Bloodhound missiles) were of a similar kind to those built in the United Kingdom.

With such a large proportion of the British Army committed abroad, relatively few structures in the United Kingdom are directly related to its front-line role in the nuclear age. It continued to use barracks and other establishments which dated from the 19th century, though most of these have been relinquished as the army has been reduced, and modern barracks and unit accommodation have been built since the

Figure 2.2
Copehill Down, Wiltshire.
FIBUA (fighting in built
up areas), the mock
German village
[18135/07]

1960s. On a few large training areas, such as Salisbury Plain, Wiltshire, and Castlemartin, Pembrokeshire, tanks rehearsed the battles that might take place on the German plains. An eerie, uninhabited mock German village (Fig 2.2) with a distinctive continental layout was imposed on the ancient landscape of Salisbury Plain, to train troops in house-to-house combat. The Territorial Army, which in the event of war was to reinforce the BAOR, also often remained in buildings built for its predecessors, many of which were in city or town centres with little room for vehicles. More recently, units have tended to be moved to the outskirts and provided with garages.

In the years just after the Second World War some new structures were built to meet the Army's continued responsibility for home defence. In the late 1940s air defence was overhauled, with the construction of reinforced anti-aircraft operations rooms to control detached gun sites encircling major conurbations (*see* Chapter 7). The Army also provided coastal defence but, beyond the refurbishment of a number of control rooms such as that at Landguard Fort, Suffolk, the wartime system remained unaltered and in 1956 it was stood down, with the consequent abandonment of many 19th-century fortifications and associated barracks. The Army also took the lead in the defence of key points, such as communications centres or critical defence installations, against saboteurs or small disruptive attacks, but the infrastructure required was modest (Fig

2.3). In the event of major threat, regional military commanders were to be subordinated to the civil regional commissioners (*see* Chapter 9), and were provided with one or two rooms in their specially reinforced headquarters. Finally, the Army may also have been able to use redundant Home Office bunkers, with some otherwise unaccounted for building work being related to military use.

The long haul

The defining document of British Cold War policy was the 1957 Defence White Paper, *Outline of Future Policy*, which recognised that the conflict would be a long haul and would need a continuing high financial commitment to pay for technologically complex weapons. It also accepted that there was no defence against nuclear weapons except strong deterrent forces. Other fundamental changes to the armed forces were also required, including the ending of conscription and scaling down of overseas commitments. It also envisaged a future in which air defence fighters would be replaced by missiles.

By that time many of the complex weapons which came to typify the Cold War – jet bombers, nuclear arms, early warning systems and guided missiles – had become available in quantity and were brought together in an all-embracing military structure. The arms race was fuelled both by a need to match the actual capability of the

Figure 2.3
RAF Neatishead, Norfolk.
Fixed defences on most
military establishments
were restricted to temporary
field works made of
sandbags or prefabricated
concrete positions such as
this Yarnold sanger. The
perimeters of many
installations were secured in
the 1980s by stronger
fencing and barbed wire,
primarily against the threat
of terrorist attack.
[AA98/05752]

opposition and by the lack of accurate information. The Soviet Union adopted various strategies in order to appear more prepared than it actually was, for example, by flying the same Bison bombers repeatedly over the reviewing stand at the July 1955 Moscow Air Show: this spectacle bred US fears of a 'bomber gap' and later a 'missile gap', thereby justifying increased defence spending. In 1957 the West received another dramatic shock when the Soviet Union launched the first Sputnik (the first man-made satellite to orbit the earth), as many feared that it might well be a nuclear missile. Development of a US intercontinental missile was still some years away, though intermediate range missiles Thor and Jupiter were soon to be available, and negotiations began to effect their deployment in Europe so that they would be within range of the Soviet Union (*see* Chapter 3).

Throughout the Cold War in Europe Berlin remained a flashpoint where a minor dispute could rapidly escalate into a conflict between the superpowers. Krushchev summed up the position with typical earthiness, saying, 'Berlin is the testicles of the West, every time I want to make the West scream, I squeeze on Berlin'. As a matter of prestige East Germany (GDR) also wanted full control of its capital, and the first secretary of its Communist Party (Walter Ulbricht) believed it was impossible to build a truly socialist state with a western enclave

in its midst. In 1958 Moscow threatened that, unless the western Allies withdrew from Berlin, the Soviet Union would conclude a treaty to hand over its rights in the city to the GDR. This did not happen and, three years later, Krushchev hoped he could bully the young and newly-elected US President John Kennedy into giving up Berlin. The response was not only a reaffirmation of the United State's commitment to the city, but also an increase in US arms expenditure. Krushchev conceded that the West could not be peaceably removed from Berlin.

Early on Sunday 13 August 1961, to stop the damaging haemorrhage of its skilled citizens to the West, the East Germany authorities began to erect a barrier between themselves and the western sectors. This first crude wall of building blocks and barbed wire became, after successive rebuilding in the following decades, an almost impenetrable barrier: the Berlin Wall. In East German propaganda it was the 'anti-fascist protection wall'. Although regarded with horror by western politicians, it reduced uncertainty and brought stability to a potentially dangerous situation. Some tension remained, however, and in October a dispute over western access rights into East Berlin led to a two-day stand-off between US and Soviet tanks either side of the crossing known as Checkpoint Charlie. The world looked on apprehensively, knowing that a single shot by a jumpy soldier could lead to a wider conflict.

Cuban missile crisis

On the other side of the world, and close to the mainland of the United States, the Caribbean island of Cuba had been seized in 1959 by the revolutionary communist government of Fidel Castro. Economically isolated by the United States, Cuba looked to socialist countries for trade and support. An attempt by Cuban exiles in 1961, aided by the US Central Intelligence Agency (CIA), to invade the island at the Bay of Pigs met with disastrous results for the attackers. When Cuba discovered, through illicitly obtained CIA documents, that 'tougher measures' would be taken unless Castro was removed by October 1962, Krushchev proposed to place Soviet missiles on the island to safeguard it. The United States discovered the plan and, on 22 October 1962, President Kennedy announced that any attack launched from Cuba would be regarded as an attack from the Soviet Union. The United States then began a naval blockade of Cuba. Missile-sized crates were seen on board Soviet ships, and US spy planes confirmed that Soviet missiles were in place.

Tension rose further on Saturday 27 October when a United States U2 spy plane was shot down over the USSR, and the nuclear forces of both sides were placed on high alert. The world held its breath – a nuclear war had never seemed closer. The following day, however, Krushchev agreed to remove the missiles and bombers from Cuba, in return for which the United States secretly undertook to withdraw its Jupiter missiles from Turkey.

Equilibrium

The Cuban crisis highlighted the dangers of the United States policy of 'tripwire response', in which any aggression could too easily result in massive nuclear retaliation. This led to the strategy of 'flexible response', whereby 'communism' would be contained by a combination of economic, political and military means, and any attack would be met with a graduated response to allow time for negotiations. The unity of NATO itself was challenged in 1966, however, by the withdrawal of France under President General de Gaulle. This had an immediate effect in Britain and West Germany, as United States stores and squadrons had to be removed from French soil and redistributed elsewhere.

During the 1960s and the early 1970s the United States was enmeshed in the war against communist North Vietnam. The inability of its armed forces and modern weapons to defeat a guerrilla army was a severe blow to US military pride in the eyes of the world and to the reputation of the US Army at home. The Soviet Union was also faced with a challenge to its authority within its sphere of influence as, in spring 1968, Czechoslovakia began to make liberal reforms in defiance of the Kremlin. Following the 'Brezhnev doctrine', which demanded absolute obedience, Moscow ordered Warsaw Pact forces onto the streets of the Czechoslovakian capital, Prague, thereby crushing any hope of change.

During the Cold War the Middle East was an area of almost continual conflict. It was of prime strategic interest to the West, both for its oil and for access to the Suez Canal. Britain and France had long-standing influence in the area, but the new state of Israel looked to the United States for support, while Israel's hostile Arab neighbours armed themselves with weapons from the eastern bloc. One of the most serious clashes was the Six-Day War of June 1967, when Israel launched pre-emptive strikes against its neighbours. The United States raised the alertness of Strategic Air Command, more as a warning for the USSR to stay away than with an intention to aid Israel directly. During the first hours of the war the Israeli air force destroyed almost all the enemy fighters while they were still on the ground, many lined up parade-ground fashion. One result of this was the widespread construction of hardened aircraft shelters (HASs) which are now an almost universal feature on military airfields (*see* p 64).

After the nerve-racking confrontations of the early 1960s, the end of the decade was marked by a thaw in relations between the two superpowers, leading to a period of détente during the early 1970s. Soviet premier Brezhnev and US President Nixon both wished to ease the tension and Strategic Arms Limitation Talks (known as SALT) began, with SALT I being ratified in 1972: it resulted in an agreement to reduce anti-ballistic missile systems and to limit the number of offensive missiles and bombers. Outwardly relations in Europe also improved, largely through the *Ostpolitik* – positive approach to trade and diplomacy with East Germany – of West German leader Willy Brandt, who agreed to recognise the post-war borders within Europe and allowed the East improved economic access to the West. Around this time East Germany began a massive programme of building military infrastructure, which it may have funded with the help of the new money it was earning as a result of *Ostpolitik*. Elsewhere in the world, particularly in the Middle East and Africa, confrontations continued and were made more deadly to the local populations as the superpowers supplied their proxies with arms.

The second Cold War

Despite negotiations towards a second round of SALT agreements, by the late 1970s relations between the superpowers again began to worsen. From the middle of the decade many in the West wished to link the promotion of human rights to any negotiations with the Soviet Union, which greatly irritated the Soviet leaders. In 1977 the Soviet Union began to upgrade its intermediate range missiles in eastern Europe with the introduction of SS-20 missiles. The West perceived these as upsetting the balance of deterrence, because they were more accurate than their predecessors, had a greater range and enabled the use of multiple warheads. The system was also fully mobile and therefore difficult to find and destroy.

To counter the SS-20s, in 1978 NATO requested that US Pershing II missiles should be deployed in Europe, and a year later it was decided that cruise missiles, then still under development, should be added. Cruise missiles were small pilotless aircraft which had a range of 1,500 miles (2,500km), with the possibility of 50 per cent landing within 39ft (12m) of their target. Technologically they brought together major advances in warhead miniaturisation and in the design of engines and guidance systems. They, and the Pershing II missiles, were designed to free manned aircraft from attacking fixed military targets, releasing them to hunt down the SS-20s. The ability to launch a first strike could now be seen to have passed to the West. Relations were made worse by the Soviet invasion of Afghanistan on 29 December 1979 and, within the countries of the Warsaw Pact, opposition to the communist system (particularly by the increasingly effective Solidarity movement in Poland) created further uncertainty. Western politicians watched anxiously to see how the Soviet Union would react.

At the same time, western political leaders openly hostile to the Soviet Union (particularly US President Reagan) had come to power. In Britain, the Conservative Party was returned to power in 1979 with a commitment to strengthen Britain's defences, and announced the following year that the ageing Polaris submarine-launched missile system was to be replaced by United States Trident missiles. After a major Home Defence review it recommended that UK spending on civil defence should rise from £29.2 million per year in 1981 to an average of £63.1 million, peaking at £69.4 million in 1984–5. Over the same period local authority spending on civil defence was projected to double from £8.4 million per year to £16.7 million. Nuclear weapons and civil defence again became major political issues and the Government issued advice to the public on protection methods, including the pamphlet *Protect and Survive*. Membership of the Campaign for Nuclear Disarmament (CND) also rose steadily and its publications, such as *Protest and Survive*, challenged the official message (Figs 2.4 and 2.5).

It was against this background that the Cold War entered one of its most dangerous periods (Fig 2.6). The ageing members of the Soviet Politburo, particularly under Soviet premier Yuri Andropov, were deeply worried by President Reagan's strident anti-communist rhetoric. Reagan substantially raised the technological and financial stakes of the Cold War by the biggest peacetime rearmament programme in the United States, although most of the weapons were the culmination of work initiated by previous administrations, the policy of rearmament having been set in train by President Jimmy Carter. Programmes included new B-1 bombers, Trident 2 submarines, the introduction of Peacekeeper (MX) and cruise missiles and, most costly of all, the Strategic Defense Initiative (SDI) or 'Star Wars'. The last was intended to protect the United States with a shield of orbiting satellites, using laser beams to destroy incoming warheads. As it would have been enormously expensive to develop and install, it would have been unlikely that the USSR would have been able to match the system technologically or economically, and the Soviet leadership became convinced that the West was planning a pre-emptive nuclear attack.

Under an operation codenamed 'Ryan', Soviet agents were instructed to be extra vigilant in watching for signs of unusual activity in the West. Tension came to a head on 1 September 1983, when Korean airliner KAL-007 was shot down by an air defence fighter after straying into Soviet air space, killing all 269 people on board. President

Reagan seized on this as an event which unmasked the callous disregard for human life by what he called the 'evil empire'. The USSR was also aware that in November NATO was planning a major exercise, Able Archer 83, to test nuclear command procedures: was this, wondered the Soviet leadership, a cover for a pre-emptive strike? Fear and unease further increased when, on 24 October, 146 US Marines and twenty-seven French paratroopers were killed by a bomb in Lebanon. Two days later the United States invaded the Caribbean island of Grenada, an event preceded by increased numbers of cipher messages between Washington and London. These incidents had also caused an increase of activity at US bases. The USSR would have been aware of the messages, if not of their content: it could easily have interpreted either or both as preparations for war.

Conscious of Soviet unease about the forthcoming exercise, and probably in receipt of intelligence that Soviet forces had moved on to the alert, NATO scaled down

its exercise. In the ensuing months nervousness among the Soviet leadership subsided, partly helped by the death of Andropov in February 1984 and the subsequent replacement of the leaders of the intelligence services.

Figure 2.4
In the early 1980s, and for the first time since the 1960s, civil defence booklets for the general public were issued under the emblematic Protect and Survive symbol. Active distribution of the pamphlet was one indicator Soviet agents might look for when trying to predict a pre-emptive strike by NATO. [BB017251]

Figure 2.5
Mosley Street, Manchester. In the 1980s many local authorities, usually controlled by Labour, declared themselves to be 'nuclear free zones' and refused to co-operate with national civil defence exercises. [AA99/03274]

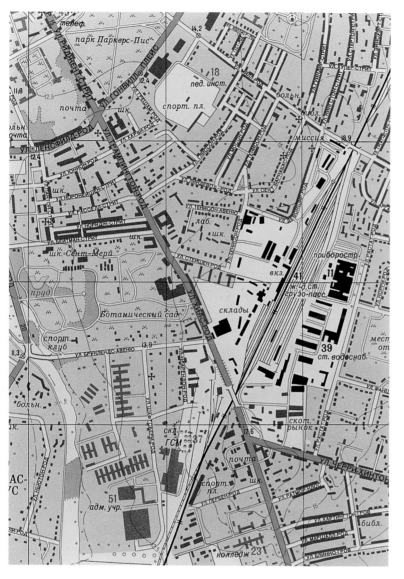

Figure 2.6
Soviet map of Cambridge,
dating from 1989. Detailed
plans for military
operations were constantly
prepared by the Soviet
Union and by the West.
Huge stocks of such detailed
maps discovered in eastern
Europe suggest that the Red
Army had plans for the
United Kingdom beyond
nuclear annihilation. One
surprising omission from
this map is the protected
regional seat of government
(see Fig 9.2). [Cambridge
N-31-133 1.10000.
BB013791]

The end

The Soviet reaction to Able Archer 83 shook President Reagan, who had not believed that Soviet fear of a pre-emptive attack was so great, and he almost immediately adopted a more conciliatory approach. The potentially disastrous events of the early 1980s, combined with the poor state of the Soviet-bloc economy, convinced the younger members of the Politburo that a dialogue with the West was essential. The death of Andropov's successor, Konstantin Chernenko, in March 1985 brought Mikhail Gorbachev to power (Fig 2.7). Gorbachev, a committed Communist, wished to overhaul the Soviet system through *perestroika* (restructuring) and *glasnost* (openness). Abroad, he and his ministers renewed contacts with the West, culminating in the summit meeting with Reagan in Octo-

ber 1985 at which it was agreed to work towards arms reduction. Between then and the next summit, in Reykjavik, private discussions and public statements ushered in the INF (Intermediate-Range Nuclear Forces) and START (Strategic Arms Reduction) treaties. At Reykjavik Gorbachev promised far-reaching cuts in Soviet conventional forces, but negotiations on a treaty to eliminate all nuclear weapons by 2000 failed when Reagan refused to stop SDI research, though the US Congress did reduce its funding. A year later, in December 1987, the INF Treaty was signed, and led to the withdrawal and destruction of SS-20s and of cruise and Pershing II missiles in Europe.

The signal from the Kremlin that reform was in the air at home and abroad had repercussions throughout eastern Europe. In 1989 Hungary began to dismantle the section of the Iron Curtain which separated it from Austria. This had unforeseen consequences for East Germany, as East German citizens were able to pass through Hungary and on to West Germany where they had an automatic right to citizenship. The East German government, one of the staunchest supporters of Moscow and a regime that had repeatedly shown its willingness to shoot fugitives, was faced with demonstrations in its major cities. Reformers from within the ruling Socialist Unity Party ousted their hard-line leader, Erich Honecker, and prepared to ease travel restrictions in an attempt to stem the flood of refugees. Following what hindsight has shown to have been a series of poorly co-ordinated events, a radio broadcast on the evening of 9 November 1989 announced that the border would be opened for 'private trips abroad'. No clear timetable or regulations were given and, as crowds began to gather at the Berlin crossing points, the border guards began to let people through. Across eastern Europe the communist governments fell in quick succession; usually peacefully, though in Romania the secret police bloodily tried to suppress the revolution over Christmas 1989.

Following the effective dissolution of the Warsaw Treaty Organisation in 1989 more than half a million Soviet troops were gradually withdrawn from eastern Europe, hastened by the break-up of the Soviet Union itself in December 1991. In the West this was matched by a large withdrawal of forces from Germany. The reductions were formalised by the Conventional Armed Forces in Europe (CFE) Treaty in November 1990, which agreed to limit the quantity of offensive weaponry, including tanks, combat aircraft and attack helicopters (Fig 2.8). Those signing up to the treaty included the USSR, the US and many European countries. The vast amounts of weapons and ammunition to be destroyed, combined with new environmental legislation, led to the creation of the demilitarisation facilities designed to dispose of dangerous and toxic military waste which are now a feature of some military depots.

The new world order, which began to emerge during the 1990s, is demanding highly mobile forces able to react both to geographically limited conflicts and as a defence against 'smart' weapons which can easily seek out fixed targets. The rigidity of the Cold War military order, however, is symbolised by its bases, which were literally set in concrete.

Figure 2.7
Mikhail Gorbachev
[© Alun Bull]

Figure 2.8
Castlemartin Range,
Pembrokeshire, Chieftain
tank. Across Europe many
serviceable armoured
vehicles have been towed
onto ranges and used as
targets to reduce stocks in
line with Conventional
Armed Forces in Europe
Treaty conditions. [© Roger
J C Thomas]

The intelligence war

MI6 Secret Intelligence Service building, Vauxhall Cross, London. In 1989, the activities of Britain's secret intelligence services were, for the first time, placed under statutory control. This new accountability was symbolised by a new, highly visible, headquarters by the River Thames. It was designed by Terry Farrell, one of Britain's leading urban architects. [BB98/12930]

Until the late 19th century, spying, or intelligence gathering, was largely restricted to information which could be collected by 'secret agents' or by legitimate military missions. During the First World War the range of sources was extended by the introduction of aircraft and wireless communications, which opened up the possibility of eavesdropping on the enemy.

After the First World War intelligence gathering began to acquire its own dedicated physical infrastructure, including radio stations set up to monitor foreign wireless traffic and later to broadcast false messages into enemy radio nets. Clandestine activities were often conducted from large country mansions surrounded by groups of anonymous-looking ministry timber huts, such as the code-breaking centre at Bletchley Park, Buckinghamshire. Bletchley housed the Government Code and Cypher School, the predecessor of the Government Communications Headquarters (GCHQ). After the war it moved to London and then, in 1952, to its present home in Cheltenham. Other intelligence-gathering bodies were scattered around the capital, but have recently been consolidated into a smaller number of locations.

As the Cold War intensified and the warning time of an attack decreased, it became crucial to be able to monitor the Warsaw Pact countries continuously for any sign of abnormal military activity,

RAF Chicksands, Bedfordshire. FLR-9, Flare 9 (the elephant cage), antenna was constructed from prefabricated parts imported from the United States. Its circular shape allowed it to detect signals coming from all directions and to determine their precise bearing. The maximum diameter of the array was 1,209ft (368.6m). It was one of five built worldwide. [15458/05]

which might indicate an imminent pre-emptive strike. Increasingly sophisticated systems were developed to monitor and analyse signals intelligence, often rendering it impossible to draw a distinct line between information gathered over the long term by early warning radar or other detection systems and intelligence-gathering stations. Some of these, like 'Cobra Mist', had a dual role, including the monitoring of aircraft and test launches from missile ranges (*see* Chapter 6).

Listening facilities, which had been directed against German forces on the eastern front, were reoccupied and re-equipped to eavesdrop on a new enemy. The former communications and intercept station at RAF Cheadle, Staffordshire, remained in service to support the work of GCHQ. RAF Chicksands, Bedfordshire, passed to the United States Air Force and, in 1963, was updated with the construction of a massive circular AN/FLR-9 antenna based on a wartime German design (the *Wullenweber*). Its main function was to relay secure radio communications for the US and its allies, but it was also used to intercept electronic signals traffic. At its centre was a round single-storey brick building which housed the receiving equipment, linked to the listening post by an under-ground cable tunnel, 0.62 miles (1km) long. Surrounding the central building was a concentric array, built from a framework of Douglas Fir, which was in turn encircled

by a steel-lattice array and two outer rings of cylindrical steel antennae. The United States Navy operated a similar facility on a former wartime airfield at Edzell, Angus. Another major US monitoring post and relay station, operated by the National Security Agency, remains active at Men-with Hill, North Yorkshire, its equipment shielded from the weather by white golfball-like domes. Also covered by domes is the US communications relay station at RAF Croughton, Oxfordshire, where some of the domes are a less conspicuous brown colour.

Spy flights over Warsaw Pact territory were regularly mounted from the United Kingdom by both British and United States aircraft. At first standard aircraft types were used, but specialised high altitude reconnaissance aircraft were regularly deployed with the result that dedicated facilities came to be needed. From 1982, the SR-71A Blackbirds were sent from their home base in California to RAF Mildenhall, Suffolk, where two shelters were built to protection them from the weather. One peculiarity of this aircraft was that it constantly leaked fuel, so that the structures had to incorporate open sides and drains.

In the same year the 19th Reconnais-sance Squadron was activated at Alcon-bury, Cambridgeshire, flying TR1 recon-naissance aircraft. These ungainly aero-planes, with a 103ft (31.39m) wingspan, were provided for training purposes with five steel-framed hangars clad in corrugated sheeting. A remarkable feature of the buildings is their upward opening, tri-partite, horizontally hinged doors. Soon afterwards work began on thirteen extra-wide hardened aircraft shelters (HASs) (*see* Chapter 4, Fig 4.16) to accommodate the TR1s, and an associated hardened squadron headquarters. Other special features of these shelters include T-shaped roof ventilators, and entry from the right-hand side; at the back, the jet efflux was vented through an opening to a blast deflector fence via a rolling steel blast door mounted on runners which rolled along rails. In the late 1980s a massive concrete two-storey bunker was built to house a centre for processing and analysing information collected by the aircraft and an avionics maintenance section. The structure was large enough to accommodate a 'drive-

RAF Chicksands, Bedfordshire. The taller antenna, AS-1555, measured 105ft (32.1m); the shorter antenna, AS-1556, 35ft (10.7m). The reflecting screen of vertical wires, antenna AS-1558, was 120ft (26.6m) high. [BB94/12098]

through' access roadway and an indoor vehicle or trailer decontamination point.

The growth in remote intelligence-gathering techniques did not make the spy redundant, first hand reports remaining vital: at one time the sites described in this book would have been prime targets. Agents would not wish to draw attention to themselves and commonplace objects in a townscape such as bollards, lamp posts or monuments in public places could take

RAF Edzell, Angus, Scotland. US Navy communications and intercept station. The operations buildings are inside the Wullenweber-type array. [D/10678]

Left:
RAF Alconbury, Cambridgeshire. One of the thirteen extra-wide hardened aircraft shelters built for the TR1 tactical reconnaissance aircraft. [AA023776]

Below:
A TR1 tactical reconnaissance aircraft sitting inside of one of the specially constructed extra-wide hardened aircraft shelters. [G30435/8]

RAF Alconbury, Cambridgeshire. The massive hardened bunker was constructed in the late 1980s to service the electronic components of the TR1s and to process their reconnaissance data. It is capped with rough concrete burster cap that was designed to absorb the impact of a missile before it penetrated to the bunker's roof. [AA023747]

on a new significance as illicit meeting or pick-up points. Espionage was also waged from anonymous suburban addresses such as the Ruislip (West London) home of the Soviet spies Peter and Helen Kroger, where residents were only alerted to their neighbours' shadowy activity by dramatic revelations or arrests.

Audley Square, London. A light blue chalk mark scrawled on this lamppost indicated to Soviet KGB agents that a package awaited collection from a dead letter box. [BB00017]

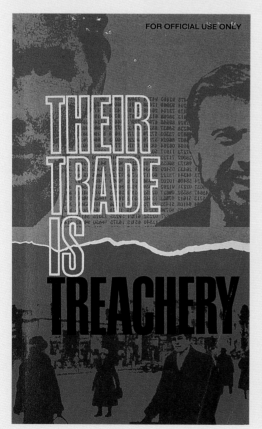

FOR OFFICIAL USE ONLY

THEIR TRADE IS TREACHERY

Far left:
Their Trade is Treachery: *booklet issued to public servants in the 1960s warning of the methods used by hostile intelligence services [BB99/06347]*

45 Cranley Drive, Ruislip: home of the American communist spies Lona and Morris Cohen, alias Peter and Helen Kroger. After their arrest in 1961 a large cache of espionage equipment was found in the house. [BB000177]

3

MAD – 'Mutually Assured Destruction'

One of the defining features of the Cold War was the stockpiling, by East and West, of ever larger and more advanced nuclear arsenals, providing each side with the potential to annihilate life on Earth many times over. It was argued in the West that as long as parity was maintained neither side would risk launching a pre-emptive attack – a policy that became known as Mutually Assured Destruction (MAD). Tension rose when either side perceived that the other was gaining a technological advantage that might upset the balance by facilitating an unanswerable first strike.

Despite their awesome power, nuclear weapons are fragile and vulnerable. They are not like the large high explosive bombs of the Second World War, which could be kept in almost any conditions. Nuclear weapons require sophisticated storage facilities and constant maintenance. They are also hugely expensive objects because they contain precious raw materials and need highly skilled labour to assemble them. The special facilities that were built to maintain and deploy Britain's nuclear deterrent forces are the subject of this chapter.

V-bomber airfields

Britain's airborne deterrent was carried by the V-force – Valiants, Victors and Vulcans. Its introduction not only represented an extraordinary technological achievement in the development of aircraft and weapons, but also required a massive investment in airfield infrastructure.

Ten main (Class 1) airfields were provided (Fig 3.1), all of which, except RAF Gaydon, Warwickshire, were pre-war permanent airfields with large aircraft hangars and domestic accommodation. The main alteration required was the provision of new runways about 9,000ft (2,743m) long and up to 200ft (61m) wide, capable of taking aircraft weighing 89 tons (91 tonnes).

The redevelopment of RAF Finningley, South Yorkshire, completed by 1957, is typical of the modifications carried out on 1930s permanent airfields (Fig 3.2a). The most noticeable change to the plan was the extension of the runway to 8,993ft (2,740m) and the creation of parallel taxiways on each side. To the west of the runway four hardstandings or dispersals were laid, each capable of holding four aircraft. To ensure that the latter could be airborne at short notice accommodation for their crew was built next to the hardstandings.

Next to the officers' mess was an operations and briefing block as well as a flight simulator (Fig 3.2b). To accommodate the many people required to keep the V-force operational round the clock the pre-war housing estate was greatly enlarged, new barracks were built and new wings added to the officers' mess. The concrete aprons around the hangars were relaid and enlarged, and an avionics building was erected to maintain the complex electrical and electronic flight systems (Fig 3.2c). In order to improve access to the hangars the 1930s watch office and associated buildings were demolished and a new air traffic control building was erected (Fig 3.3). The earlier bomb stores were largely replaced by unit stores where the nuclear weapons were held and maintained (*see below*). Less obvious changes to the airfield included new handling facilities for bulk fuel.

The post-war period also saw a growth in aircraft navigation and communication aids, some of which were outside the perimeter of the airfield. The ground-based elements of these systems, often relatively flimsy metal structures, are particularly vulnerable to clearance as new systems are introduced or when sites are about to be closed (Fig 3.4).

The archaeological remains of these sophisticated technological monuments may be no more than concrete bases or unremarkable single-storey buildings. One of the more widespread systems was Gee-H, a navigation aid for Bomber Command aircraft operating over Europe. The transmitters (Fig 3.5) were installed in a series of 'chains': the South Western Gee Chain, for example, consisted of a master station at RAF

Figure 3.1
Map showing the location
of V-bomber main and
dispersal airfields and
atomic bomb stores in
February 1962.

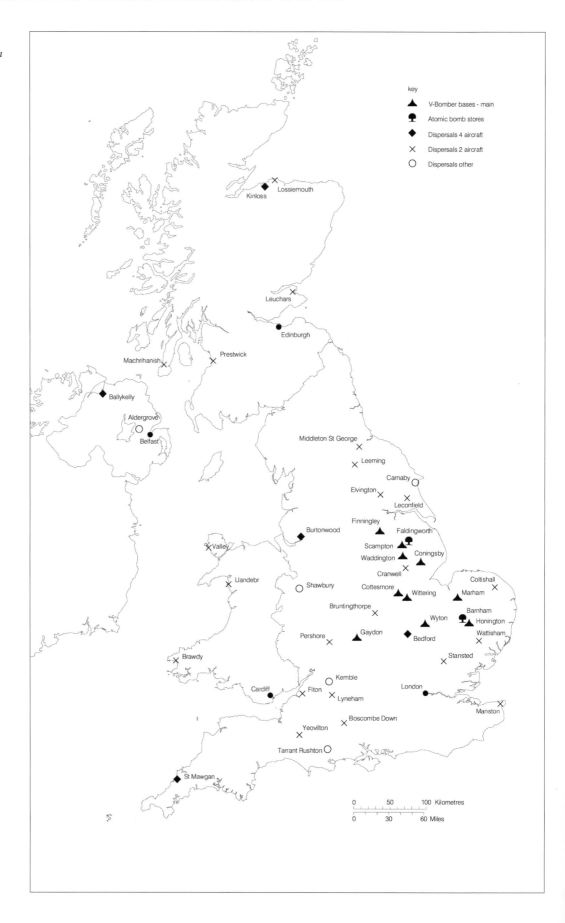

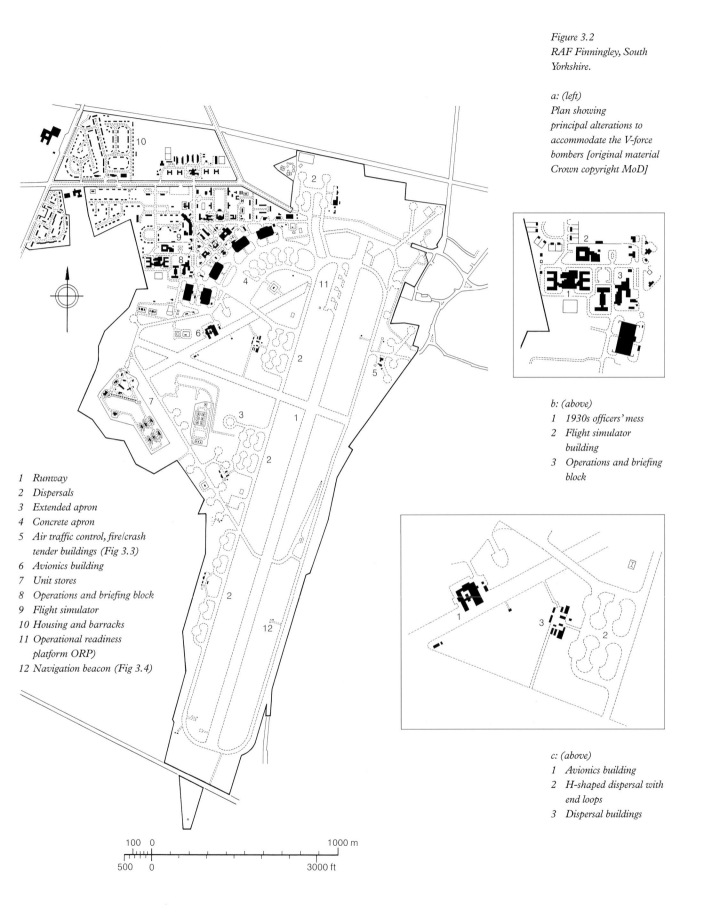

Figure 3.2
RAF Finningley, South
Yorkshire.

a: (left)
Plan showing
principal alterations to
accommodate the V-force
bombers [original material
Crown copyright MoD]

1 Runway
2 Dispersals
3 Extended apron
4 Concrete apron
5 Air traffic control, fire/crash
   tender buildings (Fig 3.3)
6 Avionics building
7 Unit stores
8 Operations and briefing block
9 Flight simulator
10 Housing and barracks
11 Operational readiness
   platform ORP)
12 Navigation beacon (Fig 3.4)

100 0   1000 m

500 0   3000 ft

b: (above)
1 1930s officers' mess
2 Flight simulator
   building
3 Operations and briefing
   block

c: (above)
1 Avionics building
2 H-shaped dispersal with
   end loops
3 Dispersal buildings

Figure 3.3
RAF Finningley, South
Yorkshire. Type 2548a/55
air traffic control building,
1955. This was the
commonest form of post-
war military control tower,
known as a split vertical
control type. Local aircraft
movements were conducted
from the upper storey, while
approach control was dealt
with on the floor below.
(No. 5 on Fig 3.2a)
[277H/3]

Figure 3.4
RAF Finningley, South
Yorkshire. Navigation
beacon, digital resolution
direction finding building
(No. 12 on Fig 3.2a)
[277H/19]

Sharpitor on Dartmoor, Devon, and secondary stations at RAF Sennen, Cornwall, RAF Folly, Pembrokeshire, and RAF Worth Matravers, Dorset (RAF Folly, however, was quickly replaced by RAF St Twynnells, where the standard Gee-H buildings are extant).

The pattern of refurbishment varied in detail according to local circumstances, but was broadly similar at all sites apart from Gaydon (*see* Fig 3.8), which was the only temporary wartime airfield selected to take V-bombers and required considerably more work. As there were no suitable hangars a new type of prefabricated steel structure was developed, known as a Gaydon hangar, which is typical of this period. New support buildings were also needed, and many were

Figure 3.5 (far left)
Gee-H transmitter [© C J Lester, Society for Lincolnshire History and Archaeology]

Figure 3.6
RAF Wittering, Peterborough UA.
a: (left)
Control tower [AA99/09832]

b: (below)
Gaydon-type hangar [AA99/09854]

Figure 3.7
RAF Wyton,
Cambridgeshire.
Photograph factory. By the
mid-1960s a single sortie by
a Victor could produce
10,000ft (3,048m) of film
for processing.
[AA99/09797]

Figure 3.8
RAF Gaydon,
Warwickshire. Air
photograph showing eastern
end of the airfield in 1971
[OS/71 061 V frame 484,
12 April 1971. Reproduced
from Ordnance Survey air
photos on behalf of the
Controller of Her Majesty's
Stationery Office © Crown
copyright Licence No GD
030859/02/01]

1   *Control tower*
2   *H-shaped dispersal*
3   *Compass swinging*
    platform
4   *Gaydon hangars*
5   *Operational readiness*
    platform (ORP)
6   *Domestic*
    accommodation

cast on site using the Laing 'Easiform' system (No. 6 on Fig 3.8). The design of the control tower foreshadowed that of most major post-war towers, having a fully-glazed visual control room above the approach control room. The only other tower of this specific type was erected at RAF Wittering, Peterborough (Fig 3.6a), which was the first operational V-bomber base. Although a pre-war airfield, Wittering had primarily been a night fighter station; it therefore lacked the hangar accommodation associated with the bomber bases, and a Gaydon hangar was erected to provide extra space (Fig 3.6b). The most significant impact on the landscape as a whole, however, was made by runway extensions, with public roads having to be realigned at, for example, RAF Scampton, Lincolnshire, and the dispersal airfield at RAF Shawbury, Shropshire (*see below*).

Amongst the Class 1 airfields RAF Wyton, Cambridgeshire, fulfilled a unique role as the home of Bomber Command's strategic photographic reconnaissance squadrons, which operated specially adapted

Valiants, Victors, and Canberras. To support this activity a photograph-processing factory was built immediately to the south of the station (Fig 3.7).

V-bomber airfields were prime targets for pre-emptive attack. At first, aircraft were placed on dispersed hardstandings on the main bases to reduce take-off time. In order to minimise the risk of the whole force being destroyed, however, a series of dispersal airfields was developed from 1958 (*see* Fig 3.1), and fully armed bombers were sent to them in periods of tension. Around thirty airfields were used in this way, though their distribution periodically changed.

Variations in the layout of the airfields reflect varying deployment strategies for the nuclear forces. In 1957 two categories of warning were devised: strategic, where 75% of the force was brought up to readiness within twenty-four hours; and tactical, which called for aircraft to be maintained at fifteen minutes' readiness for up to a week, and forty minutes' readiness for up to a month. On the main bases up to four aircraft were

Figure 3.9
RAF Wittering,
Peterborough UA. Four
Vulcan B-2s on an
operational readiness
platform [14133509 ©
The Flight Collection]

generally held on each dispersal area. Two forms of these distinctive dispersals are encountered: a simple 'H' shape, as at Gaydon (No. 2 on Fig 3.8), Scampton and Wittering; and a more flexible form with turning loops on either side as at Cottesmore, Suffolk, and Finningley (*see* No. 2 on Fig 3.2a). Where space was restricted, loop-type hardstandings for two aircraft were used. Next to the hardstandings were electrical junction boxes that provided power for the aircraft via quick-release cables.

Each dispersal was provided with crew accommodation, with the larger buildings built of prefabricated concrete panels and the smaller ones of brick. By the late 1950s, with the threat of attack by ballistic missiles, it was necessary to improve take-off time even further. To achieve this it was proposed to build operational readiness platforms (ORPs) at the ends of runways on the Class 1 and dispersal airfields (Fig 3.9 *and see* No. 11 on Fig 3.2a, No. 5 on Fig 3.8), though actual construction was probably not completed until 1963; previously such features were only found on fighter airfields. In February 1962 there was a further reduction in reaction time, as the main bases were required to keep three fully armed aircraft at fifteen minutes' readiness – a policy known

as 'quick reaction alert' (QRA). With crew strapped into their aircraft, known as 'cockpit readiness', take-off time could be reduced to three minutes. Other modifications to the layouts of the dispersal airfields to speed up aircraft movements were also planned, probably in 1959, with a proposal to build turning loops at the end of the runways at Leeming, North Yorkshire and Pershore, Worcestershire (Fig 3.10).

The dispersal airfields generally had runways of similar length to those of the main stations but the other facilities, intended to support the crew close to their aircraft for up to a month, were more rudimentary, sometimes consisting of no more than a caravan or crew room, communications links to Bomber Command and a telelink to the cockpit. One of the larger dispersals was RAF Carnaby, East Riding of Yorkshire (Fig 3.11). At RAF Bedford, Middleton St George, Cleveland, and Pershore similar facilities were provided, though in some places the layouts of the existing airfields led to minor variations. No facilities were provided for the storage and maintenance of nuclear weapons: if a second strike was possible additional bombs would be provided from the parent station or an overseas unit.

Figure 3.10 (opposite) RAF Pershore, Worcestershire. V-Force dispersal airfield showing characteristic single long runway, with a detached dispersal area to the bottom left. Photograph taken by a reconnaissance Canberra of 58 Squadron based at RAF Wyton. [F21 58/RAF /4596 31 frame 0040, July 1961 © Crown copyright MoD]

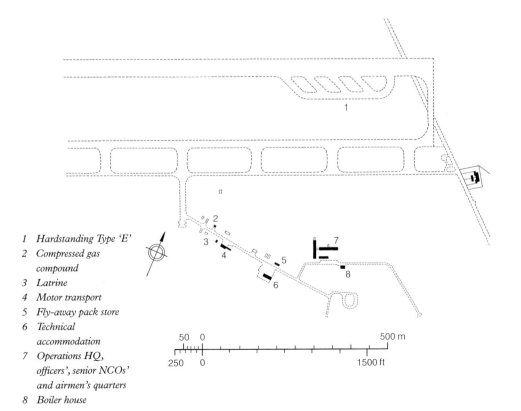

1 Hardstanding Type 'E'
2 Compressed gas
   compound
3 Latrine
4 Motor transport
5 Fly-away pack store
6 Technical
   accommodation
7 Operations HQ,
   officers', senior NCOs'
   and airmen's quarters
8 Boiler house

50   0   500 m

250   0   1500 ft

Figure 3.11 RAF Carnaby, North Yorkshire. Section of the airfield showing hardstanding Type 'E' and layout of crew area. It was unusual: in the juxtaposition of Thor and Bloodhound missiles, and in the presence of the airborne nuclear deterrent on the same site. [Redrawn from Air Ministry Drg No. 622/60K March 1960. Original material Crown copyright MoD]

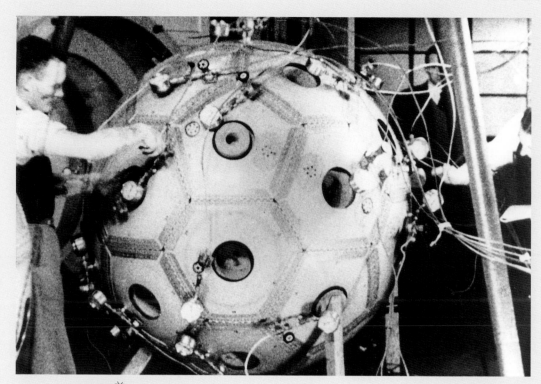

Figure 3.12a
'Blue Danube'. Frame from a cine film showing the outer high explosive lenses. Scientists are shown practising fitting detonators. The sphere, sometimes referred to as the 'physics package', is about 5ft (1.52m) in diameter. [© Crown copyright. Photo courtesy of AWE]

Figure 3.12b (below) Components of an implosion-type atomic bomb [from B Cathcart, 1994, Test of Greatness: Britain's Struggle for the Atom Bomb ©John Murray (Publishers)Ltd]

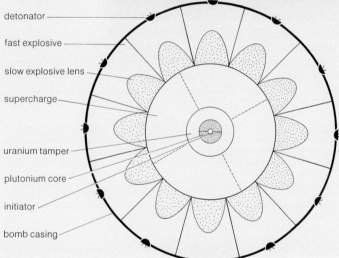

detonator
fast explosive
slow explosive lens
supercharge
uranium tamper
plutonium core
initiator
bomb casing

The British nuclear deterrent

The first nuclear weapon issued to the RAF in 1953 was code-named 'Blue Danube' This appears to describe not one bomb, but a series of closely related weapons that were subject to continuous modification. The atomic bomb dropped on Hiroshima in 1945 relied on propelling two sub-critical masses together in a device resembling a gun barrel. The bomb that destroyed Nagasaki worked on the implosion system and it was this device that provided the model for the post-war British bomb.

Table 3.1 Summary of main British free-fall nuclear weapon types

Name	Length	Diameter	Weight	Service
Blue Danube	24ft (7.3m)	5ft (1.52m)	10,000lb (4,636kg)	1953–1962
Red Beard 1	12ft (3.66m)	3ft (0.91m)	2,000lb (907kg)	1961–1972
Violet Club	24ft (7.3m)	5ft (1.52m)	10,250lb (4,649kg)	1958–1959
Yellow Sun MkI	21ft (6.4m)	4ft (1.22m)	7,000lb (3,175kg)	1959–1962
Yellow Sun MkII	21ft (6.4m)	4ft (1.22m)	7,000lb (3,175kg)	1961–1972
WE-177 B	11ft 1in (3.37m)	16½in (0.42m)	950lb (431kg)	1966–1995
WE-177 C	11ft 1in (3.37m)	16½in (0.42m)	950lb (431kg)	1966–1998
WE-177 A	9ft 4in (2.84m)	16½in (0.42m)	600lb (272kg)	1972–1992

The sub-critical plutonium fissile core at the centre of the device (Figs 3.12a and b) was machined to form a hollow sphere, in the middle of which was a neutron source. The sphere was surrounded by precisely-machined lenses of high explosive. When initiated, a spherical pressure wave was produced, imploding the sub-critical core and thereby forming a critical mass resulting in the nuclear explosion. To detonate the high explosives lenses the bombs were equipped with elaborate interlocking fuzing systems which both ensured that they detonated when required and guarded against unscheduled detonation (munitions have fuzes, household appliances have fuses.) These complex sub-assemblies included small radar that detected height above the ground, so that the bombs could be triggered in the air to maximise blast damage. Alternatively, they could be activated at a set height by barometric switches, which served as a back-up if the radar failed or were jammed. Mechanical timed and impact fuzes could also be selected as the preferred method of detonation or could function as a reserve. To power these electrical systems the bombs were fitted with batteries and turbo-generators.

Blue Danube was a large device (Table 3.1). By the late 1950s a second-generation British atomic bomb, 'Red Beard', was in production. It was far smaller and could be carried by a wider range of aircraft.

In the late 1950s a more powerful warhead, known as 'Violet Club', was devised and fitted into existing Blue Danube casings. The issue of this bomb to the RAF began in March 1958. It was superseded in the following year by an improved version – 'Yellow Sun' Mark I. Britain's first H-bomb or thermo-nuclear weapon, 'Yellow Sun' Mark II, entered service with the RAF in 1961. Shortfalls in the British stockpile were at this time made good by the availability of United States' nuclear weapons held on a number of RAF bases.

The H-bomb which formed part of the British arsenal for the longest period was the WE-177. The first version, WE-177 B/C, was introduced in 1966 and a smaller variant, WE-177A, was in service by 1972.

Storage and handling of nuclear weapons

The first British nuclear bomb was 'Blue Danube' (Fig 3.13), for which two specialised storage and maintenance facilities were built – one at Barnham, Suffolk (a former open bomb store) and one at Faldingworth, Lincolnshire (a wartime airfield). Both sites were a long way from their nearest airfields and were designed to service bombs for a number of squadrons. The detailed regulations for the handling of this weapon are not available, but something of the procedures may be reconstructed by analysis of the site plans and structures.

The sites have virtually identical five-sided plans: each covers 23 acres (9ha), and has a similar range of buildings (Fig 3.14). Their boundaries give two layers of security. The perimeter is defined by a high, wire-mesh fence surmounted by barbed wire; mid-way along the sides are projecting bastions enabling the whole length of the fence to be observed from illuminated inner patrol paths (Fig 3.15a), themselves watched from towers placed at the corners. The inner boundary consists of concrete panel fencing capped with barbed wire. At Barnham the guardroom and associated buildings were originally between the inner and outer fences (Fig 3.15b) but they were later moved outside the perimeter (Fig 3.15c), creating a sterile area in which dogs could be set loose.

Most of the support buildings outside the main storage area were occupied by the RAF Police, the only personnel permanently stationed at Barnham. They included a guardroom, mess, dormitory, gymnasium and police dog section, all built from Seco hutting – a prefabricated building system of hollow plywood beams and columns. The inner compound was entered through a pair of electrically-operated sliding gates set on rails which remain in the road surface. Within the main storage area the buildings fall into three main categories: non-nuclear component stores, fissile core stores, and maintenance buildings. Both sites retain elements of ornamental tree planting, including limes and poplars, whose regular spacing suggests more concern for the human working environment than for camouflage.

Non-nuclear component stores

The main function of the non-nuclear stores was to hold the outer casings and the high

Figure 3.13 (above) 'Blue Danube'. Each bomb was 24ft (7.3m) long, 5ft (1.52m) in diameter, weighed 10,000lb (4,636kg) and cost about £1 million. This particular weapon is being prepared for testing at Orfordness, Suffolk. [© Crown copyright. Photo courtesy of AWE]

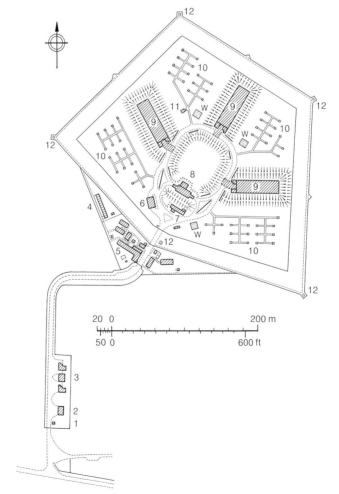

1 Picket post
2 Motor transport garage
3 Standby generators
4 Dog compound
5 Guardroom, barracks, mess room, fire station, etc
6 Inspection and repair workshop
7 Storage building
8 Storage building
9 Atomic bomb stores
10 Fissile core stores
11 Inspection room
12 Observation towers
W Water tanks

Figure 3.14 Barnham, Suffolk. Site plan [original material courtesy of K and A Eldred]

Figure 3.15
Barnham, Suffolk.
a: (far left)
Inner patrol path and
watch tower
[AA98/07801]

b: (left)
Air photograph showing the
site as it was in 1956
[1540/RAF/1778 frame
0128, 16 Jan 1956. ©
Crown copyright MoD]

c: (below)
Air photograph taken in
1998, showing how the
southern boundary has
been pulled in to place the
ancillary buildings outside
the sterile area [15881/12]

explosive part of the bomb. The casings could be split into three parts – the tail unit containing parachutes and gas bottles to extend its fins, the central section holding the explosive lenses, and the nose cone housing radar units and other electronics. Both Barnham and Faldingworth were provided with three almost identical stores (Type D-D), arranged around an internal loop road, and each within a 14ft (4.4m) high earth traverse. The stores are rectangular, have reinforced-concrete frames, precast concrete block walls and flat concrete roofs.

As Blue Danube was a heavy and bulky weapon the entrance to each store has a heavy lifting crane (Fig 3.16). It is supported on a reinforced-concrete gantry to which is attached a rolled steel joist runway beam for a 10 ton (10 tonne) hoist. The doorway is 10ft (3m) wide and 12ft (3.6m) high. Flanking the entrances are rooms which originally contained heating and air-conditioning plant to maintain a stable environment, and a raised air extraction duct is placed asymmetrically on the roofs of the stores. The main storage area measures 190ft 2½ in (58m) by 60ft (18m) and is eleven bays long by three bays wide, the central bay being narrower than the others.

Figure 3.16 (above)
Barnham, Suffolk. Lifting
gantry and entrance to
non-nuclear component
store [AA98/07818]

The layout of the stores suggests that bombs were received on pantechnicons – very large trucks – and off-loaded onto trolleys for storage, while their proportions show that the bombs were held partly disassembled. This not only avoided the obvious dangers of storing assembled nuclear weapons, but also enabled easy access to their individual components; the maintenance of each required different skills and facilities.

Fissile core stores

The fissile cores were stored in small kiosk-like buildings (hutches), of which each site has fifty-seven: forty-eight Type A (Figs 3.17a–d) and nine Type B stores (Fig 3.17e). At Barnham they are organised in four unequal groups, while at Faldingworth there are five. The buildings within each group are linked by walkways from which short spurs lead to the individual stores.

The Type A buildings were designed to hold a single core (Fig 3.17d) but the Type B stores are slightly longer, being intended to hold two cores (Fig 3.17e); they also have small waist-high wooden counters next to the doors. Both varieties are constructed from solid concrete blocks and are rendered with cement inside and outside. The design drawing shows a variety of irregularly edged roof plans, designed to cast a tree-like shadow. This form of roof was used within the airfield stores areas at Honington, Suffolk, Marham, Norfolk, Waddington, Lincolnshire, and Wittering, Peterborough (Fig 3.17c, *see below*), while a simple rectangular roof plan was used at Barnham (Fig 3.17a) and Faldingworth.

The stores were similar to those intended to hold conventional explosives. All were protected by copper earthing straps, and the electrical fuse boxes and switches were mounted externally. Inside, cabling was sealed in small-bore pipes, and lit by sealed bulkhead lights. The outward-opening doors were secured with combination locks, but there also appear to have been electrically-operated spring-loaded bolts so that the doors could be secured from a central control panel that also indicated if the door was open. The control panel itself may have been in the guardhouse. The doors were marked with a black radiation sign and star, both on a yellow background (Fig 3.17b).

The fissile cores were held in a stainless steel vessel set into a keyhole-plan cavity in the centre of the solid concrete floor. Unusually, some of the vessels remain in place at the bomb store for RAF Wittering (Fig 3.18): they are 2ft (610mm) in diameter and 1ft 11in (590mm) deep, and were sealed by lids rotated into place on supporting lugs and locked into the main vessel by three nibs. At some point during the operational life of Barnham the holes of the Type B stores were filled in and covered by gritless asphalt, but at Faldingworth the holes were

Figure 3.17
a: (opposite right)
Barnham, Suffolk.
Fissile core storage building
Type A [AA98/07811]

b: (above left)
Door of fissile core store
[AA98/07805]

c: (above right)
RAF Wittering,
Peterborough UA
Fissile core store building
Type A [AA99/09822]

d: (far left)
Fissile core store building
Type A [original material
courtesy of K and A
Eldred]

e: (left)
Fissile core store building
Type B [original material
courtesy of K and A
Eldred]

Figure 3.18
RAF Wittering,
Peterborough UA. Stainless
steel vessel for fissile core
[AA99/09826]

Figure 3.18
RAF Wittering,
Peterborough UA. Stainless
steel vessel for fissile core
[AA99/09826]

left open. The significance of these alterations is unknown. Both Barnham and Faldingworth had enough holes to store a total of 132 cores. This was probably in line with the original intention to produce a stockpile of 200 atomic weapons, however, far fewer warheads for Blue Danube were issued to the RAF between 1957 and 1961. It is therefore likely that only a handful of weapons were ever stored at Barnham and Faldingworth, and that the capacity of the stores far exceeded the number of warheads. Together with the special unit stores on airfields, bomb stores may therefore have been part of a deadly game of nuclear brinkmanship to mislead the Soviets about the size, location and readiness of the British stockpile.

Maintenance buildings

Deep maintenance and refurbishment was carried out at Barnham and Faldingworth, as well as the storage of nuclear weapons. This required environmentally controlled examination areas for the dismantling of sensitive components. This was particularly nec-

essary with Blue Danube, which needed a lot of maintenance to keep it ready for service.

The principal maintenance buildings on each site, designated storage buildings C–D (see No. 8 on Fig 3.14) were opposite the main gates, behind high, earth traverses. Their construction is similar to that of the non-nuclear component stores, with a reinforced-concrete frame and panels infilled with breeze-block. The buildings could be entered from either end, while the layout of the access roads made it possible for bombs to be brought from the stores and returned directly to them, and to be received from and dispatched to the main gate.

Entry into each building was controlled by air locks which were arranged so that the inner doors could not be opened before the outer doors were closed. The air locks were only 20ft (6m) long – too short to take a fully assembled Blue Danube. All doors leading into the main servicing area were secured by combination locks. The air locks gave access to a large central bay, which at Faldingworth was empty, apart from three small benches along its southern wall and a runway beam which ran the full length of the building's ceiling and supported four hoists. Behind the building was a 'plant room' containing electrical gear and a photographic darkroom, neither of which could be entered from the main servicing bay. The presence of a darkroom suggests that X-ray equipment was being used to detect minute cracks in the casing for the high-explosive lenses surrounding the core.

Each site also had a building for the periodic inspection of the cores, supplemented, from 1959, by identical inspection and repair workshops. Unlike the earlier structures, they were brick-built and were lit by tall windows. They had double doors at either end, and along one side were single-storey buildings housing an office and workshops. It is not clear whether their construction coincided with the introduction of a new weapon type.

Airfield unit stores

Apart from RAF Wyton, the main V-bomber airfields were provided with a storage area for nuclear weapons, known under the anonymous title of 'unit stores'. Most still lie on active airfields and have therefore been unavailable for detailed analysis. Three distinct types are found. Some of the earliest were built at RAF Wittering to receive Blue

Danube in November 1953. These stores comprised a central spine road with single branches leading off to mounded bomb stores: the fissile cores were stored in individual hutches (*see* Fig 3.17d). Wittering was also the Bomber Command Armament School and additional buildings may have been provided for the training of personnel in the use of the new weapons.

More typical of the units store areas found on the main airfields is the one at RAF Gaydon which was about one mile (1.6km) from the airfield (Fig 3.19). The site was laid out to minimise the amount of handling and bombs could be towed around the site on a trolley. Partly assembled atomic weapons were brought in by truck, taken to the D1 building for assembly and then moved to the D2 mounded stores for long-term storage: up to thirteen cores could be held in individual cubicles encased in a long earthwork bank (Fig 3.20). The stores, which were at the centre of loop roads, were designed to offer more protection than those at Barnham and Faldingworth, to counter the danger of aircraft crashes and fuel spillages that were a hazard so close to an active airfield. Inside, the bombs were kept on their trolleys and the environment was controlled by equipment housed in a self-contained plant room attached to one side of the stores. Other buildings were provided for servicing and testing the components of the bombs.

Other unit store areas were similar to those at Gaydon, though the local landscape demanded minor variations in plan. The unit stores at RAF Finningley show how the layout evolved to serve one of the main V-bomber bases (Fig 3.21). The stores formed a self-contained compound behind a double

Figure 3.19 (below left) RAF Gaydon, Warwickshire. Atomic bomb store. The D1 building used for assembling bombs is to the top left. Pairs of D2 mounded stores line the road to the right. The long narrow buildings in the centre were built later, to store National Film Archives. [18538/24]

Figure 3.20 (below) RAF Gaydon, Warwickshire. On most airfield sites the fissile core stores were set in an earthen bank (see No. 8 on Fig 3.23).

perimeter fence. Weapons were brought to the D1 building (Fig 3.22a) for assembly before being taken to the D2 mounded stores (Fig 3.22b); these could hold two Blue Danube or four Red Beard bombs but only a single H-bomb, as these had fissile material built in making it too hazardous to have two in one store. Periodically the bombs, or sub-assemblies, might be taken to other buildings for testing. The fissile cores were stored separately in thirteen small hutches set into an earthwork mound (No. 8 on Fig 3.21). In Blue Danube the gauntlet containing the core was inserted during flight, but in later weapons it was probably installed in the stores area before they were issued for use. It was perhaps this change in handling procedure that prompted the construction of a fuzing shed (No. 7 on Fig 3.21) and other structures at Finningley around 1959.

The Faldingworth stores are unusual because they also functioned as the opera-

tional stores for RAF Scampton, and therefore had a similar range of assembly and test buildings as those found at Finningley. In the late 1950s a third type of nuclear weapon store, known as the supplementary storage area (SSA), was built on a number of V-force airfields. At Scampton, which lacked a nuclear weapons store, a free-standing SSA was built (Fig 3.23), but at other airfields such as Coningsby, Cottesmore and Wittering, SSAs were added to existing nuclear weapons stores.

The stores comprised individual chambers, 36ft (11m) × 18ft (5.5m), encased in an earthwork bank, with between twelve and twenty-four chambers on a single site. This massive increase in storage capacity reflects the increase in the number of British warheads, from thirty in 1960 to 310 by 1964, as well as novel handling procedures for new generations of weaponry. At a small number of airfields (Honington, Marham and Waddington) USAF-style 'igloos' were built to hold US nuclear weapons that were allocated to the RAF but guarded by US personnel; similar to facilities built for the USAF Strategic Air Command (see Chapter 4).

For more than thirty years the WE-177 and its variants (see The British nuclear deterrent pp 28–9) formed the RAF's principal nuclear weapons. Although far smaller than the earlier generation of weapons they required the same level of security and environmentally controlled storage conditions, and existing facilities were used where possible. During the 1980s, however, prompted by the need for airfields to be able to work under full nuclear, biological and chemical (NBC) conditions (see Chapter 4), vaults for WE-177s were placed in the floors of a number of hardened aircraft shelters (HASs) such as those of the Tornado squadrons at Marham. This innovation, which made it possible to winch the bombs up out of the vaults directly onto the aircraft, not only reduced reaction time but also removed the need for the hazardous journey from the bomb store to the aircraft. Bomb stores were not built entirely underground, mainly because building and maintaining underground bunkers is very expensive; the stores were also places of work, so there needed to be relatively easy access to the cores for routine checking. Perhaps naively it was not expected that bomb stores would be attacked, and the intention was to move the bombs to the airfields in times of tension. The next generation of bomb stores was placed in earthen mounds.

Figure 3.21 (below) RAF Finningley, South Yorkshire. Type B1 unit stores [redrawn from Air Ministry Drg No. H&V 8561B/54. Original material Crown copyright MoD]

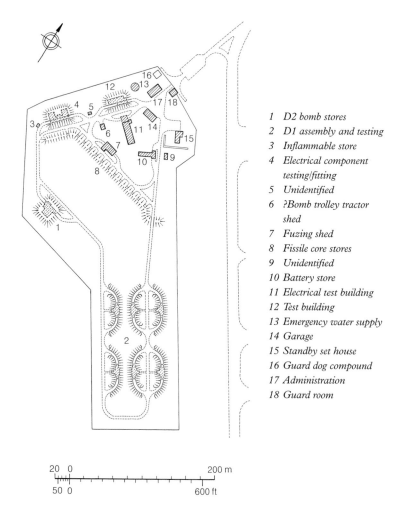

1 D2 bomb stores
2 D1 assembly and testing
3 Inflammable store
4 Electrical component testing/fitting
5 Unidentified
6 ?Bomb trolley tractor shed
7 Fuzing shed
8 Fissile core stores
9 Unidentified
10 Battery store
11 Electrical test building
12 Test building
13 Emergency water supply
14 Garage
15 Standby set house
16 Guard dog compound
17 Administration
18 Guard room

20 0   200 m
50 0   600 ft

Figure 3.22
RAF Finningley, South Yorkshire.
a: (left)
Type D1 mounded preparation building special weapons store [277H/33]

b: (below)
Type D2 special weapons store [redrawn from Air Ministry Drg No. H&V 8561B/54 24.12.54. Original material Crown copyright MoD]

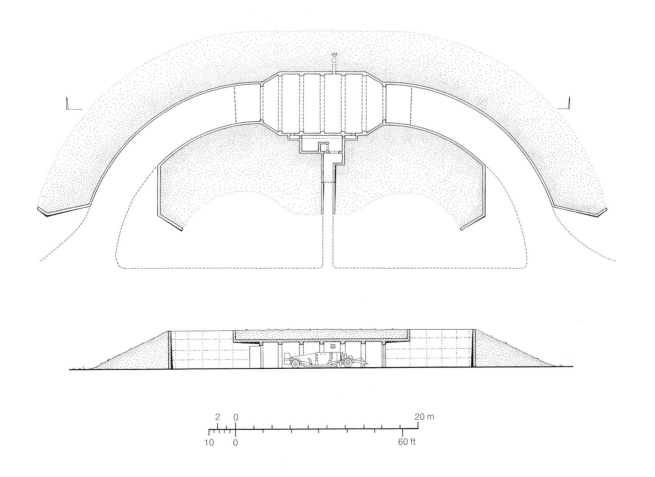

Figure 3.23
RAF Scampton,
Lincolnshire.
Supplementary storage area
[12854/28]

Figure 3.24 (below)
Thor missile No. 90 at
RAF Tuddenham, Suffolk.
Supporting the missile is its
road trailer. [AIR 27/2964
© PRO]

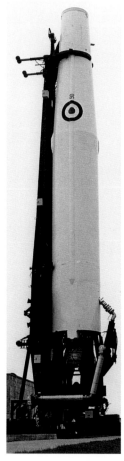

Thor intermediate-range ballistic missiles

Manned bombers were particularly vulnerable to attack and, inspired by the German V-2 rocket of the Second World War, East and West looked to rocket systems to deliver weapons of mass destruction. In 1954 the USAF made its intercontinental ballistic missile (ICBM) programme its top priority. In the following year it was realised that the Soviet Union would soon deploy an intermediate-range ballistic missile (IRBM) to threaten Europe and Japan, and renewed impetus was given to the United States IRBM programme as a stopgap until the ICBM was operational; one result of this was the USAF project named Thor (SM-75).

The first Thor test flight, in January 1957, ended prematurely in an explosion on the launch pad and it was not until September, after the fifth test flight, that the programme was judged successful. Almost immediately thereafter, US unease about the progress of the Soviet missile programme was confirmed by the successful launch of *Sputnik I*, and US President Eisenhower ordered the Thor programme into full production.

Thor was a rocket, powered by a mixture of liquid oxygen and rocket grade RP-1 (kerosene) (Fig 3.24). It stood 65ft (20m) tall and had a maximum diameter of 8ft (2.5m). Its flight path was controlled by an inertial guidance system that used linked gyro-compasses to detect changes in acceleration as a means of monitoring its precise location, and allowed adjustments to be made to its course. This allowed the weapon to deliver its W-49 (1.44 megaton) warhead to a maximum range of 1,500 miles (2,410km) with an accuracy of two miles (3.2km). Thor was deployed in Britain from 1959 to 1963, when most of the missiles were airlifted back to the USA. An original training version is on exhibition at the RAF Museum in Hendon, another has been recently obtained from the United States for the National Space Centre at Leicester and a third example is at the Cosford Aerospace Museum, Shropshire.

Deployment in Britain

If Thor missiles were to reach targets in the Soviet Union they had to be fired from somewhere in Europe or Japan, and a host country had to be found quickly. Britain was keen to accept the weapons as they would provide a ballistic missile system at least five years before the projected British 'Blue Streak' system and would also enable British forces to gain experience of handling strategic missiles. In February 1958 it was agreed that sixty Thor missiles would be deployed in Britain and that they would be divided between four main bases: at Feltwell in Norfolk, Hemswell in Lincolnshire, Driffield in the East Riding of Yorkshire and Dishforth in North Yorkshire. Sixteen subsidiary or 'satellite' bases were also identified, though they differed from those finally selected (Table 3.2 and Fig 3.25).

It was agreed that the United States would supply the missiles and all essential support equipment, while provision of bases and infrastructure was left to the British. The RAF manned the squadrons, but the warheads remained under United States control (Fig 3.26). The missiles would only be launched following the agreement of both governments, which was theoretically

Table 3.2 Deployment of Thor missile squadrons (main bases in bold) (*see also* Fig 3.25)

Site	Squadron No.	Arrived	Stood down
Feltwell	77	Sep 1958	Jul 1963
Mepal	113	Jul 1959	Jul 1963
North Pickenham	220	Jul 1959	Jul 1963
Shepherds Grove	82	Jul 1959	Jul 1963
Tuddenham	107	Sep 1959	Jul 1963
Hemswell	97	Jul 1959	May 1963
Caistor	269	Sep 1959	May 1963
Bardney	106	Jul 1959	May 1963
Ludford Magna	104	Jul 1959	May 1963
Coleby Grange	142	Sep 1959	Apr 1963
Driffield	98	Nov 1959	Jun 1963
Carnaby	150	Aug 1959	Apr 1963
Catfoss	226	Nov 1959	Jan 1963
Breighton	240	Aug 1959	Jan 1963
Full Sutton	102	Nov 1959	Apr 1963
North Luffenham	144	Feb 1960	Aug 1963
Folkingham	223	Feb 1960	Aug 1963
Polebrook	130	Dec 1959	Aug 1963
Harrington	218	Dec 1959	Aug 1963
Melton Mowbray	254	Dec 1959	Feb 1963

ensured by a dual key system involving British and United States officers sitting together with different launch keys. What was not mentioned publicly was that the agreement was to last for only five years.

In April 1958 it was confirmed that Feltwell would be the site of the first Thor squadron and the final selection of its satellite stations was listed. As the scheme (code-named 'Emily') developed it was also con-firmed that all the missiles were to be sited in eastern England, between Yorkshire and East Anglia. Generally, none were to be in the same place as the V-bombers, although at RAF Carnaby and RAF Breighton, both in the East Riding of Yorkshire, they were on the same sites as Bloodhound missiles, which were partly intended to protect the Thor missiles (Fig 3.27).

Thor missile sites

Hardly any Thor missile main bases survive intact as field monuments despite the fact that it is scarcely forty years since they were

Figure 3.25 (below left) Map showing distribution of Thor missile sites (see also Table 3.2)

Figure 3.26 (below) Thor missile squadrons were manned by the RAF but there were contemporary concerns, reflected in this cartoon, about who in fact controlled the missiles. [Sunday Express, 2 March 1958 © Copyright Sunday Express]

"There is a demand by the natives that missile bases should be manned by R.A.F. personnel. Very well . . ."
Sunday Express, March 2nd, 1958

built. Only at North Luffenham, Leicestershire, do all the structures or their footings remain. At Hemswell and Feltwell the main buildings survive, some converted to other uses, but Driffield has been entirely cleared. Despite extensive research on both sides of the Atlantic, no detailed technical drawings showing site layouts and structures within them have been found, but the physical layout of the sites can be recovered by archaeological fieldwork using such contemporary documents as are available.

The final selection of main stations – Feltwell, Hemswell, Driffield and North Luffenham – reused pre-war permanent airfields. These offered a reasonable standard of accommodation for personnel, and large hangars that could be adapted for missile servicing. At each site one existing hangar was designated a receipt, inspection and maintenance building (RIM) used for all the missiles in the complex. From the outside the hangar appears little altered, except that the original doors were welded shut and had smaller vehicle-sized openings cut through them. Inside, however, considerable alterations were made to create environmentally-controlled servicing bays for the missiles and support equipment (Fig 3.28). Around the walls single-storey, brick maintenance bays with false ceilings were constructed, those for handling more sensitive components (propulsion and propellant workshop, guidance laboratory and calibration laboratory)

Figure 3.27 (above) RAF Breighton, East Riding of Yorkshire. In the foreground are the remains of the Bloodhound missile site and to the rear the Thor missile emplacements. Also visible is the layout of the underlying Second World War airfield. [17142/14]

Figure. 3.28 (right) RAF Feltwell, Norfolk. Interior of RIM, showing modifications to the 1930s C-type hangar, including the insertion of compartmentalised servicing rooms. Mobile servicing equipment for the missiles was also stored in this building. [AA99/02003]

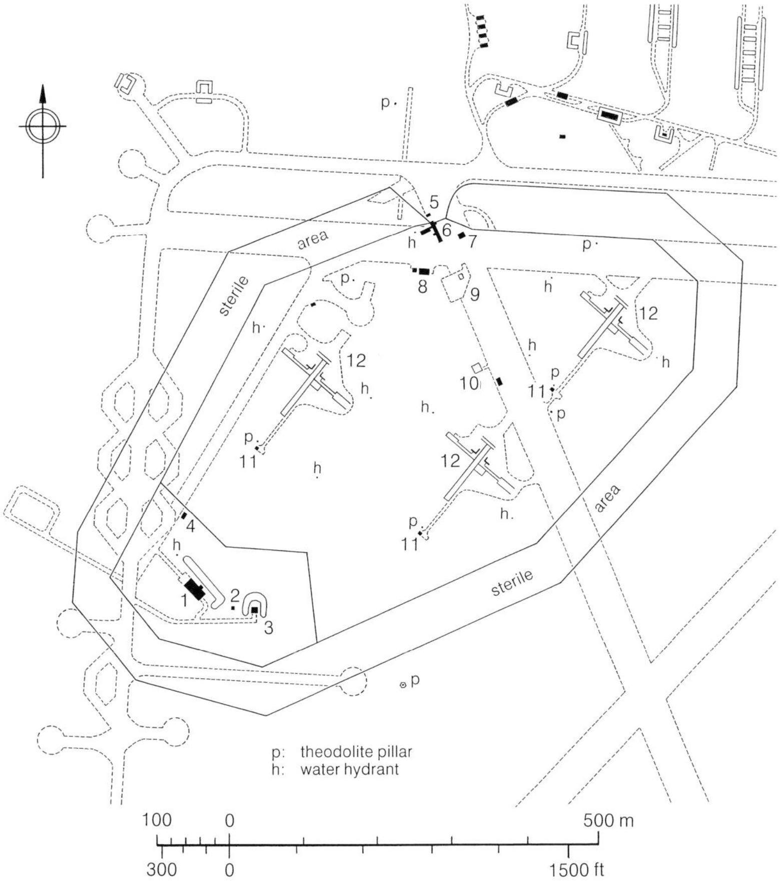

Figure 3.29
RAF Driffield, East Riding
of Yorkshire. Plan of Thor
main station emplacement
area [redrawn from PRO
AIR 27/2804]

1 *Surveillance and*
  inspection building
2 *Pyrotechnic store*
3 *Classified storage*
  building
4 *Picket post (USAF)*
5 *Police car shelter*
6 *Guard room (RAF)*
7 *Fire tender garage*
8 *Fuel tank and generator*
9 *Launch control area*
10 *Water tank*
11 *Long-range theodolite*
   buildings
12 *Launch emplacements*

p: theodolite pillar
h: water hydrant

having large air-conditioning pipes mounted on their roofs. The large open area in the hangar was used for servicing missiles and ground equipment, and above it a pair of runner beams were fixed to the roof to support lifting hoists. Large, flat, wall-mounted heaters were added, new lighting was installed and maintenance walkways were suspended from the roof trusses. The RIM building also contained the squadron's offices and a missile control centre which was permanently manned by an RAF missile controller and USAF authentication officer who had radio links to their respective headquarters. Adjacent to the RIM building was another hangar used as the technical storage building, while at Feltwell, which was the training school for Thor, a third hangar contained a launcher erector used for training.

Launch emplacements

On the opposite side of the airfield were three missile launch emplacements, which were common to all Thor sites. Next to them was a separate fenced enclosure entered through double gates with a small guard post, which was under the control of the USAF 99th Munitions Maintenance Squadron which had responsibility for the warheads. Within the compound were a surveillance and inspection (S and I) building and a classified storage building, each partly surrounded by earthwork traverses. The S and I buildings were steel-framed with windowless walls formed from Hy-rib wire mesh sprayed with concrete, and consisted of a one-bay working area with a hoist and doors at either end. Here the warheads were checked before issue and minor maintenance work was carried out. The classified storage building was a two-bay structure that may have been used to store warheads mounted on handling trollies.

The area occupied by the launch emplacements was almost identical at the main and satellite stations (Fig 3.29) though the latter were each provided with a one-bay classified storage building and a pyrotechnic store, usually placed at least 656ft (200m) from the centre of the nearest placement and shielded by E-, F- and T-shaped earthworks. The classified storage buildings are similar in construction to the S and I buildings. Surviving painted notices at Breighton state that the maximum amount of explosives permitted in the building was 800lb (363kg) and

Figure 3.30
RAF Mepal,
Cambridgeshire. Theodolite
pillar. To the rear are the
walls of one of three
emplacements.
[AA98/07841]

lay-by capable of holding both a missile on its trailer and its immediate support vehicles. There was also a single garage for a police vehicle and the whole area was well lit at night. Inside the gate was a standard Air Ministry prefabricated timber hut accommodating the guard and crew rooms, squadron office and telephone exchange. Opposite was a fire tender garage, though on many sites this was later made redundant by a mains fire-fighting system. Close to the main gate, but not less than 700ft (213m) away from a missile, was the launch control area (LCA) – an open area of concrete on which were placed the control trailer, a checkout trailer, four mobile generators and a 5,000 gallon (22,730 litre) oil tank.

that a two-man policy operated in the building – a stipulation which always ensured that no one would be left alone near a nuclear warhead. The pyrotechnic stores are small single-cell buildings with one doorway and were probably used to store rocket igniters; earthen banks separated them from the classified storage buildings.

The buildings and emplacements lay in an irregularly shaped compound surrounded by a pair of fences between which was a sterile area (Fig 3.29). Outside the main gate was a

The precise procedures for initiating a launch sequence are not available but the survival of fixed survey positions demonstrates the attention paid to the exact siting of the missiles so that their trajectories could be calculated. In addition to standard Ordnance Survey triangulation pillars there were other features peculiar to Thor sites, including long-range theodolites mounted on concrete pillars about 13ft (4m) tall (Fig 3.30) and set at a distance from the emplacements. Three pillars survive at Feltwell but elsewhere no

Figure 3.31
RAF North Luffenham,
Leicestershire. Survey plan
of Thor missile
emplacement No. 3

1 *Long-range theodolite building*
2 *Theodolite pillar*
3 *Shelter causeway*
4 *Shelter rails*
5 *Launcher erector mounting* (see Fig 3.33b)
6 *Blast wall*

7 *Short-range theodolite platform*
8 *Shelter door runners*
9 *Fuel catch pit*
10 *Liquid oxygen dump pit*
11 *Liquid oxygen tank catch pit*

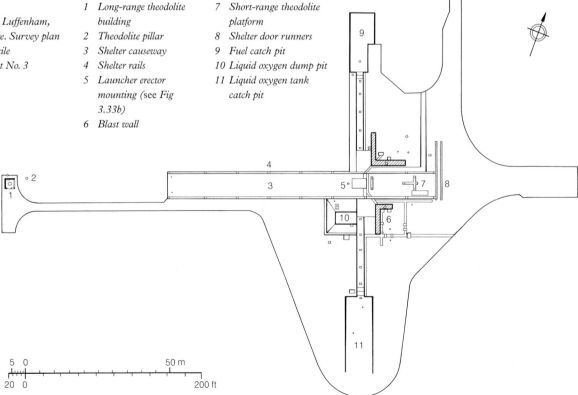

more than one has been found. Rusting bolts on top of the pillars suggest they were originally capped with a plate on which the instrument was mounted. Around the pillars brass survey studs were set into the ground at the four points of the compass and there was originally a light, metal framework on which the operators stood.

Each emplacement was also equipped with an array of survey positions (Figs 3.31 and 3.32). At one end was a brick theodolite house, though such structures rarely survive as more than foundations. In the centre of each theodolite house was a pillar for mounting a theodolite, and there were large openable windows though which the missile could be sighted; there was another theodolite pillar in front of the building, though again few remain. At the opposite end of the emplacement, beyond the blast walls, was a metal platform on which were mounted two short-range theodolites that were centred over brass studs set into the concrete beneath.

At the centre of each Thor emplacement was the launcher erector (Figs 3.33a–c), which was securely fixed to a metal cage set in concrete. Here missiles, which were usually stored horizontally on their trailers under retractable sheds, were raised to a vertical

position, still on their handling trailers. The kerosene and oxidiser, liquid oxygen (LOX), which fuelled the rocket, were kept apart at either end of the emplacement to prevent spontaneous combustion (Fig 3.33b). They were conveyed to the rocket along pipes suspended in concrete conduits. Sawn-off stainless steel fittings indicate the side of the pad used to handle the supercool liquid oxygen, which has a boiling point of -183 degrees centigrade. A LOX dump tank was provided close to the erector in case the fuel needed to be rapidly discharged from the missile. Other features found on the pads include open channels, originally covered by metal grilles, which carried cabling and pressurised gas pipelines from the support trailers, which in turn stood behind L-shaped blast walls in positions marked by painted lines. Truncated sections of hollow-section steel tubing set into the concrete show the locations of lamp standards (Fig 3.33c).

The relatively insubstantial and vulnerable nature of emplacements reflected the fact that the system was deployed as cheaply and rapidly as possible and was a one-shot system (no reloads). Planning also recognised that Thor was a stopgap, with an operational life of no more than about four years.

Figure 3.32
Reconstruction of Thor
missile emplacement

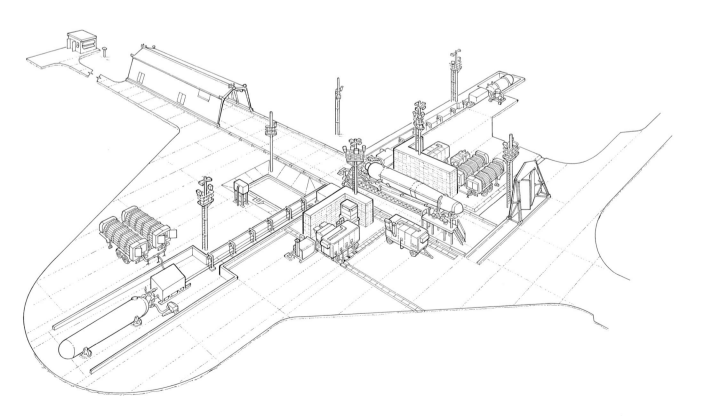

Figure 3.33
a: (above)
RAF Mepal,
Cambridgeshire. Remains
of launcher erector. Below
was a steel cage, known as
a grillage, set in concrete.
The fittings were supplied
direct from the United
States. [AA98/07832]

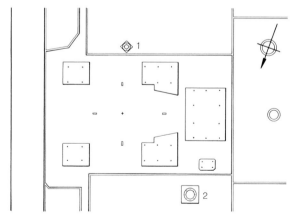

1   *Stainless steel liquid*
    oxygen pipe
2   *Steel kerosene pipe*

b: RAF North Luffenham,
Leicestershire. Thor missile
emplacement No. 3: detail
of launcher erector
mounting

c: RAF Tuddenham, Suffolk. Thor missile in its horizontal storage position with its protective shelter rolled back. In the foreground are trailers which housed a sub-station, electrical and air conditioning equipment. On the platform, next to the missile's nose, two short-range theodolites are visible, and in the background two missiles stand erect. [AIR 27/2964 © PRO]

Life on a Thor station

In addition to accommodating technical support the main stations also provided housing for the people who worked there, though other nearby airfields might also have been used. Housing needs could usually be met from existing buildings, although at Feltwell some new houses were built. Personnel stationed at subsidiary sites were transported from their accommodation by bus. The only member of staff in permanent residence was the commanding officer, who was normally provided with a detached house and garage some distance from the missile site (Fig 3.34).

Life on these often remote stations is documented in the operations record books for the squadrons, which are preserved at the

Figure 3.34
Tuddenham House, Cavenham, Suffolk. Commanding officer's house at RAF Tuddenham [B98/10460]

Public Record Office. Most months were routinely spent practising bringing the missile to readiness and counting down to launch. This monotony was broken by intrusions onto neighbouring sites to test their security, by periodic protests by peace campaigners and, more disturbingly, intelligence concerning possible attacks by militant Irish nationalists, the Irish Republican Army (IRA).

Between April and August 1963 Thor was phased out, having served its purpose, North Luffenham being the last site to be closed. The emplacements were quickly dismantled, salvageable items recovered and the remainder of the metal fittings removed as scrap, leaving the bare concrete remains we find today. The last operational Thor missile was airlifted from Britain on 27 September 1963. In the United States, however, Thor variants continued in use as research rockets and satellite launchers, and were later converted into anti-satellite weapons which remained in use until 1975.

The Thor emplacements also illustrate the global distribution of some Cold War structures. At Vandenburg Air Force Base, California, three emplacements survive which are laid out almost identically to those in the UK. They were originally constructed for training RAF crew in launch procedures. Similar facilities were later created on Johnston Island, in the South Pacific, to support the anti-satellite programme.

Proposed silo-based IRBM 'Blue Streak'

At the same time as the Thor missiles were being deployed, the independent British intermediate-range ballistic missile (IRBM) 'Blue Streak' was under development. The proposed deployment followed a similar pattern to that of Thor. Sites in eastern England were preferred (particularly those which were already owned by the Air Ministry) as the Home Office wanted to avoid the proliferation of nuclear target areas.

Various launch facilities were discussed, including a mobile system similar to that used by wartime V-2s and a proposal to launch missiles at sea, from either floating platforms or submerged silos. The scheme eventually adopted used an underground silo and, rather than have the missiles raised to the surface on a massive hydraulic lift, as were contemporary US Titan I missiles, it was decided to design a silo from which the missile could be 'hot launched' (Fig 3.35a).

The design of the silos posed severe challenges. Each was to be capable of withstanding a one-megaton explosion within half a mile (0.8km) and to be able to recover from a near miss within a day. Accordingly, the outer walls of the silo were to be 5ft (1.5m) thick reinforced-concrete, to protect against the effects of the electromagnetic pulse (EMP) released by a nuclear explosion, and were to be encased by ½in (13mm) of mild steel. The top was to be sealed by a massive, rail-mounted concrete lid weighing 400 tons (406 tonnes). Two of the most difficult problems were posed by the rush of hot gases (the efflux) from the missile when launched, and the simultaneous noise reverberation that could shake the missile to pieces. The first was overcome by incorporating in the silo a U-shaped shaft (Fig 3.35b), one end of which held the missile while the other allowed the efflux to escape, and noise reverberation was countered by an acoustic lining of diamond-shaped cones.

The interior of the silo was to be divided into seven levels – at the base were the fuel storage tanks, with plant rooms, small servicing bays and crew and control rooms above. This differed from later US practice of having the control post in a separate capsule away from the silo. It appears that an unmanned variant of the structure may have been considered, as a number of disused Rotor bunkers (see Chapter 5) were identified as possible launch centres.

The silos were to be placed in groups of five to ten, with central technical and domestic sites, and dispersed at about 6-mile (10km) intervals, as it was calculated that by this means only one silo in a group of six would be destroyed by a twenty-megaton warhead. As sixty Blue Streak missiles were proposed, silo construction would have been a massive engineering project and the last site would not have been operational until 1 July 1969, but the programme was abandoned almost immediately, in April 1960. Before that, however, trial boreholes had been drilled at Duxford, Cambridgeshire (conveniently close to the de Havilland factory at Stevenage), and elsewhere.

In addition, staff at the Rocket Propulsion Establishment at Westcott, Buckinghamshire, had by 1958 begun work on the design of the silo, a one-sixtieth model of which was built, together with a one-sixth scale mock-up of the launch shaft and efflux tube, for live firing tests (Fig 3.36). Internationally these trials were groundbreaking, and produced designs for the first

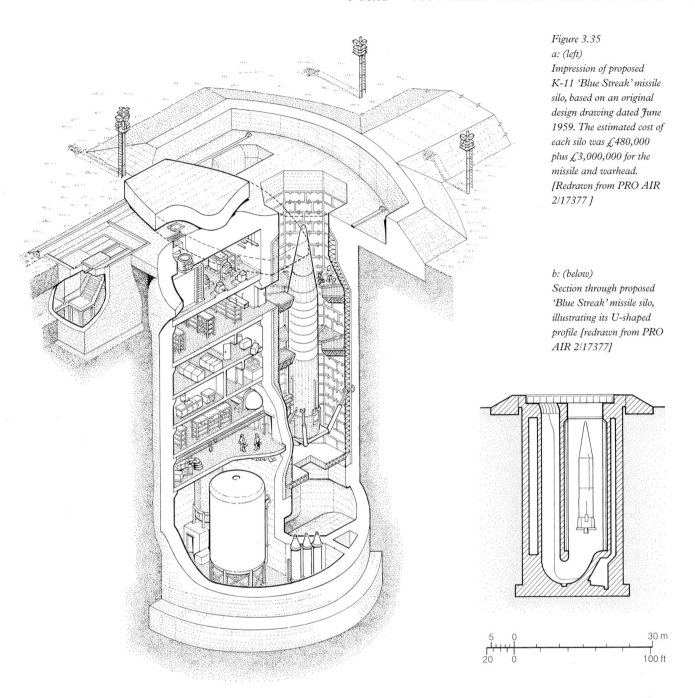

Figure 3.35
a: (left)
Impression of proposed K-11 'Blue Streak' missile silo, based on an original design drawing dated June 1959. The estimated cost of each silo was £480,000 plus £3,000,000 for the missile and warhead. [Redrawn from PRO AIR 2/17377]

b: (below)
Section through proposed 'Blue Streak' missile silo, illustrating its U-shaped profile [redrawn from PRO AIR 2/17377]

practical 'hot-launch' silo. Although never built in Britain, the design was adopted for the United States Titan II missile silo (*see* Fig 11.4).

'Blue Steel'

Even before the first British nuclear bombers were in service it was recognised that they would have a limited lifespan, as Soviet air defences were constantly being improved. As

early as 1954 the Air Ministry set up a study for the design of a 'stand-off' bomb that could be launched many miles from its target. The main contractor for this weapon, known as 'Blue Steel', was A V Roe of Woodford, Cheshire.

Blue Steel was a difficult weapon to handle and maintain, requiring specialised equipment and structures (Fig 3.37). It had its own inertial navigation system, automatic pilot, flight computer and electrical power

Figure 3.36
Westcott, Buckinghamshire.
Some of the surviving
fragments of the ⅙ scale silo
mock-up. To the rear is a
section of the efflux tube,
and in the foreground part
of the U-bend.
[BB99/04750]

Figure 3.37
RAF Museum, Hendon. A
'Blue Steel' missile loaded
on an AEC Mandator
transporter: note the lifting
beam used to move the
missile. Blue Steel was 35ft
(10.7m) long with a
maximum diameter of 4ft
2¼ in (1.28m) and had a
fuelled weight of 17,000lb
(7,711kg). Fifty-seven
rounds were ordered at an
estimated cost of
£21,200,000, but probably
no more than forty were
deployed. [MP 00087 ©
RAF Museum Hendon]

supply for heating and operating its control mechanisms – effectively it was a small aircraft. Storage and maintenance of the warhead took place in existing unit stores areas but additional special facilities were required for fuelling its rocket engine. As the time taken to fuel and arm the missile was between four and fifteen hours, and the thermal battery which powered the warhead took up to thirty minutes to insert, the credibility of the system as part of a quick reaction deterrent is questionable.

Blue Steel was deployed on only two V-bomber airfields, Scampton and Wittering, although in times of tension fully fuelled and armed weapons would have been flown to dispersal airfields. The missile entered service in autumn 1962 at Scampton and became fully operational during 1963 with, ultimately, a total of forty aircraft able to carry it.

Perhaps because of the urgent need to deploy Blue Steel, its servicing facilities at Scampton were nearly all built from prefabricated components. The main servicing and storage building (Fig 3.38a) was formed from two modified, prefabricated steel-framed 'T2-type' hangars of wartime design, linked by a flat-roofed, drive-through connection. Alterations to the standard T2 pattern include the use of aluminium cladding and the provision of two-storey office accommodation. In the central section of the building the missiles were lifted from transporters on to steel-framed stillages, or storage racks, by an overhead gantry crane. They could then be moved to the opposite side of the building, where photographic evidence shows engines being serviced. The hangar was equipped with enclosed electric safety lighting and large wall-mounted heaters, while its ceiling and walls were sealed with insulated panels to reduce heat loss and to help prevent dust getting in. The hangar was connected to the avionics building, which had been built a few years earlier and was also used for servicing, the work being conducted in self-contained workshops probably using free-standing test consoles. The darkrooms provide the only clear evidence for specific activities but the corridors in the various functional areas are painted in different colours.

Specially designed side-loading transporters (Fig 3.37) were used to move the missiles around the site, including taking them to the detached fuelling area. Apart from the kerosene tanks, this consisted of a steel-framed, aluminium-clad shed where the missiles were filled with the highly volatile fuel (Fig 3.38b). One side of the building forms a large space with concertina doors at either end, while the remainder of the structure is divided into ten bays, each of which could accommodate a missile. An earthenware drain runs round the interior to carry water used to sluice away spilt fuel to an external sump and filter. After fuelling, missiles were taken to a waiting bomb trolley before being moved to an aircraft.

Figure 3.38
RAF Scampton,
Lincolnshire.
a: At the bottom left is the
'Blue Steel' storage and
servicing building,
adjoining which is the
1950s avionics building. In
a separate compound is the
control tower and fire
station; at the top right is
the fuelling building (Fig
3.38b). [12869/48]

b: 'Blue Steel' fuelling
building and office
[AA99/06116]

Figure 3.39
RAF Wittering,
Peterborough UA.
a: Exterior of 'Blue Steel'
storage and servicing
building. Missiles were
transferred in the upper
annex from the airfield
transporters onto their
storage stillages and then
moved into the main
storage area. Beneath are
the garages for the
transporters.
[AA99/09838]

At Wittering there was more time to pre-pare for the deployment of Blue Steel. Here too, the new servicing and storage facilities were placed next to the existing avionics building. The new two-storey structure was far more elaborate than that at Scampton. Its lower level is divided into thirteen bays and was probably used to house handling equip-ment, including missile transporters and trolleys (Fig 3.39a). The missiles were stored and serviced on the upper level, which took the form of a steel-framed hangar. Handling procedures also differed from those at Scampton, as the missiles were transferred from airfield transporters on to the storage stillages by overhead cranes in a receiving bay, separated from the main servicing hangar by a sliding concertina door. The interior specification was generally as high as that at Scampton (Fig 3.39b). At other air-fields periodically visited by Blue Steel armed aircraft the only infrastructure put in place was a high test peroxide defuelling pit, used to dump this volatile chemical in an

b: 'Blue Steel' storage and
servicing building. Interior
of annex showing gantry
crane and entrance to main
storage area [AA99/09834]

emergency. High test peroxide, or hydrogen peroxide, acts as the oxidant for the rocket engine and is highly volatile.

Despite the heavy investment in ground facilities at Wittering, the Victor Blue Steel squadrons based there were disbanded in the last few months of 1968, as the Victors were not suitable for the low-level flying required to evade Soviet radar. Low-level flying also reduced the range of the missile to 25–50 miles (40–80km) which led in part, by December 1970, to the complete withdrawal of Blue Steel squadrons.

Polaris

As early as 1960 plans to commission an upgraded version of Blue Steel had been cancelled, on the understanding that the US Skybolt missile would be made available to the British. When the United States halted development of that system in late 1962 Britain was potentially left without a credible deterrent. As a result of negotiations between British Prime Minister Harold Macmillan

and US President John F Kennedy, however, the Polaris submarine-launched ballistic missile was secured, on the understanding that the missile would be supplied from the United States and the submarines and warheads would be designed and manufactured in Britain. As a result, the strategic 'quick reaction alert' passed from the RAF to the Royal Navy in 1969. The geography of the strategic deterrent moved to Scotland and was centred around a home port at Faslane and the armament depot at Coulport, both in Strathclyde, and the major refit yard at Rosyth, Fife, though there were some support facilities in England (Fig. 3.40).

Aspects of the close, though at sometimes strained, links between Britain and the United States in the deployment of nuclear weapons have been described in this chapter, including the construction of Thor missile sites and storage areas for US nuclear weapons allocated to British forces. The next chapter describes facilities built in England specifically for US forces, many of which were designed to hold nuclear weapons.

Figure 3.40
Chatham, Kent. The nuclear refuelling depot, including the 120-ton crane and 10-storey office block at the centre of the picture, was one of the few installations built in England to support the nuclear submarine fleet. Photographed at the time of its completion in June 1968, it has now been demolished. [G12455/13]

4
The United States 'umbrella'

The Cold War was marked by the superpowers' permanent stationing of large military forces in the countries of their alliance members. In the United Kingdom, units of the United States Air Force (USAF) dominated, while its army was heavily committed to West Germany. This large, sometimes contentious, presence of the USAF reflected both Britain's geographic strategic importance and the 'special relationship' between the two countries. What the USAF built was distinctive, and directly echoes shifting American and NATO strategy, as advancing technology determined how a conflict between the superpowers might be fought. And although the bases left impressive reminders on the post-war British landscape and building them cost millions of dollars, they were only one element of the global build-up aimed at providing the 'nuclear umbrella' under which the West was to be shielded.

Strategic Air Command

From the late 1940s, the United States began a policy of 'containment' to prevent the perceived worldwide threat of communism. In a pre-nuclear age such a policy would have meant huge commitments of manpower and conventional armaments. In the wake of the Korean War, and particularly after the election of US President Dwight D Eisenhower in 1952, the strategy was maintained but, under his 'New Look' policy, more emphasis was placed on the early use of nuclear weapons and massive retaliation should the Soviet Union threaten western interests. This strategy depended on advanced technology, but required less manpower. Aircraft of the USAF Strategic Air Command (SAC) were central to this policy and they needed bases close to the Soviet Union, since aircraft could not yet cover the distance there from the US. Britain had a stable and sympathetic government, and offered sufficient proximity to the USSR without the risk of being quickly overrun.

Discussions about the stationing of USAF bombers in Britain began in 1946 and soon after a number of aircraft passed through on training flights, although there was no permanent presence until the Berlin crisis of 1948. After temporary deployments at the Lincolnshire bases of Scampton and Waddington the USAF had, by 1950, three bomb groups – ninety aircraft – established at Sculthorpe and Marham, both in Norfolk, and at Lakenheath in Suffolk; all three had been redeveloped during the last months of the war to be designated very heavy bomber bases. Reconstruction had concentrated on providing new runways, perimeter tracks and hardstandings; at Lakenheath more than one million square yards of concrete, between ten and twelve inches deep, was laid. Few new structures were built except for the control towers (Fig 4.1).

As the divisions between East and West hardened, the United States realised that purpose-built airfields would be required. SAC was concerned about the vulnerability of its existing stations in eastern England, and began negotiations to establish its main bases further west, centred on Oxfordshire. Four airfields were selected: two – Brize Norton and Upper Heyford, Oxfordshire – were pre-war permanent airfields, while the other two, at Fairford, Gloucestershire, and

Figure 4.1
RAF Lakenheath, Suffolk. Very heavy bomber station, Type 294/45 control tower. Next to the tower were the fire party rest room, crash tender and ambulance garage and night-flying equipment store. To the right, to provide added protection, there are semi-movable blocks. [MF 98/00244/16A]

Greenham Common, West Berkshire, were temporary wartime constructions with limited infrastructure. It was estimated that it would cost between £2 and £2.5 million to rebuild each airfield.

The principal operational requirements for their long-range bombers was a main runway up to 10,000ft (3,048m) long and enough strengthened hardstandings to hold a bomb wing of forty-five aircraft. Such standings come in a variety of shapes, including truncated triangles, diamonds, 'spectacles' and characteristic circles, known as 'SAC bubbles', some created by infilling the 'eyes' of earlier spectacles (Fig 4.2).

A 'wing' was usually the largest organisational unit to occupy a single airfield. Administratively it was broken down into 'squadrons' some of which might be responsible for tasks other than flying, such as maintenance or security. Squadrons might, in turn, comprise a number of 'flights'. On some smaller airfields and installations a squadron might be the highest organisational unit.

While the runways and standings were being built, SAC units were sent on periodic deployments, in turn, to Bassingbourn, Cambridgeshire, and Mildenhall, Suffolk, and even when the main bases were complete, SAC units were still regularly deployed to Lakenheath, Mildenhall and Sculthorpe. In addition to these facilities, further dispersal fields were required, where reinforcements might be sent in times of tension. Because such fields were sometimes nothing more than a long runway and hardstandings they were called a basic operation platform (BOP). At RAF Elvington, North Yorkshire, a new 10,152ft (3,094m) runway and a massive 49-acre (19.8-hectare) rectangular concrete apron was laid (Fig 4.3a). The only new buildings were a combined headquarters building and crash tender shed (Fig

Figure 4.2
RAF Greenham Common, West Berkshire. A 9,000ft (2,743m) runway was built, with two 1,000ft (305m) overshoots, parallel taxiways and paved hardstandings, together with a new control tower, three hangars, and accommodation for 1,500 personnel. In the foreground is the site of the new 1950s munitions area, later incorporated into the 1980s cruise missile complex. [15691/03]

Figure 4.3
RAF Elvington, York.
a: SAC dispersal airfield.
The former technical area is
occupied by an aviation
museum.

b: (below)
Prefabricated crash tender
shed; a building typical of
many 1950s USAF bases.
[AA98/12474]

4.3b), an approach control room, a control tower (Fig 4.3c), a pump house, and fuel tanks that were supplied by a pipeline from Goole, East Riding of Yorkshire. No accommodation or munitions stores were provided, reflecting the role of Elvington as a forward operating base. Despite the exten-

sive works, however, the site was never occupied. Similar reconstruction was carried out at Chelveston, Northamptonshire, and at Bruntingthorpe, Leicestershire, which SAC occupied for a short time between 1959 and 1962.

From their home bases in the United States aircraft were deployed overseas on ninety-day rotations, and this is reflected in the infrastructure of the foreign airfields. Most heavy maintenance was undertaken in the United States, but aircraft might require routine or emergency attention while overseas. At many airfields the existing hangars were either inadequate or too small and a specific hangar type, known as a 'nose dock', was evolved; probably designed by the British Government's Ministry of Works for the USAF, along similar lines to a wartime hangar used to service Sunderland flying boats. The Ministry of Works, a wartime creation, was responsible for providing all types of accommodation for government departments and for allocating rationed building materials. As the name suggests, these nose dock structures sheltered the front section of an aircraft to make it possible to work on its

nose and engines under cover. In common with other hangars of the period, the group built at Upper Heyford (Fig 4.4a) are aluminium, whereas the pair at Alconbury, Cambridgeshire, are of a slightly different design and are steel-framed (Fig 4.4b). Others were built at Lakenheath, Mildenhall and Sculthorpe. Another distinctive hangar typical of this era – the Luria – was a steel-framed and steel-clad structure, 320ft × 160ft (97.5m × 48.8m), wide enough to house the B-47 Stratojet or KC-97 refuelling tanker. Two were built at Fairford and three at Greenham Common (Fig 4.4c). One of the latter was destroyed in an accident and replaced by a concrete-framed hangar, with a distinctive raised central ridge and a range of two-storey offices or workshops along one side (Fig 4.4d). A similar hangar was constructed at RAF Bruntingthorpe, Leicestershire, which was redeveloped for the USAF between 1957 and 1958. Other hangars and sheds on USAF airfields were produced by the Butler Manufacturing Company of Kansas City.

Standard British-designed brick control towers were erected (Fig 4.5) at the four main bases. These well-constructed buildings are the exception, however, as the symbolic might of SAC was expressed by its aircraft rather than through architecture.

c: (left)
Control tower
[AA98/12476]

Figure 4.4
a: RAF Upper Heyford,
Oxfordshire.
Aluminium nose docking
shed [AA98/12356]

Figure 4.4
b: RAF Alconbury,
Cambridgeshire. Steel-
framed nose docking sheds,
one with a SAC shield on
its gable. They were last
used as stores. [3020/18]

c: RAF Greenham
Common, West Berkshire.
Luria-type hangar
[BB94/19193]

d: This hangar at RAF
Greenham Common was
errected after its
predecessor was destroyed by
a B-47 jettisoning its
external fuel tanks in
February 1958.
[AA000541]

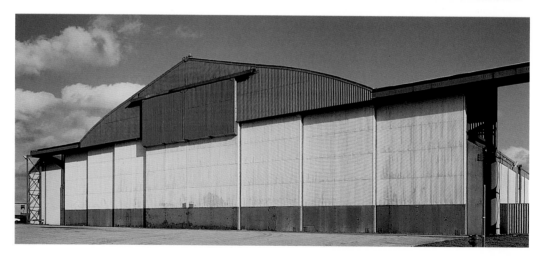

Militarily, it was imperative to make the bases operational as quickly as possible and utilitarian prefabricated structures were preferred; a variety of materials and construction methods were used, and many components came from the United States. At Chelveston and Elvington (Fig 4.3c) tall, open, steel-framed control towers were built, while at Alconbury the tower has a similar framework but is encased in pressed-steel sheeting. New fire stations, often placed close to the control tower as at Alconbury, Elvington (Fig 4.3b), Bentwaters and Shepherds Grove (both Suffolk), were constructed from long prefabricated concrete blocks 36in × 10in (900mm × 250mm) with

Figure 4.5 (above left)
RAF Greenham Common,
West Berkshire. Type
5222A/51 control tower.
Identical towers were
erected at all the SAC main
bases. [AA000524]

Figure 4.6 (above)
Boiler house of the 1950s
at Greenham Common,
showing the walls clad in
pressed-steel panels
[304H/33A]

Figure 4.7
RAF Greenham Common's
domestic area as
reconstructed during the
early 1950s. In the
foreground are the
distinctive rows of barrack
blocks for the SAC crew.
[15288/38]

a slight pinkish tinge. These blocks are found in other structures of the period, including the inspection building in the bomb store at Shepherds Grove. Elsewhere, steel-framed structures clad in pressed-steel sheets were used (Fig 4.6), or concrete walls cast on site with pitched roofs of corrugated metal or asbestos sheeting.

At first, domestic accommodation at the four main SAC bases was often rudimentary, limited to wartime Nissen huts, and there were hardly any recreational facilities. In 1955 the commander of SAC, General Curtis Le May, acknowledged that for his bombers to be fully effective he needed to look after the welfare of the crew. On the main bases in England the greatest need was for better barrack accommodation for the crew engaged on ninety-day tours (Fig 4.7). USAF barracks at this date set new standards in service accommodation, replacing large open dormitories with double bedrooms that afforded an unprecedented degree of privacy. In the mid-1950s conventional housing estates were built at a number of bases, including Lakenheath, Sculthorpe and Upper Heyford; constructed by the British government in exchange for American tobacco, they became known as 'tobacco houses' or 'surplus commodity houses', a total of 1,500 of which were built.

To speed up construction, four US Engineer Battalions carried out most of the work on the new SAC bases. Correspondence between the British Air Minister, Aidan Crawley, and the United States' ambassador sheds interesting light on the role of a military institution – the USAF – as a means of social transformation and on British attitudes in 1950. Crawley expressed concern both about the use of American labour and, in particular, the presence of 'coloured troops', at a time when the USAF was pursuing a policy of racial integration.

United States 3rd Air Force

From 1951, the command of USAF units in England was split between the 7th Air Division, which was responsible for units allocated to the SAC units, and the 3rd Air Force, which controlled units committed to a tactical role in Europe. The airfields allocated to the 3rd Air Force were mainly temporary wartime ones, many of which had been abandoned in 1945. The aircraft operated by the 3rd Air Force were smaller than those of the SAC, generally fighter-bombers used to defend the SAC bases, provide

escorts, or attack tactical targets in Europe. Like the deployments of SAC, those of the 3rd Air Force operated from a small group of key airfields – Manston in Kent, Bentwaters (see Fig 4.13), Shepherds Grove and Woodbridge (Fig 4.8), all in Suffolk, and Wethersfield in Essex. Most required considerable work before modern jet aircraft could be introduced, the minimum usually being provision of new runways at least 8,000ft (2,438m) long, bulk fuel handling facilities and accommodation. Where possible existing structures were reused, the wartime control towers at Bentwaters and Woodbridge being retained and extended. Surviving T2 hangars might be reused or brought from elsewhere, although at Bentwaters small hangars of corrugated sheeting, just large enough to house a single fighter, were built. At some airfields, such as Wethersfield, existing wartime spectacle-shaped hardstandings were also reused. At Woodbridge, however, the need to hold a fighter wing consisting of seventy-five aircraft led to the laying of new Y-shaped hardstandings. Reserve fields were also identified and at Carnaby, East Riding of Yorkshire, work started on building hardstandings for a complete fighter wing, but was stopped before the scheme was completed.

USAF activity has been identified on around thirty airfields in England during the 1950s, but with very varied levels of intensity. The USAF also operated a major supply base at Burtonwood, Cheshire, large munitions stores at Welford, West Berkshire (Fig 4.9) and at Framlingham, Suffolk, as well as having food depots, hospitals, communications and intelligence gathering centres (see pp 14–18), and a variety of other facilities (see Chapter 6).

Munitions storage areas

The first type of atomic bombs carried in Britain by USAF aircraft were of the 'Fat Man' type, and were similar to the bomb dropped on Nagasaki. No facilities associated with these weapons, either assembly sheds or bomb loading pits, have been identified by fieldwork, even though from the early 1950s special weapons stores (Fig 4.10a) were provided at all the SAC main and 3rd Air Force bases where nuclear weapons might be deployed. They were surrounded by a single or double perimeter fence, overlooked by distinctive octagonal guard towers – examples of which survive at Alconbury (Fig 4.10b), Shepherds Grove

Figure 4.8
RAF Woodbridge, Suffolk.
An example of a wartime
crash airfield modernised in
the later 1950s. This view
shows the single runway,
Y-shaped hardstandings
and, towards the bottom,
the detached igloo group.
[Sortie 231/4236, frame
149, 23 Jul 1963, V2 ©
Crown copyright MoD]

Figure 4.9
RAF Welford, West
Berkshire. Ammunition
store for the USAF laid out
over a wartime airfield.
[Photo by Aldon P
Ferguson]

was through a pair of sliding, blast-proof, steel doors, often shielded by a detached concrete and earth revetment on the opposite side of the access road. Internally the igloos were featureless except for a large lifting hook set in the ceiling, safety lighting and heating, and all were earthed against lightning strike. They offered flexible storage spaces and could easily accommodate SAC's largest weapon, the Mark-17 hydrogen bomb which measured 24ft 9$\frac{1}{2}$in (7.6m) in length.

Within each group, one igloo usually contained an internal reinforced-concrete vault, with a safe-like door. The vault may have been intended to house separate capsules that contained the fission elements of many 1950s United States atomic weapons, which were inserted into the weapon only in time of war. At Upper Heyford, an apparently unique capsule store was built – a double-storey reinforced-concrete structure with blind metal-framed windows designed to give the impression of an insignificant structure. Some SAC secondary or dispersal fields, such as Chelveston, were provided with igloos, but they were not a universal feature.

At Upper Heyford there were at first twenty-seven igloos – more were later added – and there were fuzing sheds normally associated with conventional bombs. Other airfields also have large igloo groups, which were probably designed to hold war reserve stocks or to be activated in times of tension, although their peacetime role might suggest little need for a special weapons store (such as Alconbury or Lakenheath), or only a limited need (such as Bentwaters). At the fighter bases of Shepherds Grove, Wethersfield and Woodbridge smaller groups of four igloos were built, and there were also four at

and Upper Heyford – and access was through a single gateway controlled by a security post. The stores vary in size and complexity, with some groups providing extra capacity for war reserves, as well as the immediate needs of the home base.

At the main base of Greenham Common (*see* Figs 4.2 and 4.22a) the munitions store consisted of five bomb storage magazines, an isolation magazine, a semi-sunken maintenance and inspection building, workshops and offices. Similar provision was made at Upper Heyford (Fig 4.10a). The magazines, commonly known as 'igloos', comprised a rectangular reinforced-concrete box, 80ft × 22ft (24.4m × 6.7m), covered in earth. Entry

Molesworth, Cambridgeshire (*see* Fig 4.27), which was primarily a transport base.

What the USAF termed 'surveillance and inspection' of the weapons was usually carried out in a double igloo unit, often set away from the main group (*see* Figs 4.10a and 4.22a). At a number of airfields, and perhaps representing a second phase of activity, single igloo units were constructed: those at Alconbury contained six cells and those at Bentwaters eight, while at Upper Heyford two units were built, one with eight cells and the other with thirteen. A variety of other buildings are also found in the munitions store areas including, at Bentwaters, a large, mounded, double-storey inspection building with heavy lifting cranes. Smaller inspection buildings, stores and security posts complete most storage areas.

Igloo-type stores are also found on several RAF airfields, including Honington, Marham, Waddington and Wittering. Some were built to hold US nuclear weapons allocated to the RAF, and might also have acted as reserve stores for the USAF.

'Reflex alert' and draw down

By 1958, policy changes, the prospect of new delivery systems (including the long range B-52 Stratofortress), the introduction of Thor and Jupiter missiles (*see* Chapter 3), the entry into service of the RAF's nuclear armed V-force, and the decreasing threat of a pre-emptive attack, resulted in Strategic Air Command's presence being gradually scaled down. Under a scheme known as 'reflex alert' far fewer USAF aircraft were stationed overseas, but those that were had to be kept at a higher state of readiness (Fig 4.11). These changes effectively ended the first major phase of United States Cold War building activity in the United Kingdom.

The early 1960s saw further reductions as the first intercontinental ballistic missiles became operational, and overseas base closures were announced under President Kennedy's economy drive. SAC bombers on 'reflex alert' made their final regular visits to Britain in 1965. The overall reduction in

Figure 4.11
RAF Greenham Common, West Berkshire. This view shows the distinctive shapes of the hardstandings laid during the late 1950s to hold bombers while on 'reflex alert'. Taken in June 1962, this photograph shows a squadron of B-47 Stratojets preparing to take off. [58/5225 F22, frame 0062 © Crown copyright MoD]

numbers was, however, less marked, as in 1966 France withdrew from NATO and a number of units which had been in France were reallocated to vacant or underused bases in Britain. This did not lead to much new building work, although new munitions lockers were built at the recently closed explosives factory at Caerwent, Monmouthshire. A number of RAF airfields were also identified as 'co-located operating bases' (shared by USAF and the host nation) for use in time of war, though dedicated infrastructure at these bases was usually restricted to stores for pre-positioned war materials and fuel.

New strategy, new threats

The 1960s also saw a shift in US, and later NATO, policy away from the suicidal strategy of Mutually Assured Destruction (MAD) to one of 'flexible response', whereby any Soviet expansion or aggression would be met with a graduated retaliation. One element in this strategy was the basing of sophisticated 'swept wing' F-111E bombers at RAF Upper Heyford in 1970. These aircraft, with terrain-following radar and electronic surveillance systems, had a 24-hour, all-weather flying capability. Their primary role was to carry NATO's intermediate-range nuclear weapons, and throughout the 1970s they represented one of the key assets of the NATO the alliance.

Construction work to accept this new

fighter was at first modest. To maintain their deterrent effect, these aircraft needed to be ready for immediate take-off. A 'quick reaction alert' area was established, comprising nine weather shelters, brick crew quarters, and a steel Brunswick watchtower (*see* Fig 4.17f). Because the aircraft were permanently armed, the whole area was regarded as a nuclear weapons storage facility and was protected by a double security fence with guard posts. The aircraft shelters (Fig 4.12) are open ended; they are formed from four trusses spaced at 20ft (6m) intervals, with a span of 79ft 4in (24.2m), the roof and side walls being clad in corrugated asbestos. At the rear are blast deflectors to draw away the efflux from the jet engines. The shelters offered little more than protection against the weather, although they were originally provided with earth traverses. Nearly identical structures are found at the other F-111 base at Lakenheath and similar structures were built at Bentwaters, Wethersfield and Woodbridge in the late 1950s, though they were smaller and had gambrel roofs: with two slopes on either side, the lower slope being steeper than the upper. Each of those bases had eight shelters: at Woodbridge they were built in two groups of four, while at the other two airfields they were arranged in a single group and had associated crew quarters (*see* Figs 4.8 and 4.13). All were enclosed by fences, which suggests they were reserved for armed aircraft.

Figure 4.12
RAF Upper Heyford,
Oxfordshire. Early 1970s
'quick reaction alert' area,
showing an F-111 weather
shelter with a jet efflux
deflector to the rear
[MF98/00246/1A]

Hardened airfields

Little new building work appears to have taken place in the late 1960s and early 1970s, as USAF's attention had been focused elsewhere during the Vietnam War and relations between the superpowers had improved. Israel's audacious pre-emptive attack on the airforces of her Arab neighbours during the 1967 Six-Day War had, nevertheless, highlighted the vulnerability of aircraft parked either in the open or unprotected shelters. From the early 1970s, under the European Defence Improvement Programme, NATO adopted a policy of providing protected structures for its frontline squadrons and their essential facilities – a

critical factor under the flexible response strategy – to ensure that sufficient forces could survive a pre-emptive attack to strike back. This marked the beginning of the largest airfield refurbishment programme since the 1950s.

Activity was concentrated on existing USAF bases, but became more intense. NATO was also concerned about the increase in the numbers of forces in eastern Europe, and USAF in Europe (USAFE) was strengthened by the deployment of specialised aircraft types. To meet the threat of Warsaw Pact armoured spearheads, Fairchild A-10 Thunderbolts, specifically designed to operate at low level to destroy armoured vehicles, were stationed at

Figure 4.13
RAF Bentwaters, Suffolk. This site was hardened in the late 1970s and early 1980s to accept A-10 Thunderbolts. To the right are the early 1950s munitions igloos and behind them eight weather shelters, to the rear of which are the hardened squadron facilities. On the left hand side of the airfield is the technical area and to its right the domestic site.
[12647/46]

Bentwaters (Fig 4.13) and at its neighbour at Woodbridge, in 1979, though in wartime they would have moved to forward operating locations in West Germany.

NATO funds were at first directed at hardening essential frontline bases in West Germany. The first airfields in the United Kingdom to be provided with hardened facilities were those of the USAF, where the United States was able to fund the work. Construction started in 1977 at Bentwaters, Lakenheath and Woodbridge, and three years later at Upper Heyford and Alconbury, and the co-located operating base at the Royal Aircraft Establishment, RAE Boscombe Down, Wiltshire.

Hardened Aircraft Shelters (HASs) are the most distinctive structure built during this period, and around 300 were constructed on airfields in England. They were usually built on the opposite side of an airfield to the technical and domestic accommodation and were generally arranged in squadron groups of between eight and thirteen shelters (Fig 4.14). New taxiways and hardstandings were also usually required to link the shelters to the runway.

The first generation of HASs built in

West Germany were known as theatre air base vulnerability (TAB-V) shelters, originally designed to house the McDonnell Douglas F-4 Phantom. Each was designed to withstand a direct hit from a 500lb (226kg) bomb, or a near miss from a larger one. They are mostly semi-circular structures with a floor width of 48ft (14.6m) and an overall internal length of 100ft (30.7m), and were built of corrugated-steel supporting a reinforced-concrete skin. The rear wall was blank, while the open front was closed by a pair of recessed doors that swung inwards against the side walls. This arrangement was later modified by remounting the doors to open outwards, to accept the F-15 fighter.

All the shelters built in the United Kingdom, whether on USAF or RAF bases, are of standard NATO designs, of which there are three types. The first (Fig 4.15a) is 124ft (37.8m) long, with a floor width of 82ft (25m), and is 33ft (10m) tall; it is more substantially built than the earlier continental designs. The most distinctive feature of this type is the pair of reinforced-concrete panel doors, each weighing about 85 tons (83.5 tonnes) supported on a framework of steel girders that was designed to transfer an equal weight to each of the rail-mounted runners. Other distinguishing features are the ten U-shaped tubular vents along the roof ridge, a blast-proof personnel entrance in the left-hand side and a simple concrete jet blast (efflux) deflector projecting from the centre of the rear wall. The second type has a smaller floor area, 120ft × 71ft (36.6m × 21.6m), and a pair of wing-like upward pointing jet blast deflectors (Fig 4.15b); examples have been recorded at Boscombe Down, Lakenheath and Upper Heyford. Most shelters were allocated to an individual aircraft, the details of which, along with the name of the chief of the dedicated maintenance crew, was often displayed on one of the doorframes. The third type (Fig 4.15c), found on most RAF airfields including Coningsby, Honington, Marham and Wattisham, has integral ground equipment annexes (GEA) and a different design of efflux deflector. In the late 1980s, as part of a NATO programme, a number of HASs at Lakenheath and Marham were modified by the installation of nuclear weapons vaults, thus rendering the old storage areas obsolete. An apparently unique HAS variant was built at Alconbury in the mid-1980s, where thirteen extra-wide HASs were constructed to house U2 or TR1 reconnaissance aircraft (Fig 4.16, see also p17).

Figure 4.14
RAF Upper Heyford, Oxfordshire. 'Quick reaction alert' area. This self-contained complex of hardened aircraft shelters is surrounded by a double fence and has its own entry control point and squadron headquarters. Aircraft from this unit would have been amongst the first to respond any Warsaw Pact attack. [18537/18]

Figure 4.15
RAF Honington, Suffolk.
a: (above)
Hardened aircraft shelter
with ground equipment
annexe [G26415/3]

b: (left)
Standard efflux deflector
[AA98/12346]

c: Wing-like jet efflux
deflector [AA98/12349]

*Figure 4.16
RAF Alconbury,
Cambridgeshire. In the
foreground and to the right
is the group of extra-wide
HASs built for the TR1.
Beyond, the smaller
standard NATO HASs are
visible. [15779/05]*

To maintain the offensive capability of an airfield it was seen as essential to provide protected accommodation for other structures. One example was the handling and storage of fuel, which was delivered to the airfields through underground pipelines and often stored in vast tanks. At Greenham Common there were eight underground 1,000,000-gallon (4,546,000-litre) tanks. From these the fuel was moved to the waiting aircraft by bowsers and on a number of bases, including Alconbury and Bentwaters, hardened fuel tanker shelters were placed close to the aircraft standings. Each USAF squadron had a hardened headquarters building, which might be attached to a conventional unhardened office built for peacetime use or might be a detached structure. The filtered environment of the building, with its decontamination rooms, was intended to provide a sanctuary for the crew to rest, eat and change, as well as to receive their mission instructions. Many were carpeted throughout. Similar hardened structures are found on RAF airfields, where they are known as personnel briefing facilities.

Other hardened structures reflected the specific function and aircraft types allocated to a given base. At Upper Heyford and

Lakenheath large avionics buildings (Fig 4.17a) were built to maintain the complex electronics of the F-111s and to process reconnaissance data. They housed life support systems, decontamination rooms, electronics workshops and photographic darkrooms, and had equipment storage and handling areas. The critical importance placed on the global surveillance data gathered by the TR1 reconnaissance flights from Alconbury was expressed by the construction, during the late 1980s, of a massive avionics and reconnaissance interpretation centre. It is a semi-sunken two-storey structure, with a 'drive through' roadway incorporating

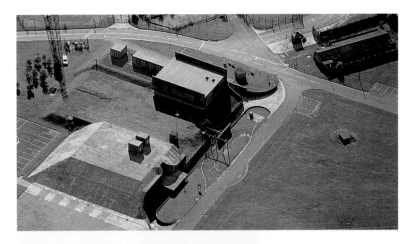

Figure 4.17
a: (above)
RAF Upper Heyford, Oxfordshire. Two-phase hardened avionics centre. The extension was primarily used to process and analyse photographic reconnaissance data. [18518/20]

b: (left)
RAF Alconbury, Cambridgeshire. Compressed air bottles on the lower floor of the TR1 avionics building; they were used to re-establish the overpressure in the building when the outer doors were opened. [AA023791]

c: (below)
Entry area of the hardened airfield battle command headquarters at RAF Upper Heyford. Beneath the roof vents is the plant room. [MF98/00246/2A]

a vehicle or trailer decontamination point, protected internally by a very substantial 'portcullis' type blast door supported on a hydraulic release mechanism. Beyond were large rooms filled with computers used to download and analyse data. Personnel had to repeatedly venture out to retrieve the reconnaissance pods – and the raw data they contained – from the aircraft, and evidence of this activity is the extensive suite of stainless steel decontamination rooms by the main

Figure 4.17
d: (above)
RAF Upper Heyford,
Oxfordshire. Main
operations room of the
hardened airfield battle
command headquarters
[AA98/12396]

e: (right)
Hardened
telecommunications
exchange
[MF98/00246/5A]

f: RAF Alconbury,
Cambridgeshire. Bomb
stores, showing a typical
entry control post. To the
rear is a Brunswick steel
observation tower.
[302K/15]

entrance. If the bunker had to be used after a nuclear or chemical attack, air pressure inside it would be maintained at a higher level than outside, to prevent the entry of poisonous gases or radioactive contamination. Each time the doors were opened the positive pressure in the outer sections of the building would be lost, but it could be rapidly re-established using large compressed air cylinders located in the basement (Fig 4.17b). In England, this feature is apparently peculiar to this structure The toilets indicate mixed male and female units, in distinct contrast to contemporary Warsaw Pact frontline facilities that were male only. On many airfields the munitions storage areas were enlarged, and the new igloos at Sculthorpe and Upper Heyford were virtually identical to their 1950s counterparts.

All activities on an airfield could be overseen from a hardened battle headquarters (Fig 4.17c). Like the squadron headquarters it was designed to be self-sufficient and contained generating plant and air filters, while entry into the building was through a suite of decontamination rooms. Raised floors and suspended ceilings were used nearly throughout to accommodate cabling and air conditioning ducts. At the centre lay the main operations room (Fig 4.17d) from where the air campaign could be directed, while other groups co-ordinated airfield defence. At Upper Heyford a room was given over to the command of the local RAF Rapier missile units. The importance of maintaining communications is reflected by the provision nearby of a hardened telephone exchange (Fig 4.17e). The exterior surfaces of most of these new facilities were treated with a dull brown chemical wash – 'Novolant' – designed to tone down their appearance from the air. At some airfields, including Lakenheath and Honington, the hardened aircraft shelters were either placed in existing woodland or surrounded with blocks of evergreen trees to further conceal their position from low-flying attackers.

Installations were also at threat from the ground, either from terrorists or from Soviet special or 'Spetnaz' forces. To counter such risks munitions storage areas, already protected by multiple fences, were provided with hardened entry control posts (Fig 4.17f) with an open fighting position on their roofs. Within the compound there might be a hardened reserve fire team facility, its walls loop-holed for close defence, and with a single or double integral garage. Pillboxes – small, partly underground concrete structures used as outposts – which had been removed after the Second World War also reappeared around airfield perimeters. The most common examples associated with USAF facilities, including Bentwaters and Lakenheath, are square in plan and are formed from prefabricated concrete panels. A novel feature in their design is a sump into which a grenade might be quickly kicked (Fig 4.18). At Woodbridge, a type similar to the British Yarnold sanger of the same era (see Fig 2.3) was constructed from circular pipe sections, but its roof was supported on six brick piers. Cruder fighting positions were also built out of timber, pressed-steel sheets and earth. Semi-movable concrete blocks are also found on some sites. They could be used to create roadblocks or, as at Lakenheath, might be placed around a building to provide added protection (see Fig 4.1); some were also stored for temporary runway repairs. Further protection was also provided by traverses formed from pressed-steel sheets filled with earth – similar to 19th-century 'Chilworth mounds' employed in some explosives factories. They were supplemented by lines of razor wire and by movement detectors, neither of which usually survives or leaves any physical trace.

During the 1970s NATO planners became increasingly worried about the growing offensive biological and chemical capabilities of the Warsaw Pact, which might be used to put key installations out of action, or make their functioning very difficult, through contamination. At Greenham Common this concern is illustrated by the wing headquarters (Fig 4.19a) which, although

not sufficiently hardened to withstand a conventional or nuclear attack, could be sealed against the local environment and was provided with a very large stainless steel decontamination suite (Fig 4.19b). Decontamination facilities for radioactive contamination are very similar, and might include external showers and internally segregated changing and shower rooms. Aircraft might also be contaminated either on the ground or during combat, and from the late 1970s wash-down or decontamination facilities were installed next to the main runway at a number of bases, including Alconbury and Bentwaters (Fig 4.19c). Such facilities comprise new hardstandings and a long earth-filled barrier approximately 6ft 6in (2m) tall on which subdued lighting was mounted. Water and chemicals to neutralise the contaminants appear to have been provided by mobile tankers.

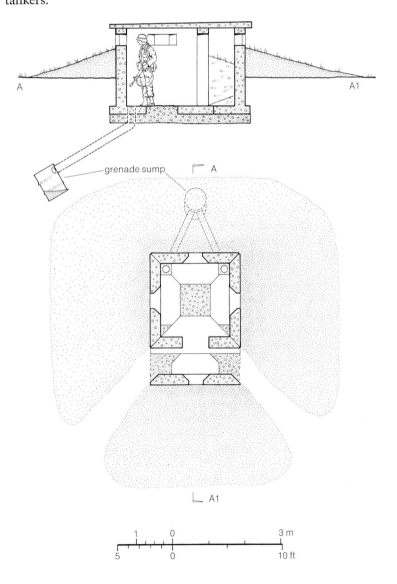

Figure 4.18
Defensive fighting position. Set into two of the corners are sumps where grenades could be quickly kicked. [Redrawn from DEX Sheet 2 of 6 8/11/86. Original material Crown copyright MoD]

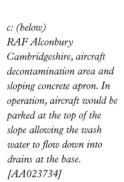

Little Americas

For over half a century the USAF bases have formed distinctive self-contained communities (Fig 4.20a). They have been called 'little Americas' and this is the impression they give, with a local dollar economy, the preponderance of American accents, cars, street names, fire hydrants, volleyball and baseball courts (Fig 4.20b). All are characterised by buildings of many different dates, including many 'temporary' wartime structures, often refurbished to a very high standard. By the 1980s, the local works services units designed the majority of buildings on bases in Britain. Buildings erected were usually of a higher quality than in earlier generations, suggesting they were there to stay. They were generally brick built, some using different coloured bricks for decorative effect, double-glazed and roofed with Eternite (asbestos cement) slates or tiles; most were single or double storeyed, although a few accommo-

Figure 4.20
a: RAF Lakenheath, Suffolk. Peace Garden, which acts as a focus for ceremonies and memorials to honour USAF personnel who lost their lives maintaining the peace during the Cold War and other conflicts. [MF98/00244/31A]

b: (below)
Baseball court at RAF Lakenheath. With the provision of social clubs and sports facilities many personnel rarely left the base area. [AA98/12323]

c: (bottom)
RAF Alconbury, Cambridgeshire. During the 1980s franchised fast food outlets such as Burger King began to offer a variety of food and recreational activities to service personnel. [GCN 29783/15]

dation blocks and mission support centres rise to three storeys. Architecturally they are low-key and undistinguished, although hipped gabled roofs were common features in the 1980s. Internal furnishings were often lavish, and included wainscot wooden panelling in senior officers' rooms and, in most cases, full carpeting. More emphasis was also given to improving the living conditions on the bases, which was reflected in new barracks, housing, shopping, fast-food outlets (Fig 4.20c), social and sports facilities. At Lakenheath (Fig 4.20d) and Greenham Common (Fig 4.21a) new 'commissaries' were built: they are wide-span steel structures with numerous shopping aisles, and are indistinguishable from any contemporary American mall.

Utilitarian buildings were typically steel-framed and clad in pressed-steel sheeting, or were constructed from breeze-blocks. As discussed above, most hardened facilities were finished in a dull brown wash, but on many bases support structures were, by the 1980s, painted cream or chocolate brown with a contrasting 'jazzy' trim (Fig 4.21b); similar schemes were also carried through to the interiors.

Figure 4.20
d: (opposite)
RAF Lakenheath, Suffolk.
A feature of United States
bases was the PX and
commissary store selling US
goods to the servicemen and
their families, who paid in
dollars. [AA98/12306]

Figure 4.21
a: (left)
RAF Alconbury,
Cambridgeshire.
Interior of commissary in
1989. Originally set up to
prevent hyperinflation in
local economies still subject
to rationing, they later
offered the comfort of a full
range of familiar imported
brands to service families.
[G29978/9]

b: Typical anonymous
1980s pressed-steel covered
support building at RAF
Alconbury, painted in
brown with a cream
coloured 'jazzy' trim. This
finish was applied to make
buildings look less obviously
military. [AA023757]

Combat art

During the Second World War, distinctive unit emblems and cartoons applied to aircraft, uniforms and buildings became part of United States Air Force culture. During the mid-1980s, officially endorsed nose art reappeared on many of the aircraft of the USAFE, intended as a means of reinforcing unit cohesion and boosting morale. Wall art in the same vein also became a common feature of many installations. Most reflected the activities of the unit, but the street-gangster style of the imagery used by many played directly into the hands of the Warsaw Pact which wished to portray NATO as an aggressive, adventurist alliance. In the 1990s, this kind of art was no longer formally sanctioned, and it has virtually disappeared from active bases.

Below: RAF Upper Heyford, Oxfordshire. EF-111A 'Raven' avionics electronics maintenance unit [MF/00246/17A18]

Above: RAF Bentwaters, Suffolk. Fairchild A-10 Thunderbolt, nicknamed the 'Warthog': painting on the door of an ammunition inspection building [AA021678]

Right: Artwork from the photograph processing area at RAF Upper Heyford, Oxfordshire. [MF98/00246/19A20]

Above: 527th Aggressor Squadron 'Bears' motif applied to hardened aircraft shelter door at RAF Bentwaters, Suffolk. This squadron operated according to Warsaw Pact tactics to provide training opponents for NATO forces [AA021675]

Above: RAF Bentwaters, Suffolk. Warthog inspecting ammunition [AA021680]

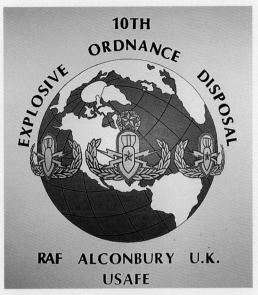

Above: RAF Alconbury, Cambridgeshire. Official unit emblem of 10th Explosive Ordnance Disposal positioned close to the entrance of a building [AA023745]

Below: RAF Greenham Common, West Berkshire. Realistic representations of cruise missile launch control centre (LCC) and transporter erector launcher (TEL) vehicles [304M/21]

Above: RAF Alconbury, Cambridgeshire. Mural in the mess of 511th Tactical Fighter Squadron 'The Vultures', showing a warthog carrying a gatling gun. A-10s or 'Warthogs' arrived in 1988 and left in 1992. [AA023744]

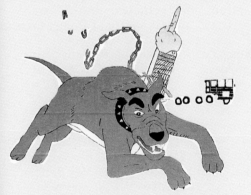

Above: RAF Greenham Common, West Berkshire. Unleashed dog with Cruise missile launcher in the background (unfinished) [304I/17A]

Left: RAF Molesworth, Cambridgeshire. Griffin emblem of 303rd Tactical Missile Wing. To reinforce the unit's historic links with the site, it took its motto 'Might in Flight' from the 303rd Bombardment Group that occupied the airfield during the Second World War. [G30076/1]

Ground launched cruise missiles

On 12 December 1979, NATO ministers took the decision to modernise nuclear forces in the European theatre by deploying Tomahawk cruise missiles and Pershing II missiles. This released aircraft from the tactical role of attacking fixed military targets, freed them to hunt out and destroy recently deployed mobile Soviet SS-20 missiles and, crucially, reassured the United States' European allies that the appropriate weapons were in place to respond to any Warsaw Pact aggression.

RAF Greenham Common

Early in the planning stage it was decided that RAF Greenham Common would act as the 'bed-down' site for the ground launched cruise missile (GLCM) system, while negotiations continued with other NATO partners (Table 4.1). An area in the south-western corner of the airfield, formerly occupied by hardstandings and the 1950s bomb store, was identified as the site for the missile shelters. Construction was sufficiently advanced by late 1983 for the first missiles to be delivered to Greenham Common, but it was not until mid-1986 that all ninety-six rounds were operational. This became the most controversial nuclear site in the country and the focus for anti-nuclear protesters (see pp 82–3).

The missiles were housed in six hardened shelters within a high security compound, known as GAMA ('GLCM alert and maintenance area' – Figs 4.22a and b). It was surrounded by a triple boundary of fencing topped with razor wire, creating two sterile strips. The main access was guarded by a hardened entry control point of a type common to other nuclear weapons stores (see Fig 4.17f), and the tall Brunswick steel tower that overlooked the compound was also typical. Additional guards could be held in the hardened reserve fire team facility with its

integral garage, and troops could also be positioned outside the compound in another hardened structure known as the combat support company building, situated close to the wing headquarters. Less visible security measures included closed circuit television cameras and radar intruder alarms.

The two launch control centres (LCCs) and four transporter erector launchers (TELs) of each flight (Figs 4.23 and 4.24) and probably two recovery vehicles were housed in one shelter – a massive reinforced concrete structure 173ft 5in × 58ft 4in (52.5m × 17.8.m) and 17ft (5.2m) high, subdivided into three lanes closed by large, pivoted, steel blast doors (Fig 4.25). The shelters' design reflected intelligence assessments that Soviet missiles might soon be able to hit a target as small as a single shelter. The doors were operated by hydraulic rams and were lowered over a pit (like a medieval drawbridge) to permit the vehicles to drive out. The reinforced concrete roof of the main structure was protected from bomb or blast damage, whether hostile or accidental, by a 8ft 6in (2.6m) layer of loose sand and a 5ft (1.5m) thick reinforced-concrete burster layer, designed to absorb the shock waves of an explosion. The slab extended 35ft 6in (10.8m) to either side of the structure in order to protect its flanks, which were also reinforced by compact sand. Pedestrian access consisted of two concrete tunnels that doglegged to a single blast door which gave entry to the shelter.

One shelter was designated for a quick reaction alert (QRA) flight (Fig 4.26). Its design differed from the others by having a permanently manned annexe on one side. This was occupied around the clock against the threat of a pre-emptive nuclear attack. On warning of such an attack the vehicles within would have driven onto the airfield from where the missiles could be launched. The annexe was a self-sufficient unit. Approximately two-thirds of its floor area

Table 4.1 Deployment of cruise missile wings in Europe

Location	Wing	No. of missiles	Activated	Operational	Inactivated
RAF Greenham Common, UK	501st	96	1 Jul 82	23 Dec 83	31 May 91
Comiso, Italy	487th	112	1 Jul 83	30 Mar 84	27 May 91
Florennes, Belgium	485th	48	1 Aug 84	31 Mar 85	30 Apr 89
Wünschheim, Germany	38th	96	15 Apr 85	31 Mar 86	22 Aug 90
RAF Molesworth, UK	303rd	64	12 Dec 86	N/A	31 Jan 89
Woensdrecht, Netherlands	486th	48	27 Aug 87	N/A	30 Sept 88

were occupied by a plant room that was protected by a blast attenuator chamber designed to dissipate the sudden increase in air pressure caused by an explosion. The remaining third of the two-level structure contained four bedrooms, a toilet, a lounge and an allied military communications panel room with direct links to its wing, USAFE and NATO headquarters.

The cruise system was designed to be mobile and elusive, deploying from hardened shelters to pre-surveyed dispersal sites. To retain its credibility, the vehicles and missiles had to be maintained at high states of readiness and serviceability. To achieve this the integrated maintenance facility and missile storage building was placed nearby and was also used for de-fuelling and refuelling the missiles. It is a three-bay, steel-framed

Figure 4.22
RAF Greenham Common, West Berkshire.
a: GLCM alert and maintenance area (GAMA) cruise missile complex. To the right is the early 1950s SAC bomb store which was absorbed into the group. [15288/33]

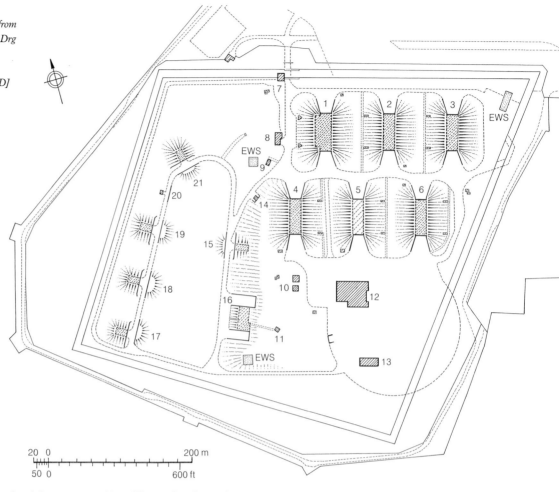

1	Quick reaction alert shelter	10	Water tank and pump house	15	Warhead store
2–6	GLCM shelters	11	MSCF tower	16	Maintenance and inspection
7	Entry control post	12	Integrated mainte nance facility	17	Food store (maintenance and inspection from 1986)
8	Reserve fire team facility	13	Missile case store	18–21	Conventional munitions stores
9	Generator house	14	Conventional munitions store	EWS	Emergency water supply

Figure 4.23
Badge of the 11th Tactical
Missile Squadron, which
operated the cruise missiles
at RAF Greenham
Common, displayed on
uniforms and unit
buildings. [AA031251]

Figure 4.25 (opposite)
RAF Greenham Common,
West Berkshire. Hydraulic
rams and vehicle bay
[AA000532]

structure clad in plastic-coated corrugated sheeting. The two-storey central bay contained workshops, storerooms and offices, and was flanked on one side by a tall, single-storey vehicle bay and on the other by the missile bay – both side bays were served by overhead gantry cranes. The support vehicles were housed and maintained outside the compound, chiefly in hangars and at a ten-bay vehicle maintenance facility. Parts of the 1950s bomb stores were renovated, the original sliding doors being replaced by hinged ones: one was used as the warhead store, and the maintenance and inspection building retained its original role. Extra capacity for maintenance was later created by converting one of the igloos into another maintenance and inspection building. The remaining igloos were used as conventional munitions stores.

RAF Molesworth

The original plan was to deploy sixty-four GLCM at RAF Molesworth; as at Greenham Common the new facilities were to be placed on the part of the airfield occupied by 1950s bomb stores (Fig 4.27). The site layout differed slightly from that of Greenham Common, but a similar range of security and servicing facilities was required. Although work began on four shelters the base was never fully activated as, on 8 December 1987, the Intermediate-range Nuclear Forces (INF) Treaty between the United States and the Soviet Union eliminated both intermediate and shorter-range missiles in Europe. The following year, a three-year withdrawal period for the GLCM system began, and the last missile left Greenham Common in March 1991.

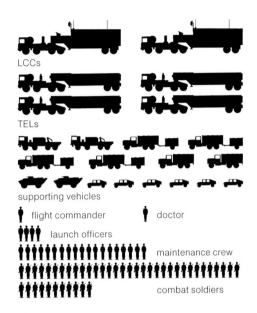

LCCs

TELs

supporting vehicles

flight commander

launch officers

doctor

maintenance crew

combat soldiers

Figure 4.24
The 11th Tactical Missile Squadron had 6 flights, each with 2 launch control centres (LCCs), with environmental support, communications and power distribution systems and weapons control equipment. Missiles were carried in 4 transporter erector launchers (TELs), 56ft × 8ft (17m × 2.4m) which weighed 80,000lb (36,287kg). Each could carry 4 missiles, giving a flight a total of 16. When deployed, 16 support vehicles and 69 men accompanied the missiles.

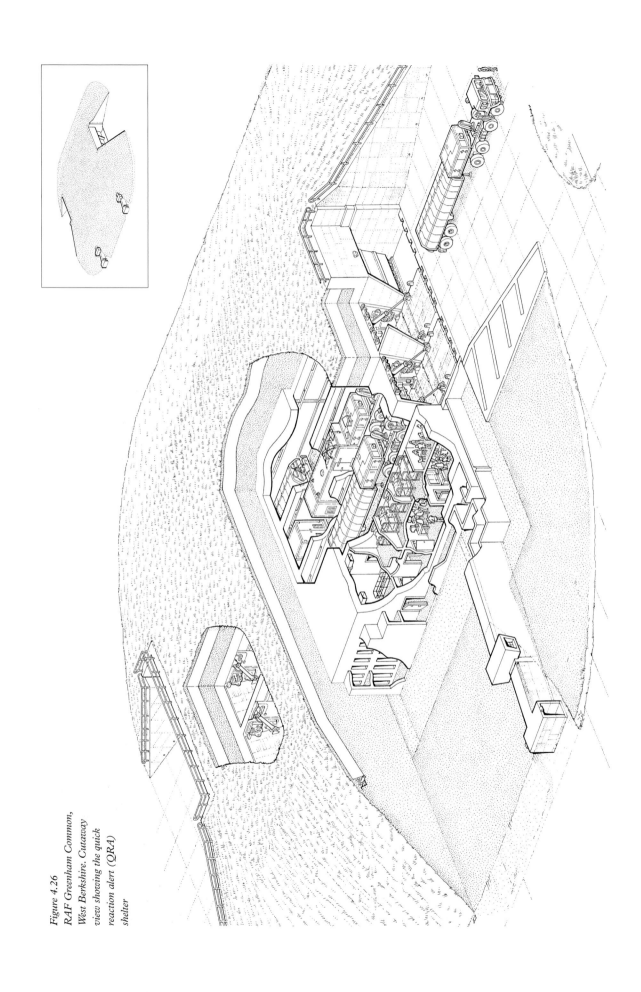

Figure 4.26
RAF Greenham Common,
West Berkshire. Cutaway
view showing the quick
reaction alert (QRA)
shelter

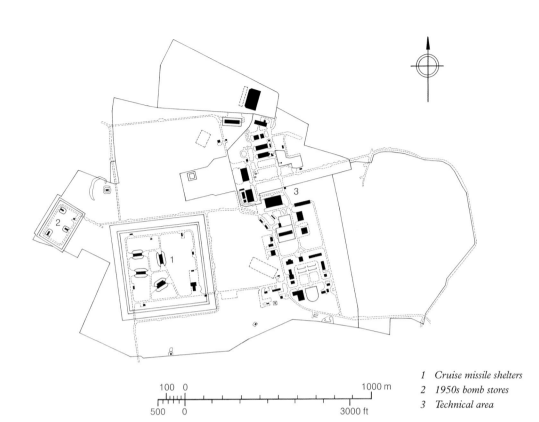

Figure 4.27
RAF Molesworth,
Cambridgeshire. Site plan
[reproduced from Ordance
Survey mapping on behalf
of the Controller of Her
Majesty's Stationery Office
© Crown copyright. Licence
No.
GD 03085G/02/01]

1   *Cruise missile shelters*
2   *1950s bomb stores*
3   *Technical area*

100   0   1000 m
500   0   3000 ft

'Draw down'

During the mid-1980s the number of USAF facilities reached its second post-war peak. The 1987 INF Treaty resulted in plans to reduce the numbers (Table 4.2). Plans were, however, soon overtaken by the collapse of the Soviet Union, which led to a major reassessment of the stationing of United States forces abroad. The result was a massive reduction, or draw down, in the United States presence in Europe, which led to many base closures. USAF flying in England is now concentrated at RAF Lakenheath and RAF Mildenhall, with occasional use being made of RAF Fairford.

Table 4.2 Principal United States Air Force bases and their functions during the 1980s

RAF Alconbury	Reconnaissance
RAF Bentwaters	A-10 tactical fighters
RAE Boscombe Down	Reserve
RAF Fairford	Airborne refuelling tankers
RAF Greenham Common	Cruise missiles and reserve
RAF Lakenheath	F-111 tactical fighters
RAF Mildenhall	Transport, reconnaissance, refuelling
RAF Molesworth	Cruise missiles
RAF Sculthorpe	Reserve
RAF Upper Heyford	F-111 tactical fighters
RAF Wethersfield	Reserve
RAF Woodbridge	A-10 tactical fighters

The peace movement

Above: The Campaign for Nuclear Disarmament logo, designed by Gerald Holton in the late 1950s. It may be read in two ways: as the semaphore signs for N and D; or as a broken cross symbolising the death of mankind and a circle representing the unborn child. The earliest badges were ceramic, a material which, it was calculated, would survive as archaeological evidence for the death of an individual even if their body was lost. [AA031252]

Overt opposition to war in Britain in the first half of the 20th century was unusual. Best known today are the 'conscientious objectors' of the two world wars though they were relatively few in number. Pacifist groups generally had little mass popular support although, during the 1930s, the Peace Pledge Union gathered thousands of signatories. After the Second World War, with the introduction of nuclear weapons and especially of Britain's nuclear deterrent V-force armed with H-bombs (*see* Chapter 3), the peace movement acquired a mass following. Peaks in support coincided with two periods of escalating political tension between the superpowers, which followed the introduction of new weapons systems.

The first was during the late 1950s and early 1960s, with the deployment of Britain's V-bombers. Thor missile sites and United States Air Force bases also attracted attention. From 1958 well-attended protest marches from London to Aldermaston became an annual feature at Easter. Elsewhere expressions of dissent ranged from large demonstrations aimed at paralysing traffic moving in and out of the bases, to lone campers. The movement was made up of many groups, including local organisations, professional groups (such as teachers or scientists) and national groups, including The Committee of 100, Direct Action Committee Against Nuclear

Warfare and (from 1958) the Campaign for Nuclear Disarmament (CND). As a whole the movement was closely allied to left-wing politics and sections of the Labour Party, and its influential supporters included Michael Foot and Tony Benn. Nonetheless, the views of some trade unionists continued to be ambivalent, as government spending on the defence industry provided many highly skilled and well-paid jobs.

Mass protest against Cold War nuclear defence policies was, at first, a distinctly British phenomenon. In the United States, with its legacy of McCarthyism and the hunt for communist sympathisers in the early 1950s, protest was stifled. In Soviet-dominated eastern Europe any sign of dissent was suppressed, and any public opposition to nuclear weapons was cynically orchestrated against the West.

Early 1980s CND badges [AA031253]

The second major upsurge in support for the peace movement came in the late 1970s and early 1980s, spurred on by discussions about Britain's intention to replace its Polaris missiles, the proposal to site cruise missiles in Europe and the possible introduction of the enhanced radiation neutron bomb. To a greater extent than in the earlier period many small local and professional groups came under the banner of CND, demanding that Britain give up her nuclear weapons and banish United States nuclear weapons from its soil. At that time the protests which received most publicity were the women's peace camps at the cruise missile bases at RAF Greenham

The peace movement has left few physical traces of its activities; its only artefacts are battered badges, tattered banners and 'underground' literature.
Right: A small selection of 1980s anti-nuclear publications [BB013803]

Above: RAF Greenham Common, West Berkshire. Temporary shelters or 'benders' in the 1980s. The potential for the archaeological remains of recently abandoned campsites to reveal something of the lifestyles of their occupants is a recognised phenomenon. The temporary shelters built by the protesters, known as benders, were flimsy structures fashioned from bowed branches and covered in polythene; their archaeological traces may resemble those left by Palaeolithic hunting shelters. Any other remains are also likely to be fragile, perhaps confined to scatters of artefacts in the topsoil and rubbish pits. At RAF Molesworth a more ambitious building, a peace chapel, was constructed.
[© Cathy Stoertz]

Left: Early 1980s leaflet announcing protests against United States bases in Britain.

Above: RAF Greenham Common, West Berkshire. Women's peace camp, 1998. Here, where the peace camp remained throughout the 1990s, the campaigners who stayed on moved to the comparative comfort of caravans. There have been proposals to erect a permanent memorial to the peace camp.
[304h/36A]

Common, Berkshire, and RAF Molesworth, Cambridgeshire, although many other installations, down to individual Royal Observer Corps posts, were picketed. Lesser known was END: the campaign group for European Nuclear Disarmament. Its existence emphasises the international character of protest at the time, which even included protests in the United States aimed at securing a nuclear freeze.

As the threat of nuclear war dwindled, membership of CND has declined, although protest against the arms trade continues.

One of the few lasting monuments to the peace movement is the Manchester Peace Garden, next to the city hall, which has a pagoda and children's play area, an open sitting area and statues.
Far left: Struggle for peace and freedom *by Philip Jackson, 1986 [AA99/03273]*
Near left: Messenger of peace *by Barbara Pearson, 1986 [AA99/03271]*

5
Early warning and detection

The task of a modern air defence system is to provide in-depth defence against attack by hostile aircraft. The system can be seen as having four main elements: detection systems; command, control and communications centres; airborne interceptors; and ground defences (Fig 5.1). The ways in which these components meshed together constantly evolved during the Cold War as defenders sought to detect and engage attackers at ever-increasing ranges, and potential intruders explored ways to defeat them. Because the means of detection were electronic, this was a battle for control of the airwaves. Not only changing perceptions of the threat – which determined changes in strategy – but also the country's ability to pay for new systems shaped Britain's air defences.

Three main periods of development can be identified. First, from the late 1940s to the mid-1950s, the main threat was piston-engined aircraft, carrying atomic bombs for use against centres of manufacturing and population. During the second phase, from the late 1950s to mid-1960s, the purpose of air defence shifted to protection of the nuclear deterrent. Finally, from the late 1960s, the doctrine of 'flexible response' stressed once again the need for air defences to counter pre-emptive attack on a wider range of targets.

Radar

The most important way of detecting hostile aircraft throughout the Cold War was radar. From its origins in the late 1930s, Britain's radar defences had, by 1945, evolved into a complex network of over 200 stations. With the end of the war and of the immediate threat of attack, most were put on a care and maintenance regime or abandoned. Thirty-six were retained, however, in a strip known

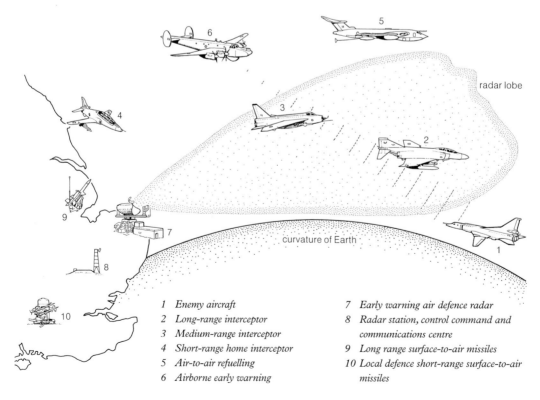

radar lobe

curvature of Earth

1 Enemy aircraft
2 Long-range interceptor
3 Medium-range interceptor
4 Short-range home interceptor
5 Air-to-air refuelling
6 Airborne early warning

7 Early warning air defence radar
8 Radar station, control command and communications centre
9 Long range surface-to-air missiles
10 Local defence short-range surface-to-air missiles

Figure 5.1
Diagram illustrating the principles of British air defence during the 1970s and 1980s. One of the major advances during this period was the introduction of airborne early warning aircraft, which extended the range of ground-based radar systems and warned of the approach of low flying aircraft.

Figure 5.2
RAF Langtoft,
Lincolnshire.
a: Ground control intercept
radar station. Late 1940s
additions include the Seco
hutting set askew to the
lane and the addition to the
wartime operations room.
[540/477, RS, frame 4001,
7 Apr 1950 © Crown
copyright MoD]

as the 'defended area', running from Flamborough Head, East Yorkshire, on England's north-east coast, right down the east coast and along the south coast as far as Portland Bill in Dorset. Ten were mostly unmanned, and the remainder were staffed only during daylight hours, because the assessment of Soviet airforce capabilities did not then include night flying.

The threat of atomic weapons called for the system to be held in a constant state of readiness and increasing aircraft speeds demanded that the time between detection and interception needed to be reduced. The previously geographically separate functions of sector operations centres (SOCs), from which interceptions over a large area of the country were controlled, was therefore combined with ground control intercept (GCI) stations, from which the fighters within a more limited area were managed. This late 1940s policy has left physical manifestations at Sandwich, Kent, and Langtoft, Lincolnshire (Figs 5.2a and b), where extensions containing additional control cabins abut the operations rooms of wartime GCI stations.

Prefabricated Seco hutting provided further accommodation which, although visible on air photographs of a number of sites, now rarely survive. To supplement radar coverage, especially for the reporting of low-level intruders, the Royal Observer Corps (ROC) was reconstituted in the late 1940s to provide direct observation of the skies (*see* Chapter 8).

b: (below)
Wartime operations room,
known familiarly as
'Happidrome' after a
popular wartime radio
show. When the photo was
taken, in 1998, the
surrounding dereliction was
typical of many former
defence sites. The late 1940s
extension is visible on the
left-hand side.
[AA98/12525]

Figure 5.3

Mobile RVT501 Mk I radar, manufactured for 'Operation Vast' (see opposite) Programme, fulfilled a similar function to the static Type 14 surveillance radar. In this view the radar aerial is shown dismounted; in operation the aerial was fixed to the cabin. This example is preserved at the Air Defence Radar Museum, RAF Neatishead. [© Roger J C Thomas]

The Rotor programme

Those modifications to the detection capabilities soon gave way to a far more ambitious programme to modernise the United Kingdom's radar defences, known as 'Rotor' *(see opposite)*. It was conceived during the late 1940s and approved by the Air Council in June 1950, and it sought to re-establish an effective air defence radar network. Not only was it the most ambitious military engineering project of the early 1950s, but it also required the co-ordination of a major manufacturing effort to produce the radar sets, 1,620 display consoles and associated plant. It also absorbed virtually all the General Post Office's cable laying capacity between 1950 and 1952. The programme aimed to place the control and operations rooms at the most vulnerable stations in large protected, usually buried, bunkers. To speed up the work, re-engineered wartime radar sets were to be used, even though their antennae rendered them vulnerable. The completion of the project was regarded as being critical to the defence of the country and, in August 1952, the Government gave it 'super priority' status, equal to that of the development of atomic weapons and guided missiles. Even

so, it suffered delays caused by shortages of the steel needed for reinforcing rods and radar gantries, and of the copper required for electrical equipment. Bad weather caused further delays, as did the commissioning of new radar and display consoles.

Operations blocks

The largest structures built during the programme – and some of the most massive constructed in the United Kingdom during the Cold War – were the operations blocks, designed to be proof against 2,000lb (907kg) armour-piecing bombs dropped from a height of 26,000ft (7,925m). In all, twenty-nine underground bunkers were built to a set of standard design types, prefixed by the letter R *(see Table 5.1 and Figs 5.4a–d)*.

The underground versions were constructed by the cut and cover method (Fig 5.5a), the depth of the excavation varying between 22ft and 65ft (6.7m and 19.8m) depending on the type of structure to be cast. To protect against ground shock (created by the detonation of a large conventional or an atomic bomb), the operations blocks were cast as monolithic structures reinforced with steel rods at 6in (0.15m)

Rotor dates and technical terms

'Operation Rotor' was designed to restore full control and reporting facilities in the late 1940s along the east and south-east coasts from the Moray Firth to Portland Bill – an area to be known as the 'Main Defended Area'. Outside that strip it was envisaged that there would be some restoration of coastal and inland cover, but excluding the Hebrides and Shetlands. Initially, Rotor relied on re-engineered wartime radar technology, and the lead contractor was the Marconi Wireless Telegraph Company. The term Rotor was used to encompass refurbished wartime stations, where there was little alteration, as well as sites which were substantially rebuilt and new sites. As the scheme was implemented there were subtle changes to the plan, while the development of new technology also led to modifications. In parallel with Operation Rotor was Operation Vast, which covered the production and allocation of radar types similar to those of Rotor but were mainly mobile rather than fixed. These units, which were compact enough to be loaded onto a single lorry, were intended to meet the needs of overseas commands and those of some allies in Europe and Commonwealth countries (Fig 5.3). The main stages of Operation Rotor are described below.

Operation Rotor 1

This referred to the original scheme, the implementation of which was split into four phases. It was in this programme that most of the heavily protected operations blocks and associated surface features were built.

Phase I All twenty-eight chain home stations to be technically restored and handed over to RAF Fighter Command.

Phase II Restoration of eight centrimetric early warning stations and six chain home extra low stations on the east and south-east coasts

Phase III Completion, by September 1953, of eleven underground ground control intercept stations in the east and south.

Phase IV Completion, by November 1954, of fourteen semi-submerged above-ground ground control intercept stations in the Midlands and the West.

Radar equipment was initially referred to as Stage 1 and Stage 2. Stage 1 described radar types that were already available or would shortly be so, and Stage 2 types that would not be available until after 1957. An unexpected technical breakthrough in the early 1950s produced a powerful new surveillance radar, known under the experimental name of 'Green Garlic', later designated the Type 80 (*see* p 104). So great were its advantages that it was termed Stage 1A equipment, and was introduced ahead of Stage 2.

Operation Rotor 2

The development of the Type 80 radar led to the revision of the Rotor programme. The intention was to install eight Stage 1A radar primarily for early warning, and twenty-one for control. Installation was to begin in 1954 and be complete by July 1956. The stations to be used had already been identified under Operation Rotor 1. Construction work was limited to the erection of the steel gantries for the Type 80 radar and of their associated modulator buildings, which housed the electrical equipment, or modulators, used to vary the transmitting frequencies of the radar. Within the operations blocks some modifications were required to allow installation of new display equipment. Work also usually involved the dismantling and removal of recently installed Stage 1 equipment.

Operation Rotor 3

In a final phase, Operation Rotor 3, radar cover was to be extended over the north and north west of Scotland and Northern Ireland, and surface and low-level cover was to be provided for the sea lanes around the west of Britain. At the completion of this operation all approaches to the United Kingdom would be covered and it would be possible to detect an aircraft the size of a small jet fighter at a range of 200 miles (321km) and an altitude of 50,000ft (15,240m). The main difference from the earlier schemes was the intention to build thirteen new radar stations, later reduced to eight. Radar were either Stage 1 equipment removed from existing sites at which Stage 1A sets had been installed, or Stage 1A radar. Following a review of the control and reporting system in 1956, Rotor 3 was never fully implemented.

Table 5.1 Summary of standard radar station building types

Type		Station function
R1	Single-storey underground bunker	Centimetric early warning
R2	Single-storey underground bunker	Chain home extra low
R3	Two-storey underground bunker	Ground control intercept
R4	Four-storey underground bunker	Sector operations centre
R5	Surface, later abandoned	Ground control intercept
R6	Two-storey semi-sunken bunker	Ground control intercept
R7	Underground equipment well for Type 7 radar	At ground control intercept stations
R8	Single-storey surface Seco huts	Ground control intercept
R9	Converted wartime operations block, later abandoned	

Additions after 1953

R10	Single-storey surface version of R1	Centimetric early warning
R11	Single-storey surface version of R2	Chain home extra low
R12	Equipment and plant room for Type 85	
R15	Data handling equipment for high speed aerial	
R17	Equipment and plant room for Type 84 radar	
R30	Modified surface wartime operation room	RAF Neatishead only

Figure 5.4
Rotor operations blocks.
a: R1 Centimetric early warning stations [redrawn from PRO AIR 20/10699]

1 *Transformer*
2 *Intercept recorder*
3 *Technical officer*
4 *Consols*
5 *Cloakrooms and toilets*
6 *Canteen and RAF rest room*
7 *WRAF rest room*
8 *Switchgear*
9 *Plant room alternators*

10 *Air coolers*
11 *Gas filtration plant*
12 *Radar office*
13 *Workshop*
14 *Track telling room*
15 *Kelvin Hughes Photo Display Unit (PDU)*
16 *GPO apparatus room*
17 *Air conditioning plant*

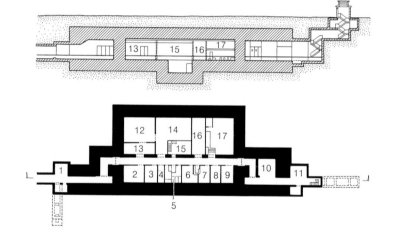

b: R2 Chain home extra low stations [redrawn from Drg No. 3/64A. Original material Crown copyright MoD]

1 *Transformer*
2 *Technical officer*
3 *Intercept recorder*
4 *WRAF toilet and cloakroom*
5 *WRAF rest room*
6 *Canteen and RAF rest room*
7 *RAF toilet and cloakroom*

8 *GPO apparatus room*
9 *Switchgear*
10 *Air coolers*
11 *Gas filtration plant*
12 *Track telling room*
14 *Radar office*
16 *Store and workshop*
17 *Air conditioning plant*

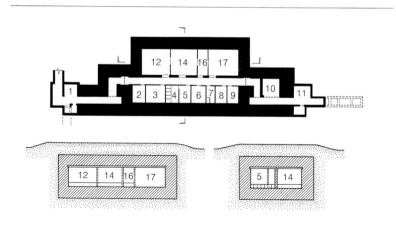

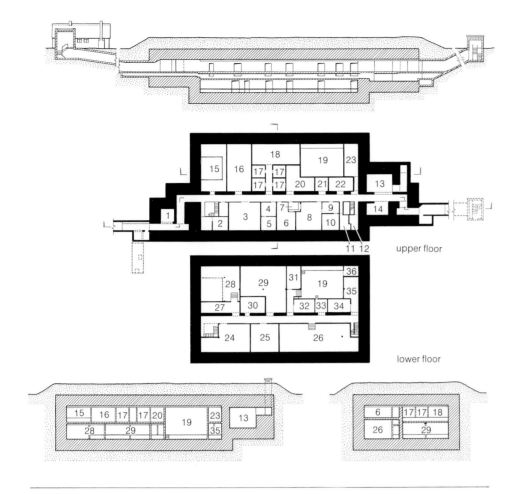

c: R3 Ground control intercept stations [redrawn from Drg No. 38/70c. Original material Crown copyright MoD]

upper floor

lower floor

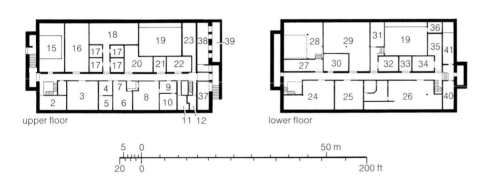

d: R6 Ground control intercept stations [Original material Crown copyright MoD]

upper floor

lower floor

1 Transformer	11 WRAF officer	22 Intercept cabin No. 4	33 Projector
2 Private branch exchange	12 RAF officer	23 Officers' rest room	34 Intercept cabin No. 2
3 GPO power room	13 Cooling plant	24 GPO apparatus room	35 Intercept cabin No. 1
4 RAF cloak room	14 Gas filtration plant	25 Radar machine room	36 Store
5 RAF toilet	15 Combined filter plot room	26 Air conditioning plant	37 Transformer
6 RAF rest room	16 Track telling room	27 VHF monitors	38 Atmospheric water coolers
7 Kitchen	17 Offices	28 Utilisation	39 Air discharge duct
8 WRAF rest room	18 Trainers	29 Radar office	40 Gas plant
9 WRAF cloak room	19 Operations room	30 Workshop	41 Switch panel and batteries
10 WRAF toilet	20 Fighter marshal	31 Store	
	21 Chief controller	32 Intercept cabin No. 3	

b: RAF Kelvedon Hatch,
Essex. The protective brick
shell was exposed in 1997
when an emergency exit
was cut through to the
upper storey.
[AA98/12611]

intervals. To allow for some movement and to aid drainage, the base of the pit might be lined with coarse gravel up to 4ft 3in (1.29m) thick, depending on the underlying geology. On this a 6in (0.15m) thick reinforced-concrete mattress was laid, over which was spread a waterproof layer. The base of the operations block was cast on top of that. The normal base thickness was 10ft (3m), although on the large R4 type (*see* Fig 5.15a) 2ft 6in (0.76m) was regarded as adequate.

The outer walls and roof were also 10ft (3m) thick and the internal walls were between 6in (0.15m) and 2ft (0.6m) wide. The exterior was coated with an asphalt damp course that was surrounded by a protective 6in (0.15m) thick brick wall (Fig 5.5b). The roof was cast using pressed-steel formwork troughs, or moulds, and was usually flush with the existing ground surface; earth up to 14ft 3in (4.34m) thick was then mounded on top. Rooms containing equipment were lined with cork and rendered with a thin skin of cement; most walls were then painted in white or cream gloss paint and exposed woodwork in light blue (also used on the lower portions of some walls).

The detailed internal configuration of the bunkers differed according to their function and is discussed in more detail below, but they share many common features. They are all rectangular in plan and are entered through doglegged passageways designed to lessen the impact of a blast wave on the relatively weak inner door. Running the length of the operations block was an offset corridor which led to the emergency exit, which in turn was protected by a staggered corridor and steel door, and usually gave access to a single flight of stairs leading to the surface.

Typically, the operations rooms were housed in the wider half of the structure and the rest rooms, lavatories, duty offices, air conditioning plant and telecommunications apparatus in the narrower part.

These structures were some of the earliest in the country to be built to house banks of electronic data-handling equipment. Special features of the design of the operations rooms and corridors which reflect this include false floors, set on steel frames supported by brick carrier walls, below which cabling and ducting could be run (Fig 5.6). Removable floor panels also gave considerable flexibility to alter the internal layout of the rooms as new equipment was introduced. The electrical processing equipment of this period relied on glass valves, which generated a terrific amount of heat. Some indication of this is the space devoted to the air conditioning and cooling plant, which was linked to forced air ducts below the floor and under the ceiling; the ducts were attached to the equipment racks and consoles by flexible metal hoses.

Figure 5.6

Cutaway view of a section of a chain home extra low R2 operations block, showing the raised floor and overhead air conditioning ducts [redrawn from Air Publication AP 2527f Original material Crown copyright MoD]

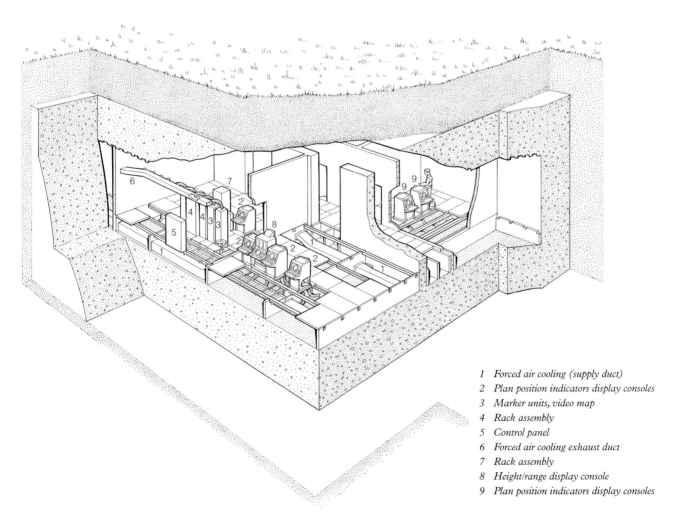

1   Forced air cooling (supply duct)
2   Plan position indicators display consoles
3   Marker units, video map
4   Rack assembly
5   Control panel
6   Forced air cooling exhaust duct
7   Rack assembly
8   Height/range display console
9   Plan position indicators display consoles

Surface structures

In contrast with many contemporary bunkers, such as army anti-aircraft operations rooms (*see below*) or civilian war rooms (*see* Chapter 9), considerable care was taken with the architectural treatment of the surface buildings on the radar sites. The guard-rooms are bungalow-like buildings (Fig 5.7); within is a single-storey rectangular building capped with a flat, concrete slab roof, above which is a pitched tile roof housing water tanks. The walls are generally of brick but, in order to blend into the local vernacular style, stone might also be used, as at Anstruther, Fife. Inside are a guardroom, armoury, store, rest room, and RAF and WRAF (Women's Royal Air Force) lavatories. Five variants are known (Figs 5.8a–e). One, such as the now demolished guardroom at Beachy Head, West Sussex (Fig 5.8c), was longer and incorporated a sub-station and switchgear; another had a bay window on one of its gable walls (Fig 5.8b). Those associated with underground operations blocks had a projecting rear annex that housed a stairwell leading down to an access tunnel. Double doors on the side of the annex allowed heavy equipment, such as consoles, to be lowered into the tunnel. Another form of guardhouse, found at Portland, Dorset, and Sopley, Hampshire, has a flat roof with a rear projecting upper storey, the one at Portland being finished in the local stone.

The use of vernacular-style surface buildings at the head of buried bunker complexes may owe its inspiration to late 1930s German designs, in particular the Wehrmacht communications centre at Zossen Wünsdorf, south of Berlin. It not only offered good camouflage, but also reflected the pre-war concerns of bodies like the Royal Fine Art Commission about the intrusiveness of new airfields into the countryside – a concern also expressed about other public architecture, such as GPO telephone exchanges. Despite this there were places, such as Hack Green, Hope Cove and Langtoft, where the small Type A bungalows (Fig 5.8e) were dwarfed by massive R6 operations blocks (*see* Fig 5.12a), destroying any pretence of concealment or aesthetics.

Despite the urgency of the Rotor programme, the construction of one of the few new radar stations in England as part of Rotor 3, on a National Trust estate at West Myne, Somerset, provoked considerable correspondence between the Air Ministry, the National Trust and the local authority about its intrusion into the landscape. The resulting compromise included a single-storey operations block with a minimal number of projections and no roof tanks, which was painted in a shade known as 'Caen Stone'. In place of the usual reinforced-concrete fence posts an angle-iron fence was erected, and was made to follow the contours of the hill; in addition, the foundation blocks for the aerial gantry were level with the ground. Elsewhere, trees (in particular poplars) were often planted to screen radar stations.

Figure 5.7
RAF Kelvedon Hatch,
Essex. Guardroom
[AA98/12614]

a

b

c

1 Veranda
2 Rest room
3 Store
4 Armoury
5 Guardroom
6 RAF lavatory
7 WRAF lavatory
8 Stairwell
9 Sub-station
10 Switch room

Figure 5.8
Diagram illustrating the
some of the variants of
bungalow-like guardrooms
(a–e) [redrawn from Drg
No. 65/46b. Original
material Crown copyright
MoD]

d

e

93

Site types

Most radar stations were designed for a specific or limited range of functions, reflected both in the types of radar found on a particular site (*see* Fig 5.10a–g), and in the range of structures required for each. The degree of protection provided was determined by geography, with sites on the east and south coast, reckoned to be closest to the potential enemy, more heavily protected than those in the west.

Radar stations may be broken down into three elements: the technical site, dispersed components and domestic accommodation. The technical site was generally defined by a chain-link fence supported by concrete posts, enclosing a guardroom, an operations block, radar arrays, a transformer building, and a sewage works. During the first phase of re-establishing the radar network, Rotor 1, all the stations were placed on or close to existing sites, and had functions similar to those of their predecessors. There are five types – chain home, chain home extra low, centrimetric early warning, ground control intercept, and sector operations centres (*see* Table 5.1).

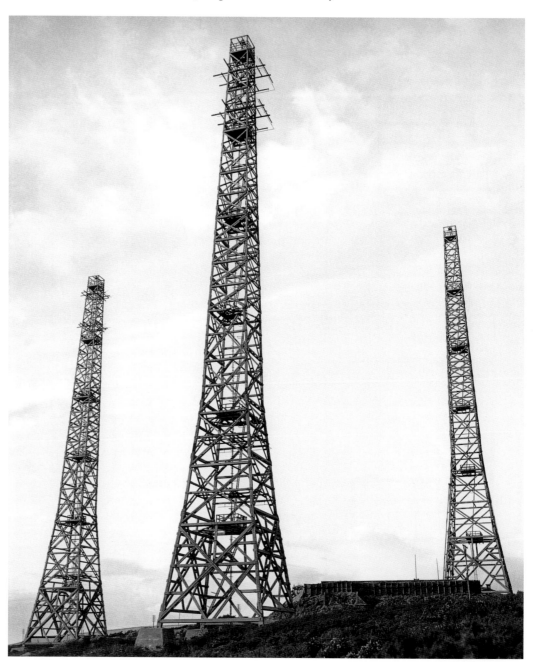

Figure 5.9
RAF Ventnor, Isle of Wight. Wooden chain home receiver masts. In the centre is the earth-covered protected receiver block.
[© Crown copyright Air Ministry. Picture courtesy of Norman Garnish]

Principal Stage radar

The Rotor programme used re-engineered wartime radar sets. At first five main radar types were associated with the Rotor 1 stations, but later these were further subdivided into production Marks with different search capabilities. The Type 7 control radar array was mounted over a subterranean well, similar in specification to the operations blocks. It had a monolithic reinforced-concrete shell, surrounded by a damp course and protective wall. The main surveillance radar was the Type 14, which was mounted on a 25ft (7.6m) steel gantry over a small building or plinth which housed turning and control mechanisms. The buildings were either of reinforced-concrete or, in less vulnerable areas, brick. Entry was by a single door which was protected from blast damage by a sliding steel door filled with sand –

an identical design to that of late 1930s RAF hangar doors (Fig 5.10e). No fixed radar arrays survive, however Type 14 plinths may be distinguished by the presence of concrete pads, to which the gantry was fixed, at each corner (Fig 5.10d). The Type 13 height-finding radar was mounted on an almost identical plinth to that of the Type 14. Similar plinths were also used to mount the Type 79 Identification, Friend or Foe aerial, which appeared from about 1954. The field remains of the Type 54 and AN/FPS-3 (AN = Authority Number) are more elusive, and consist of no more than their concrete feet and the remains of small plant buildings. Also refurbished as part of the programme, but not illustrated, was the mobile Type 11 set, which was used to counter jamming attempts at ground control intercept stations.

Chain home

The chain home stations were developed during the 1930s as part of Britain's first early warning system. Designed to detect the approach of hostile aircraft, they were used to great effect during the Battle of Britain in 1940. Initially, twenty-eight wartime stations were refurbished with little alteration to their fabric, except at stations such as Bawdsey, Suffolk, and Ventnor, Isle of Wight, where

they had more than one role. The key features of the east coast chain home stations were four 350ft (170m) transmitting towers and four 240ft (73m) wooden receiving towers. The antenna wires were strung between the towers, and the main buildings were protected by earth mounds or blast walls (Fig 5.9). On the west coast, stations used guyed steel masts for the transmitting aerials and had only two receiving masts; their buildings

Figure 5.10
Radar types

a: Type 7 control radar. The antenna was supported by a hollow cylindrical steel column mounted on a steel box which housed the turning mechanism. Also visible are the metal vents of the subterranean well that housed the transmitter, monitor receiver and other equipment, and was entered by one of two metal manholes in the roof. This radar had an effective range of about 90 miles (145km). [© Crown copyright. RAF Air Defence Radar Museum]

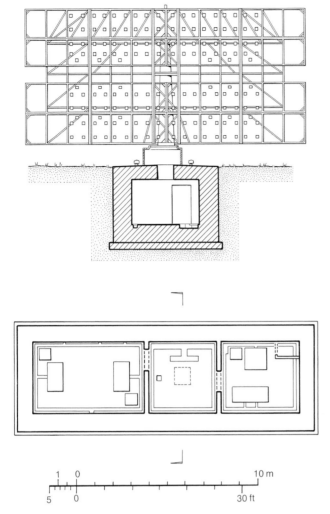

Figure 5.10
Radar types

b: (above)
Plan and section of R7
radar well. The shallow
trench running around the
edge of each room
accommodated electrical
cabling. [Redrawn from
Drg No. 3/4070. Original
material Crown copyright
MoD]

c: (right)
Type 13 height-finding
radar. This operated on a
100mm wavelength. The
head of this radar nodded
up and down.
[BB98/10067 © Crown
copyright. RAF Air
Defence Radar Museum]

were mounded in earth, scattered around the site and provided with backups to guard against loss. Very few towers or masts still exist: at Swingate near Dover two original masts survive, and at Dunkirk, also in Kent, a single tower remains, while at Stenigot, Lincolnshire, a truncated mast has been listed as 'a building of special architectural or historic importance'.

Chain home extra low

One of the weaknesses of the original chain home system was the difficulty of detecting low-flying aircraft. This was addressed during the war by the introduction of chain home extra low stations. As remodelled during the 1950s, the layout of such stations was very simple, comprising either a single Type 14 plan positioning radar, as at Goldsborough, North Yorkshire, or a Type 54 (Figs 5.10d and f). All stations were also provided with buried R2 operations rooms, which were entered through standard guardrooms (*see* Fig 5.8a). R2s were single-storey bunkers containing a typical range of services, together with a combined filter and plotting room (*see* Fig 5.4b).

Centimetric early warning

Centimetric early warning stations provided both surface and medium to high altitude coverage, and had more complicated station layouts than the chain home installations. All had Type 14 plan positioning radar and Type 13 height finders. (*see* Fig 5.9c) Some, such as Trimingham, Norfolk, and Portland, Dorset, were combined with chain home extra low functions, and were equipped with Type 54 radar; some also had US AN/FPS3 long-range search radar to extend their capability (Fig 5.10g). The availability of the United States' equipment reflected the importance of Rotor stations in protecting US airbases in Britain (*see* Chapter 4). Operations were conducted from an R1 type structure that was nearly identical to the R2, except that the plotting room (No. 15 on Fig 5.4a) contained a Kelvin-Hughes photo display system. A typical establishment of this kind would have around 245 people.

Ground control intercept

The main function of the radar stations described above was to provide early warning of the approach of attacking aircraft. Some of the ground control intercept (GCI) stations were also involved in building up the picture of air movements, and some had a special room – the combined filter plotting

d: (far left)
Type 14 surveillance radar.
This used similar electronics
to the Type 13, operating on
a 100mm wavelength. It
was used to fix the plan
position of targets.
[BB98/10069 © Crown
copyright. RAF Air
Defence Radar Museum]

e: (left)
RAF Langtoft,
Lincolnshire. Rotor-period
radar plinth showing the
sliding sand-filled door to
the left [AA98/12518]

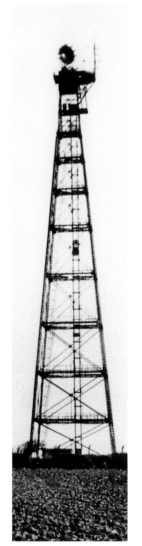

f: (far left)
Type 54. This was a
circular parabolic reflector
mounted on top of a 200ft
(61m) steel tower. The
cabin beneath the aerial
housed the transmitter and
turning gear. At the base
was a small building
housing a generator, an
alternator and switch gear.
[Neat 176/94 © Crown
copyright. RAF Air
Defence Radar Museum]

g: (left)
AN/FPS-3 long-range
search radar [© Crown
copyright. RAF Air
Defence Radar Museum]

Table 5.2 Summary of radar types used at ground control intercept stations (A–E)

Radar	A	B	C	D	E
Type 7 Mk 2	1	1	-	-	1*
Type 11 (m) Mk 7	1	1	1	-	1
Type 13 Mk 6 with A-band IFF	2	4	2	1	4
Type 13 Mk 7 without IFF	3	2	2	1	2
Type 14 Mk 8 with G-band IFF	1	1	1	-	1
Type 14 Mk 9 with G-band IFF	1	2	1	-	2
Type 54 Mk 3 without IFF	-	1	-	-	1

* remotely positioned

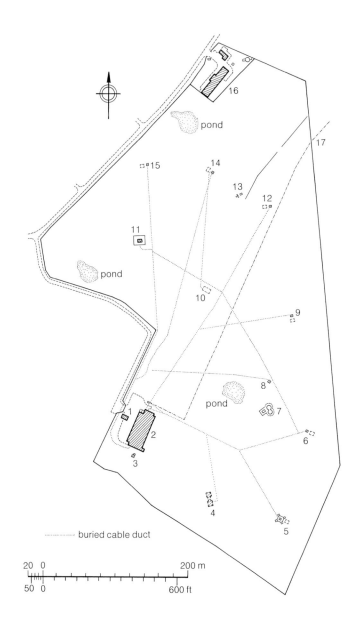

1 Guardroom
2 R6 operations block
3 Electrical sub-station
4 Type 80, not built
5 Type 14 radar
6 Type 13 radar
7 Sewage plant
8 Type 14 radar
9 Type 13 radar
10 Type 11 radar
11 Type 7 radar
12 Type 13 radar
13 Identification Friend or Foe aerial base
14 Type 13 radar
15 Type 13 radar
16 Wartime operations block
17 Buried standby power cable

buried cable duct

*Figure 5.11
a: RAF Hack Green,
Cheshire. Ground control
intercept (A) station
[redrawn from HAK Site
plan for structure R6
c1953. Original material
courtesy of Hack Green
Secret Nuclear Bunker]*

room – for the task of guiding intercepting fighters towards their target.

GCI stations were the most numerous and most technologically complex Rotor sites. Twenty-nine were built in the United Kingdom, of which eighteen were in England (although probably only sixteen of them reached operational status). Within this group there was considerable diversity, the main varieties being designated GCI A–E depending on the types and number of radar installed (Table 5.2). This lead to considerable differences in plan to accommodate different numbers of radar arrays (Figs 5.11a and b). At Bawdsey and at Treleaver, Cornwall, the picture was further complicated by their being on the same site as chain home stations. All the radar were placed on the technical sites, except in some instances, such as Bawdsey, where the Type 7 control radar was 1¼ miles (2km) from the operations block; there was a similar distance at Sandwich between the Type 7, near its wartime predecessor, and the new R3 operations block at Ash, Kent.

The range of activities carried out by the ground control intercept stations is apparent in the provision of large two-storey operations block – underground R3s in the more vulnerable eastern areas, and in the west the semi-sunken R6, the walls of which are only 3ft (0.91m) thick (Fig 5.12a and see Fig 5.4c and d). The identical purpose of the two types is evident from their almost indistinguishable floor layouts. Activity was focused on the double-storey operations room. On the ground floor was the general situation map (Fig 5.12b), together with a map displaying the disposition of fighters. 'Tote boards' on the wall presented weather information and the readiness of different squadrons. Surrounding these were the main radar consoles and on the upper level, overlooking the map tables, were the fighter marshal's cabin and more consoles (Fig 5.12c). The total cost of an R3 operations block and associated technical equipment was around £500,000. In the least threatened areas a different building – the R8 operations block – was used, as at RAF

b: RAF Langtoft, Lincolnshire. Ground control intercept (A) station. This view shows that by 1958 many of the wartime buildings and late 1940s Seco hutting had been demolished (see Fig 5.2a). At the centre left are the R6 bunker and its associated guardroom. A Type 80 radar modulator building has been built, but no radar array was installed. At the bottom, connected by the criss-cross arrangement of paths, are the radar plinths. [58/2591, V, 24 Sep 1958, frame 0010 © Crown copyright MoD]

Figure 5.12
a: (right)
RAF Hope Cove, Devon.
R6 type semi-sunken
operations block. At the
right is a doorway leading
to flight of steps to the upper
corridor; to the rear is the
raised air discharge duct.
[AA000501]

b: (below)
View of the floor of the
operation well in an R3
operations block (probably
1950s and probably RAF
Bawdsey, Suffolk)
[X60980 © Crown
copyright. RAF Air
Defence Radar Museum]

Chenies, Hertfordshire, and RAF Hartland Point, Devon (Fig 5.13). It is a large single-storey structure formed from four parallel ranges of prefabricated Seco hutting with a double-storey operations room and would have offered no protection from any form of attack. This type is also associated with later additions to the system such as Charmy Down, Wiltshire, where only footings and radar plinths survive, and where it appears that radar equipment was never installed.

Figure 5.13 (below) RAF Hartland Point, Devon. Ground control intercept (C) station. The large building at the centre is the R8 prefabricated operations block, surrounding which are the radar arrays.

Figure 5.14
Map showing the air defence sector boundaries and radar stations.
[Redrawn from PRO AIR 8/1630]

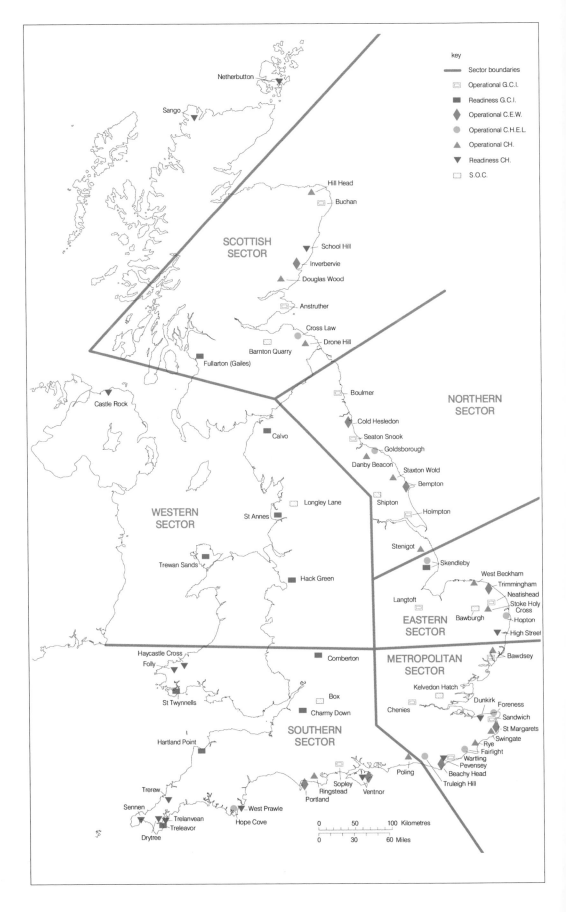

Figure 5.15
a: Floor plans and section
of R4 sector operations
centre [redrawn from Drg
Nos. 3/24H and 3/94.
Original material Crown
copyright MoD]

1	Transformer	9	RAF rest room
2	Operations room	10	Women's toilet
3	WRAF rest room	11	Men's toilet
4	Officers' rest rooms	12	GPO apparatus
5	Men's toilet	13	Air conditioning plant
6	Women's toilet	14	Air coolers
7	Kitchen	15	Gas filtration
8	Cable trunking		

b: (below)
RAF Kelvedon Hatch,
Essex, 1954. Cabins
overlooking the three-storey
operations well
[BB98/10073 © Crown
copyright. RAF Air
Defence Radar Museum]

Sector operations centres

The United Kingdom was divided into six sectors for air defence purposes (Fig 5.14), each controlled by a sector operations centre (SOC). Two were housed in wartime underground group operations centres at Box, Rudloe Manor, Wiltshire, and Longley Lane, Preston, Lancashire. The remaining four were placed in new purpose-built underground bunkers at Barnton Quarry, Edinburgh, Bawburgh, Norfolk, Shipton, North Yorkshire and Kelvedon Hatch, Essex. They were all built to a standard design of buried three-storey structure known as an R4 (see Fig 5.15a). The main block was rectangular, 120ft 4in × 60ft 9in (36.7m × 18.6m), with a small annexe attached to the bottom floor containing coolers and gas filtration plant. Entry was usually to the upper level through a guardhouse (see Fig 5.8a), as at Shipton, North Yorkshire, although at Kelvedon Hatch, where the bunker was built into a hillside, the entrance tunnel leads to the lowest level (see Fig 5.8d).

The R4 buildings were not in the same place as the radar sites and had no associated radar, since their task was to build up the picture of a raid across a sector, drawing

information from the radar sites described above. Using this information controllers of the fighters, and later of the guided weapons, would allocate targets. The structure of the bunker reflects this activity.

In the centre was the operations room, which occupied the full height of the well (Figs 5.15a and b). Information was displayed on tote boards fixed to one wall, and on an inclined map table on the floor. Round the other three walls were control cabins overlooking the displays. The most senior officers, including the chief fighter controller or guided weapons controller, battle commander and electronics officers, occupied the upper level, the remainder of which was used for telephone equipment and rest rooms, the latter divided by rank and sex, and a single small central kitchen.

The ground executive, which controlled the radar, and the air executive, which directed the airborne aircraft and interceptions, occupied the cabins in the middle level. Small duty rooms and display and communications consoles occupied the remainder of this floor. The larger area occupied by the women's lavatory on this level reflected the balance of the sexes in these roles, as well as the career opportunities which new technology had opened up in the air force for women. On the bottom floor most of the area not occupied by the operations room was used to house teleprinters, generators, and cooling and air filtration plant (Fig 5.16).

Stage 1A equipment (Rotor 2)

It was inevitable that during the programme new technology would become available. The most significant development was an experimental early warning radar known as 'Green Garlic', designated Type 80 in January 1954. It could be used either as an early warning radar or by ground control intercept stations, and its introduction marked a major advance over the modified wartime sets: increasing the range by 40 per cent, dramatically improving target discrimination (allowing operators to assess the number of aircraft in a raid), enhancing continuity of track following, and more effectively resisting jamming.

Its introduction was accompanied by new display equipment, including fixed-coil deflected-cathode ray tubes and Kelvin-Hughes photographic projectors, both of which helped to speed up control and reporting.

The programme to install Type 80 became known as Rotor 2 and was confined to existing radar stations, which were supplied with a gantry to support the aerial, and an associated modulator building (modulators varied the transmitting frequencies of the radar). Alterations were also made to the operations blocks, but have left no archaeological trace. Type 80 immediately led to the redundancy both of some recently installed equipment and of the wartime chain home stations and, owing to its improved coverage, ultimately led to a reduction in the number of stations.

The experimental Green Garlic set was built at Bard Hill, Norfolk, but no remains of it survive. The first Type 80 to enter operational service, in April 1955, was sited further south, at Trimingham, where the modulator building remains. The radar aerial was supported on a steel gantry that sat over the modulator building, which held DC supply rectifiers to convert alternating electrical current to direct current, and apparatus to ensure that the radar emitted a wave of constant frequency. A short corridor connected the modulator building to another single-storey building with separate rooms for generators and switchgear. At more vulnerable sites the building was constructed from 14in (360mm) solid brickwork; elsewhere 9in (230mm) brickwork was used. In a few places, such as Trimingham, breeze-blocks were used. The walls were finished with a painted cement render.

There are two variants of the Type 80 modulator building (Figs 5.17a–d). The earlier, associated with Mark I equipment, measures 40ft 6in × 29ft 7in (12.35m × 9.04m). The second version was associated with Mark II and III equipment (Fig 5.17e) and

Figure 5.16
RAF Kelvedon Hatch,
Essex. Original 1950s air
filtration and cooling plant
[AA001052]

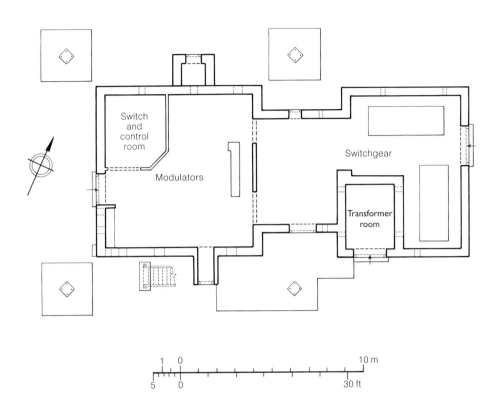

Figure 5.17
a: (left)
Plan of modulator building
for Type 80 radar Mark I

Switch
and
control
room

Modulators

Switchgear

Transformer
room

1   0   10 m

5   0   30 ft

was also later used for the Type 84 radar (*see below* and Fig 5.20a). This building was over twice as long, as well as wider, measuring 96ft × 35ft 1½in (29.26m × 10.66m), and can be recognised from the fan and filter room placed centrally on its roof and an annexe attached to the modulator room. About twenty-four Type 80s were installed but at some locations, such as Langtoft, Lincolnshire, evidence from air photographs

indicates that although the modulator building was finished the array was never fitted, probably since it was realised that Soviet counter-measures would soon be able to defeat the system. Where the Type 80 was employed on ground control intercept sites, United States AN/FPS-6 height-finding radar was also fitted (Fig 5.17f), since the earlier (Type 13) height-finding radar had a shorter range than the Type 80.

b: (above)
RAF Bempton, North Yorkshire. Centrimetric early warning station. First version of Type 80 modulator building associated with the Mark I radar [MF 98/00248/32]

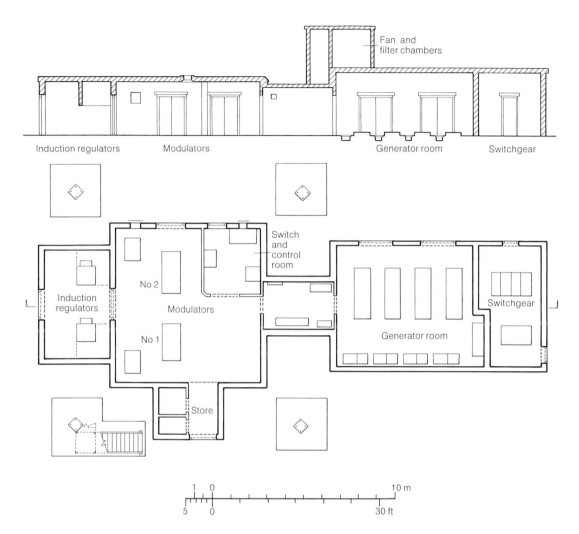

Induction regulators   Modulators   Generator room   Switchgear

Fan and filter chambers

Switch and control room

Induction regulators

No 2

Modulators

No 1

Store

Generator room

Switchgear

1 0   10 m
5 0   30 ft

Figure 5.17
c: (above)
Plan of modulator building for Type 80 radar Mark II and III [original material Crown copyright MoD]

d: (right)
RAF Hope Cove, Devon. Second version of the Type 80 modulator building associated with the Mark II and III radar. Clearly visible at the left are the annexe attached to the modulator room, and the raised fan and filter room. [AA000498]

*e: RAF Bawdsey, Suffolk.
Type 80 Mark III radar.
The aerial was a 75ft ×
25ft (23m × 7.5m) mesh
reflector, supported on a
25ft (7.5m) steel gantry.
Beneath the array was the
turntable and turning gear.
Below, in a rotating cabin,
were the transmitter,
receiver and Identification
Friend or Foe equipment.
This radar could detect a
medium-sized target up to a
maximum range of c 270
miles (434.5km) and an
altitude of 80,000ft
(24,384m) [45.
Reproduced by kind
permission of the East
Anglian Daily Times and
Evening Star]*

*f: AN/FPS-6 height-finding
radar at RAF Bawdsey
[43. Reproduced by kind
permission of the East
Anglian Daily Times and
Evening Star]*

Dispersed components

In addition to the main technical site, radar stations also had a number of dispersed components, which might be spread in an arc at a distance of more than a mile (1.6km) from the centre. They included wireless transmitter and receiver stations. At Langtoft the wireless station is a single-storey brick building with a flat, concrete roof and hinged, steel blast shutters protect its windows. Air photographs taken at the time show that at Hack Green, Cheshire, there were three wireless stations, two of which survive (though one is probably wartime in origin), and consist of a house for the standby set or backup generator, a wireless building and concrete bases for the masts. Most standby sets were detached from the main technical site, placed either on the associated domestic site or on their own. Some, such as that at Kelvedon Hatch (Figs 5.18a and b), were built in the style of a simple chapel. The one at Neatishead is almost identical, although it was roofed with local pantiles; all its woodwork and windows frames are painted 'RAF blue'.

Figure 5.18
RAF Kelvedon Hatch, Essex.
a: Chapel-like standby generator building [AA001059]

b: Standby generator building: detail of tile air vent [AA001063]

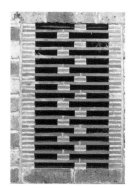

VHF transmitter stations

As part of the system to control fighter aircraft, a very high frequency (VHF)/direction finding fixer network of seventy-nine stations was established across the United Kingdom, fifty-eight of them in England. They were divided into thirteen fixer organisations: the seven on the east coast were operational, while four in the west were held on standby and the other two were held in reserve. Directional finding equipment at these sites allowed pilots to calculate their positions by transmitting a signal that was fixed by triangulation at a sector operations centre, after which the calculated location was radioed back to the aircraft. The structures themselves were a mixture of refurbished wartime sites and new buildings. Both are relatively insubstantial, the derelict and reused wartime example north of Duxford airfield, Cambridgeshire, consisting of a small ruined brick building for the electrical equipment, and a protective brick wall surrounding the standby generator.

Domestic accommodation

Many of the radar stations were built in remote rural areas where it was difficult to find lodgings for large numbers of people. A typical ground control intercept station might have about twenty-seven officers, forty-five senior non-commissioned officers, and 350 corporals and aircraftsmen/women. Their accommodation was invariably a long way from the radar station, and buses took staff to the station for their shifts. In some places it was possible to use barracks and housing at nearby airfields, but often new estates were at built some distance from the radar stations. Most of these survive, and examples include those at Hack Green (Fig 5.19), Langtoft and Sandwich. The buildings were a mixture of temporary huts and permanent brick housing estates, the latter distinguishable from contemporary council estates by the variety of house types, which were allocated according to rank and marital status. Some of the female radar operators were employed under a local service scheme, which meant that they lived at home and were not liable to be posted to other stations.

The late 1950s

After the implementation of the well-structured and layered early warning and control system provided by the Rotor

Figure 5.19
Baddington, Cheshire. Part of the housing estate that served RAF Hack Green. House types were allocated according to rank and marital status.
[AA98/08169]

programme, the picture during the late 1950s and early 1960s became far more confused as defence planners thought through the implications of the detonation of the Soviet H-bomb in 1953. This process resulted in the 1957 Defence White Paper, which marked a distinct change in British defence strategy and placed nuclear deterrence at the heart of policy.

From that time, the purpose of the warning systems was no longer to safeguard the population but, under the doctrine of 'tripwire response', to provide early warning of aggression by the Warsaw Pact in order that nuclear armed aircraft and missiles could immediately be launched against targets in eastern Europe. Remaining air defences – aircraft and surface-to-air missiles (*see* Chapter 7) – were there essentially to protect the nuclear deterrent. This period was also characterised by acute Treasury scrutiny of new projects, usually resulting in cuts. Technologically, it was a time when new radar began to replace the earlier modified wartime sets, with the prospect of yet more powerful radar co-ordinated by computers. Countering these were advances in Soviet jamming technology.

Even after the completion of the Rotor system in February 1956 there were deficiencies, including gaps in coverage and serious delays in control and reporting (the time taken for data to be transferred from the early warning radar to the sector operations centres and out to the interceptor control stations). This became more serious as aircraft speeds increased and as the first surface-to-air guided weapons – Bloodhound – were being introduced (*see* Chapter 7). Soon after the completion of Rotor 1, the 1958 Control and Reporting Plan recommended the abandonment of sector operations centres, and the designation of nine 'comprehensive' (later 'master') radar stations equipped with Type 80 radar for reporting and controlling, and with direct connections to the fighter airfields. Links were also established between a limited number of early warning stations and new tactical control radar, built to control the Bloodhound missile system (*see* p 158–9). It was also recognised that advances in Soviet electronic counter-measures would soon enable jamming of Type 80s, and a Phase 3 plan was drawn up to include the introduction of new radar systems. (It was initially called 'The Modified 1958 Plan' but, after a series of cuts, it bore so little resemblance to the original plan that it was renamed 'Plan Ahead'.)

The realignment of defence policy also coincided with a growth in civil air traffic in the late 1950s, and British Prime Minister Harold Macmillan insisted that Plan Ahead should only proceed if it improved civil air traffic control. After further delays the scheme was again modified before finally gaining approval in February 1961, the military element being known as 'Linesman' and the civil component 'Mediator'.

Air defence during the 1960s: 'Linesman'

Technologically, the Linesman project marked a break with the past and offered the prospect of a fully computerised air defence scheme based on a mainframe computer. This was made possible by the invention of the germanium transistor. Construction work associated with Linesman was modest, reflecting both improved radar technology (which enabled fewer radar to monitor a much wider area) and the reduced significance of air defence under the new deterrent strategy.

Major building projects were restricted to three existing stations at Boulmer, Northumberland, Staxton Wold, North Yorkshire, and Neatishead, Norfolk, each of which required about 300 personnel when operational. They did not conform to any standard overall ground plan, although the same radar and building types were used. Between 1962 and 1964 powerful Type 84 surveillance radar (Fig 5.20a) were installed at all three sites. These radar not only increased the range of detection but, with a peak power output of 4 megawatts (drawn from on-site generators powerful enough to provide electricity for a small town), they were able to burn through the latest Soviet jamming technology. A similar radar was also installed at Bawdsey, but in 1970 it was moved to Bishops Court, Northern Ireland (although its R17 modulator building survived and was reused by a later Bloodhound missile unit, and another was built on Cyprus. As with the earlier series of surveillance radar, the Type 84 was unable to establish height, and each site was equipped with two or three HF200 height-finding radar mounted on distinctive segmental conical metal towers (Fig 5.20b), none of which survive.

At the same time, work began on the R12 radar equipment buildings for Type 85 radar (Figs 5.21a and b) at Boulmer, Neatishead and Staxton Wold, although they were not fully operational until 1968. Like the Type

Figure 5.20
a: RAF Neatishead, Norfolk. Type 84 radar. This, the last surviving fixed Cold War radar, was a high power medium to long-range surveillance radar and could be used in three operational modes – early warning, close control of interceptors and general surveillance. The array comprises a pair of back-to-back 60ft × 20ft 8in (18.28m × 6.23m) parabolic reflector dishes. At either end of the horizontal girder are steel frameworks for mounting hornfeeds (only one of which was installed) that transmitted and received the radar beams. It was originally envisaged that the front dish would function as the main radar, while the rear dish would operate as an Identification Friend or Foe (IFF) aerial. That arrangement was not adopted, and the IFF aerial was placed above the main dish. [AA98/05747]

84 this system could draw on massive power reserves to defeat jamming, but it was also equipped with banks of transmitters and receivers which could rapidly change transmitting frequencies to deter hostile blocking attempts (Fig 5.21c). The associated R12 building is a massive rectangular reinforced-concrete structure of two storeys plus basement, measuring 192ft 3in × 156ft (58.60m × 47.55m) (Fig 5.21d). Special features to house large amounts of electronic equipment included cable ducts which were set into the ground floor, while the first floor, where the main receiver and passive tracking apparatus were housed, was set on a false wooden-tiled parquet floor. A problem with all electronic equipment at this date was the amount of heat it generated: as well as providing space for cable runs, the raised floor allowed for forced-air cooling ducts that were supplemented by further ducts hung from the ceilings in order to maintain the internal temperature at around 20°C. Some of the cooling plant (Fig 5.21e) was housed in a single-storey annexe at one side of the building.

b: HF200 height-finding radar. The nodding height finder consisted of a 35ft × 8ft (10.67m × 2.44m) perforated aluminium 'orange peel' reflector. At right angles to it is the hornfeed. The tower housed control gear and oil pumps for the hydraulic nodding mechanism. [© Crown copyright MoD]

*Figure 5.21
a: RAF Staxton Wold,
North Yorkshire. R12
building. The radar was
formerly sited on the right
hand projection.
[AA98/03658]*

*b: Type 85 radar. This was
a high-power surveillance
radar. It consisted of a
parabolic reflector dish 60ft
× 21ft 8in (18.28m ×
6.53m) with rectangular
stabilising fins. At the front
is the hornfeed and beneath
it the Identification Friend
or Foe aerial. [© Crown
copyright. RAF Air
Defence Radar Museum]*

*c: RAF Neatishead,
Norfolk. R12 transmitter
hall [Neat 174/96 ©
Crown copyright. RAF Air
Defence Radar Museum]*

1 Pressure vessel
2 Apparatus room
3 Cables
4 Main entrance and
  decontamination
5 Men's toilets
6 Battery Room
7 Type 85 transmitter
  apparatus room
8 Air conditioning plant
9 Transformers
10 Lighting
11 Direct current generators
12 Control room
13 Air intake openings
14 Filters
15 Loading bay
16 Store
17 Technical office
18 Transmitter stores
19 Loading bay
20 Transmitter workshop
21 Aerial control
22 Constant current DC
   current generator, or
   metadynes
23 Control room
24 Men's toilets
25 Toilets
26 Kitchen
27 Rest room
28 Main Type 85 receiver
   and passive tracking
   apparatus
29 Services duct
30 Air extract duct
31 GPO apparatus
32 Office
33 Receiver stores
34 Receiver workshop
35 Store

d: Floor plans of R12 building [redrawn from HQFC Drg No. 1960. Original material Crown copyright MoD]

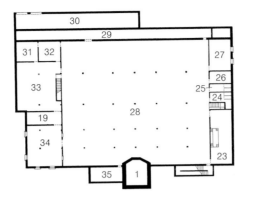

upper floor

lower floor

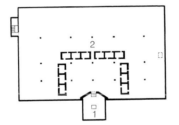

basement

In a further attempt to counter Soviet jamming, a passive detection system known as 'Winkle' was introduced between 1965 and 1968. The equipment, comprising a high speed aerial (Fig 5.22) mounted above an R15 data handling equipment building, was installed at four places: three on the same site as Type 85s and the fourth at Dundonald Hill in Strathclyde, Scotland. It was worked together with a Type 85 to establish the position of a jamming source.

At the same time as these advances were taking place the R3 Rotor period bunkers at

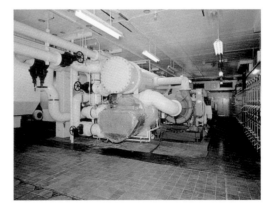

e: RAF Staxton Wold, North Yorkshire. R12. Part of the massive cooling plant [AA98/03667]

Figure 5.22
RAF Staxton Wold, North
Yorkshire. High-speed
aerial. It has a narrow
curved reflector dish. To its
front is an array of 160
receiving horns; below is the
R15 data handling
equipment building.
[© Crown copyright MoD]

Figure 5.22
RAF Staxton Wold, North
Yorkshire. High-speed
aerial. It has a narrow
curved reflector dish. To its
front is an array of 160
receiving horns; below is the
R15 data handling
equipment building.
[© Crown copyright MoD]

Figure 5.23
West Drayton. Part of the
combined military master
control centre (L1) and
civil southern air traffic
control centre [G15020/1 ©
Crown copyright]

Boulmer and Neatishead were converted to
R3As. Alterations were substantial, and
included the insertion of an additional floor
over the operations room. New buildings
were also erected at these stations, including
combined guardrooms and fire sections, station headquarters, offices and mess rooms.
As there was now less emphasis on surviv-

ability, the standby powerhouses were also
built within the stations rather than separately.

As part of the compromise involved in
integrating the military and civil systems, the
RAF master control centre (L1) originally
destined for the Rotor bunker at Bawburgh,
Norfolk, was moved to a new above-ground

structure at West Drayton (Fig 5.23). Although unprotected, this site was expected to have significant operational advantages because it was close to London's Heathrow Airport. As originally envisaged, L1 was to form a central command and control centre, with automated data-handling for receiving and distributing information from all the main radar stations. That plan proved too ambitious for contemporary computer technology, however, so L1 developed as an air defence data centre at which a picture of air activity over the United Kingdom could be built up. It was also linked to a number of continental radar, thereby forming part of the wider NATO early warning system. But it never lived up to its original expectations, and in the late 1960s it was down-graded to a tactical control centre.

The building is a typical 1960s reinforced-concrete multi-storey structure, which reflects the redefined role of air defences to confirm that an attack was underway (*see* Chapter 6) and defend the nuclear deterrent forces: if deterrence failed and the country was attacked with nuclear weapons there would be little left for the airforce to defend, so there was little point in investing in a protected control building. In contrast, the UK Regional Air Operations Centre (UKRAOC) was placed in what had been wartime underground operations centre at High Wycombe, Buckinghamshire; simply, perhaps, to save the cost of a new building.

Often, putting civil air traffic control on the same site as military operations had little effect on the appearance of the radar stations concerned. At Hack Green it only resulted in some minor internal rearrangement of equipment positions in the operations block. At Ash, which was to become one of the main approach control radar for London, the alterations were more radical. Two Marconi A264 Radar (Fig 5.24), a secondary surveillance radar, and a building to house a new microwave communications link were built; the guardhouse was remodelled, and a large administration block constructed. Similar alterations were made at Ventnor.

The Linesman project suffered a serious setback in 1966 when the R3 at Neatishead was destroyed by a fire that claimed the lives of three firemen. Nevertheless, the radar remained and the operational centre moved to Bawdsey. Operational control was restored at Neatishead in 1973, when the above-ground wartime operations room was extended and re-equipped with standby local

Figure 5.24
RAF Ash, Kent. Early 1960s Marconi T264A radar plinths [AA96/03090]

early warning and control (SLEWC) consoles, the building being designated an R30 (Fig 5.25). A similar operations room was established at Boulmer. These changes resulted in the closure of the radar stations at Bawdsey and Patrington (East Riding of Yorkshire) and their Type 80 radar.

Figure 5.25 (below)
RAF Neatishead, Norfolk. Standby local early warning and control consoles and glass tote board, displaying, for example, weather conditions and the operational status of various fighter squadrons. This room is now maintained as a museum display. [BB98/10062]

The 1970s: Towards the improved United Kingdom Air Defence Ground Environment (UKADGE)

The Linesman radar system, which was not fully operational until 1974, had been conceived as part of the strategy of 'tripwire response'. By 1967, however, NATO had moved on to 'flexible response', in which threats from the Warsaw Pact were to be met by détente, deterrence and defence. A series of reports produced in 1971, at a time when the Soviets were beginning to deploy bombers armed with long-range stand-off missiles, outlined the main weaknesses of Linesman, including its vulnerability to attack and poor coverage below 1,000ft (305m).

The final report, issued in October 1971 (*A revised plan for the UKADGE*), proposed that command should be maintained centrally at two sites – West Drayton and Strike Command HQ High Wycombe – and that control should be allocated to four control and reporting centres (CRCs) at Buchan, Bishops Court, Boulmer, and Neatishead. The plan was that all the sites would be able to exchange data by narrow-band digital links, and that the CRC would be linked on a 'ring-main' to allow one site to take over from another in an emergency. In the short term the existing radar would be maintained, but they were later to be replaced by others which were smaller and cheaper than the fixed radar of the early 1960s (Fig 5.26 *and see* Figs 5.20a, 5.21a and b). At the same time airborne early warning radar were deployed in Shackleton aircraft, stationed first at Kinloss and, from 1974, at Lossiemouth, both in Morayshire, Scotland. The airborne system not only extended coverage over the horizon but also enabled the radar to look down on low level intruders (*see* Fig 5.1).

The new network was planned to give full cover to the approaches to the United Kingdom (Fig 5.27) and to provide early warning of any attack. Unlike the previous system, it was designed to continue to operate under hostile attack and to disseminate data to co-ordinate the air defence of the country by manned interceptors, surface-to-air missiles and light anti-aircraft guns (*see* Chapter 7). Unlike the earlier systems, it was fully integrated into the wider NATO air defence system (the NATO Air Defence Ground Environment, or NADGE) and most of the funds for its installation were provided by NATO.

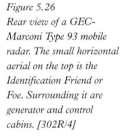

Figure 5.26
Rear view of a GEC-Marconi Type 93 mobile radar. The small horizontal aerial on the top is the Identification Friend or Foe. Surrounding it are generator and control cabins. [302R/4]

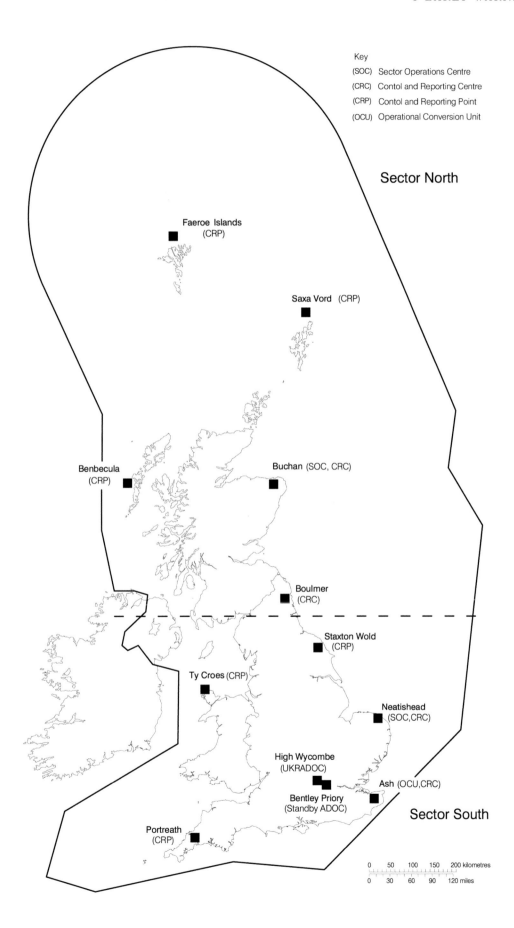

Key
(SOC) Sector Operations Centre
(CRC) Contol and Reporting Centre
(CRP) Contol and Reporting Point
(OCU) Operational Conversion Unit

Sector North

Faeroe Islands
(CRP)

Saxa Vord (CRP)

Benbecula
(CRP)

Buchan (SOC, CRC)

Boulmer
(CRC)

Staxton Wold
(CRP)

Ty Croes (CRP)

Neatishead
(SOC,CRC)

High Wycombe
(UKRADOC)

Ash (OCU,CRC)

Bentley Priory
(Standby ADOC)

Sector South

Portreath
(CRP)

0   50   100   150   200 kilometres

0   30   60   90   120 miles

Figure 5.27
Improved United Kingdom
Air Defence Ground
Environment; map showing
the extent of the United
Kingdom Air Defence
Region and principal
control facilities.

Figure 5.28
a: (above)
RAF Ash, Kent. Air intake
vents, a support building
and a slight mound hint at
what lies beneath.
[AA96/03081]

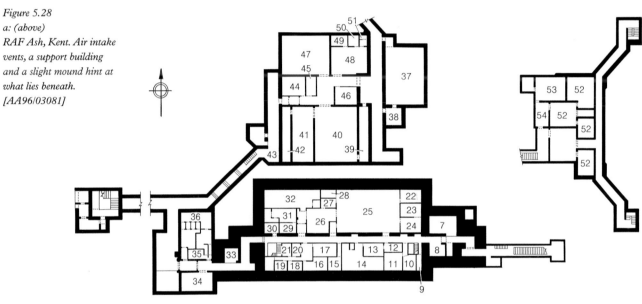

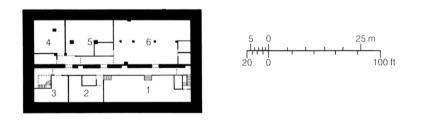

b: Plan showing the bunker
after the alterations made to
the 1950s R3 underground
operations block [original
material courtesy of ATIS
REAL Weatheralls]

1	Air conditioning plant
2	Equipment spares store
3	Store
4	UNITER room and battery bay
5	Computer room
6	Operations room
7	Cooling plant
8	Gas filtration
9–11	Toilet
12	Kitchen office
13	Kitchen
14	Rest room
15–21	Offices
22	Remote data entry terminal room
23	Large screen display room
24	Office
25	Operations room
26–31	Offices
32	Communications centre
33	Transformer
34	Unknown
35	Shelter marshal
36	Decontamination room
37	Fuel tanks
38	Unknown
39	Air extract duct
40	Generator room
41	Fan chamber
42	Air intake
43	Air intake shaft
44–50	Unknown
51	Toilet
52	Water tanks
53	Fresh air plant
54	Water plant room

c: Late 1980s air intake shaft (No. 43 on Fig 5.28b). Air intakes are to the left. [AA96/03108]

d: (below) Late 1980s entrance, providing access to the new plant rooms and operations bunker [AA96/03075]

Figure 5.29 (right)
RAF Neatishead, Norfolk.
Blast door at the entrance
to the refurbished R3
bunker. If attacked with
chemical or biological
weapons the inner doors
could be sealed, and entry
would have been through
the decontamination suite
to the left. [BB98/10053]

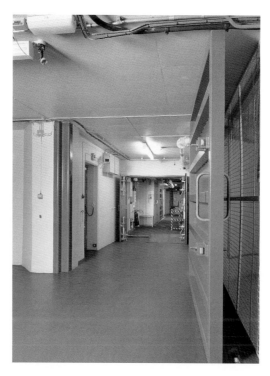

Figure 5.30 (below)
RAF Neatishead, Norfolk.
Refurbished upper
operations room. In front of
each operator is a large
circular radar screen. To
either side monitors display
written data and at the top
right is a screen providing
information on the weather,
airfield status and fighter
readiness. [BB98/10055]

The system had three elements – the fixed sector operations centres, the control and reporting centres or posts, and the mobile radar. The United Kingdom Air Defence Region was divided between North and South, respectively controlled from sector operations centres at Buchan and Neatishead. Ash was equipped to a similar standard to form the training unit, and could operate as a back-up facility in case of emergency. All elements were linked by landlines and microwave communications, with the facility rapidly to switch between control centres in case one was destroyed.

Substantial rebuilding work took place at Buchan, Neatishead and Ash, all of which had 1950s R3 (or 3A) bunkers. In line with the wish to harden these sites against attack, and in contrast to practice in the Linesman period, new plant rooms for standby generators and air intakes and vents were buried in large holes next to the existing bunkers (Figs 5.28a–c). At the original entrance a large new suite of decontamination rooms was

Figure 5.31
RAF Staxton Wold, North
Yorkshire. Linesman site
plan [original material
Crown copyright MoD]

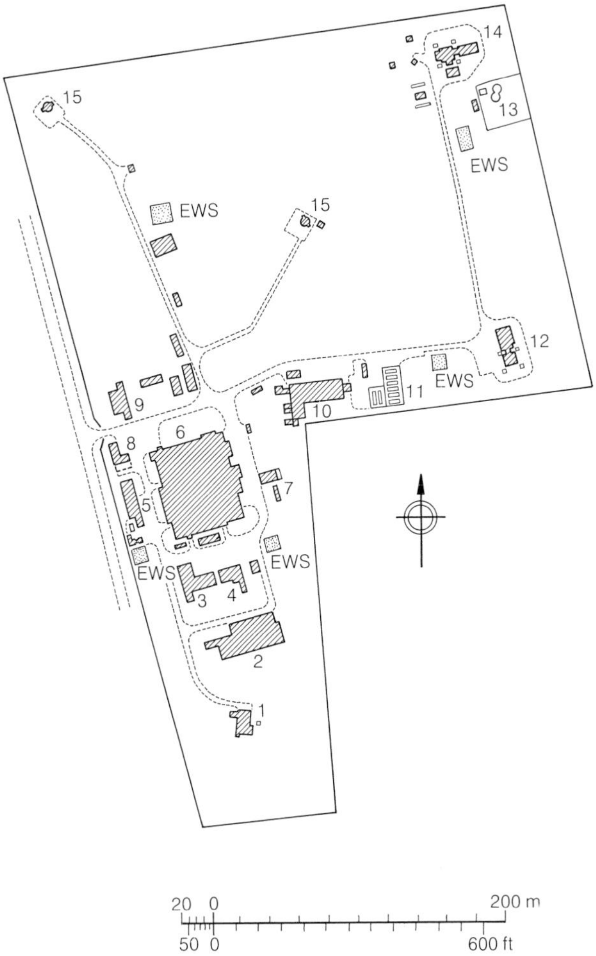

1   GPO building and mast
2   Stores
3   Administration
4   Motor transport section
5   Station headquarters
6   R12, Type 85 radar building
7   Petrol
8   Guard house
9   Married quarters
10 Power house
11 Fuel tanks
12 R15, high speed aerial building
13 Sewage works
14 R17, for Type 84 radar
15 HF200 height-finding radar
EWS Emergency water supply

added (Fig 5.29), reflecting concerns about chemical and biological agents as well as nuclear weapons. For people to sleep at times when the bunker was sealed, fold-up bunks were fixed to the corridor walls. At Neatishead the original entry through the bungalow-like guardroom was retained, but the old tunnel at Ash was sealed and a new entrance built (Fig 5.28d). The bunker interiors, although essentially keeping their 1950s layouts, were entirely re-equipped, the most noticeable change in the operations room being the replacement of the manually updated tote boards with personal electronic displays (see Fig 5.30). Within the sector operations centres various teams built up the electronic air defence picture so that other specialists, including the fighter allocator, master controller and intercept controller, were able to scramble aircraft or assign the target to a missile unit.

Below the sector operations centres in the hierarchy were control and reporting centres or posts (CRC or CRP centres were underground and posts on the surface) with display consoles identical to those in the sector operations centres. Their task was to create a local air picture of flying activity and relay it to the sector operations centres. After they had scrambled the fighter interceptors the control and reporting centres might assume the tactical control of the fighters. Staxton Wold (Fig 5.31) is typical of these smaller reporting centres. It was placed on the site of an existing radar station, at the heart of which was a new single-storey surface bunker (Fig 5.32). There was usually also a mobile 90-series radar, but it would be moved during times of tension. Most of the support buildings were brick (some, such as the stores and offices, reused existing structures) but their appearance was often softened by the addition of pitched tile roofs built over their flat concrete originals. New buildings included a combined mess and, later, a two-storey barrack block.

121

Figure 5.32
RAF Staxton Wold, North
Yorkshire. To the left is the
1980s control and reporting
post and to the right the
ball-like radome, covering
90 series radar. The control
equipment and generators
associated with the radar
are housed in the
transportable containers.
[AA98/03642]

In contrast to the earlier generation of surveillance radar which relied on enormous reserves of power to burn through jamming, new radar introduced in the late 1980s used sophisticated electronics to defeat Soviet counter-measures. To ensure their survival, these 90-series radar were fully mobile – the radar, its control cabin, generators, and other essential equipment could be loaded onto seven trucks and be away within six hours. In peacetime they were usually set up on a fixed base, but infrastructure was fairly rudimentary: at Trimingham it comprised a loop of concrete laid over and around the 1950s bunker, on which the radar and its supporting vehicles were parked. The guardroom was refurbished and used as a flight office and mess room. In the event of conflict, the radar would be moved to one of a number of pre-surveyed positions, making them more difficult to find and destroy. In addition to

the information fed from ground-based radar, the sector operations centres were also able to draw in data from airborne early warning aircraft, ship-borne radar and continental NATO radar stations.

The end of the Cold War has reduced the expectation of an air attack on the United Kingdom, and in England the system has been reduced to a single fixed command and control station at Neatishead. As a cost-saving measure mobile radar, such as the ones at Staxton Wold and Trimingham, were placed beneath weather-proof covers, transparent to radio waves, known as radomes (Fig 5.32) and their control cabins placed in breeze-block structures. The introduction of the Boeing E-3D Sentry airborne early warning aircraft reduced the reliance on ground-based radar and necessitated a major building programme at RAF Waddington, Lincolnshire (Fig 5.33).

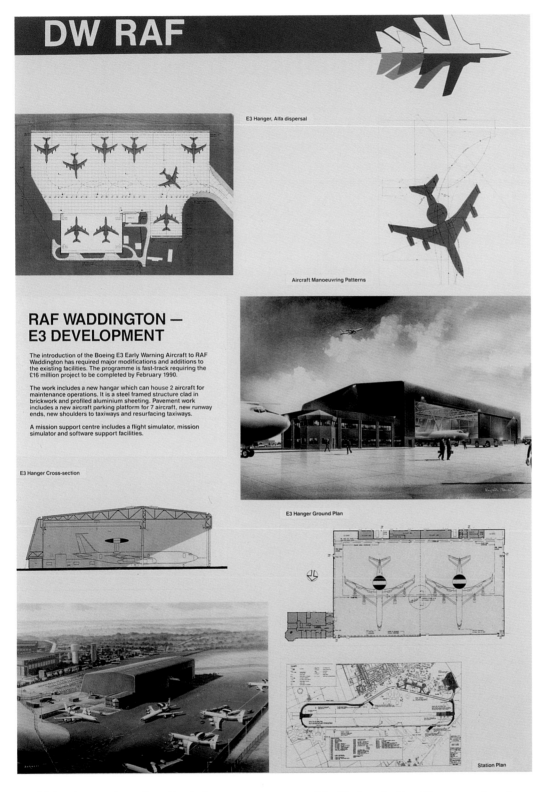

Figure 5.33
RAF Waddington,
Lincolnshire. Design
drawings and an artist's
impression of the new Alfa
dispersal built for the
Boeing E3 early warning
aircraft [ECN 821/7]

This chapter has described the systems and sites designed to guard against the threat of air attack by manned bombers. But defence planners acknowledged in the late 1950s that the Soviets would soon have the capability to launch unstoppable interconti- nental ballistic missiles. To warn of such an assault, the United States began to develop a ballistic missiles early warning system (BMEWS) and associated communications networks: they form the subject of the next chapter.

6
Warning of ballistic missile attack

Since the early 1960s various electronic systems have been used to provide early warning of ballistic missile attack. The three main systems described in this chapter are the ballistic missile early warning system (BMEWS), part of which was based at Fylingdales in North Yorkshire, over the horizon radar (OTHR), and tropospheric scatter systems, which allowed information to be passed to the political and military commanders in the United States.

Ballistic missile early warning system (BMEWS)

The ballistic missile early warning system (BMEWS) was a radar system developed in the United States during the late 1950s to provide early warning of land-based Soviet nuclear missile strikes. Its origins lay in British work during the Second World War which produced cathode ray direction finding receivers (code-named 'Oswald' and 'Willie') which could detect the launch of German V-2 rockets in Holland though they could not track them in flight. BMEWS consisted of three long-range radar sites (Fig 6.1): Thule Air Base, Greenland (BMEWS I); Clear Air Station, Alaska (BMEWS II); and RAF Fylingdales (BMEWS III). These fed information back to the computers of North American Defense Command (NORAD) which was deep inside Cheyenne Mountain, Colorado. RAF Fylingdales, on the North Yorkshire Moors roughly 8 miles (13km) south of Whitby, has been opera-

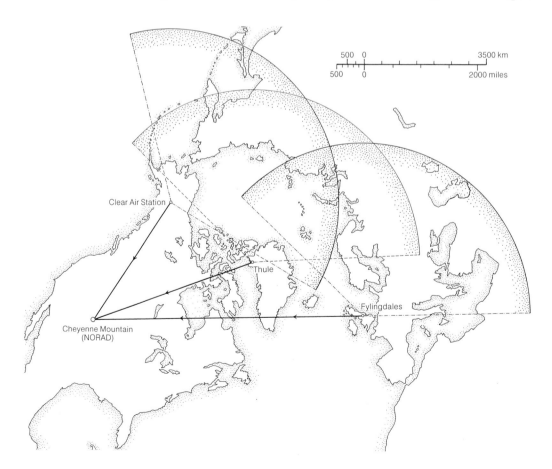

Figure 6.1
Geographical coverage of the ballistic missile early warning system (BMEWS)

124

tional since September 1963, providing early warning against missile attack on the North American continent and Western Europe.

The need to provide early warning of ballistic missile attack on the United States was first considered in 1952, but the systems then proposed were deemed unnecessary as the Soviet Union did not at that stage possess weapons of sufficient range to strike North America. Effort was therefore concentrated on a network of radar stations designed to detect Soviet bomber aircraft approaching over the Arctic. By 1957 it became clear that Soviet technology had advanced significantly. On 15 May the USSR tested the 'Mechanism' – the world's first rocket capable of functioning as an intercontinental ballistic missile; a month later they very publicly demonstrated their technological capability by launching *Sputnik* using a SS-6 (Sanwood) rocket; and in November they sent the first animal, the dog Liaka (Patch), into space in *Sputnik II*. Although the US had in the meantime begun to develop its own intermediate range ballistic missiles (IRBM), named Thor and Jupiter, and intercontinental ballistic missiles, Atlas and Titan, they were severely shaken by their opponent's capability. It was this that led to the urgent resurrection of plans for a ballistic missile defence system providing cover right across the Arctic.

The BMEWS used high-powered long-range radar operated from three sites chosen to allow monitoring of the Arctic region. The sites had to be in sparsely populated places where an area could be physically isolated (for both safety and security) and where the bedrock was sufficiently stable to carry the massive foundations of the tracker arrays. The first two sites – Thule Air Base in Greenland and Clear Air Station in Alaska – were speedily chosen and contracts were let in early 1958. The choice of the third site, which had to be further east, was more complex and, after initial consideration of Iceland, the British Government agreed to accept the system. Several locations were short-listed during 1958, ranging from the north of Scotland to East Anglia, and by September 1959 the US Department of Defense had agreed to construction within the British Army's former practical training area on Lockton High Moor, south of Whitby in North Yorkshire. The site was renamed RAF Fylingdales (though it is not actually in Fylingdales parish). During 1960 the lease to the United States was agreed by Parliament and construction of the main

building was complete by March 1963. Operations commenced on 22 July and formal commissioning on 17 September the same year. Since then the site has operated continuously, though the initial systems were replaced in 1992 by a solid-state phased-array radar (SSPAR).

Purpose of RAF Fylingdales

Unlike BMEWS I and II, BMEWS III at Fylingdales gave warning of attack by both intermediate-range and intercontinental missiles. As originally designed, depending upon the exact launch site, 15–30 minutes' warning could be given to the eastern states of the US and 2½–17 minutes to the British Isles and western Europe. This was intended to give Britain enough warning for the RAF's V-force bombers to take off, to activate the Royal Observer Corps' nuclear monitoring organisation, to allow the United Kingdom Warning and Monitoring Organisation (UKWMO) to broadcast simultaneous attack warnings on all TV and radio networks, and to sound air raid sirens.

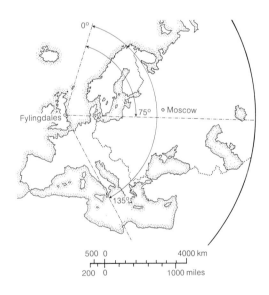

Figure 6.2
Area covered by RAF Fylingdales, North Yorkshire, showing the arc scanned by each radar array before modernisation

By the 1970s the original design had been upstaged by new types of weapon, including submarine-launched ballistic missiles (SLBM) and satellite technology. These meant that an attack could be launched from any direction, rather than from particular sites within eastern Europe (Fig 6.2). This was one of the reasons for a major modernisation of Fylingdales during the late 1980s and early 1990s, providing a new system able to detect missiles from any angle.

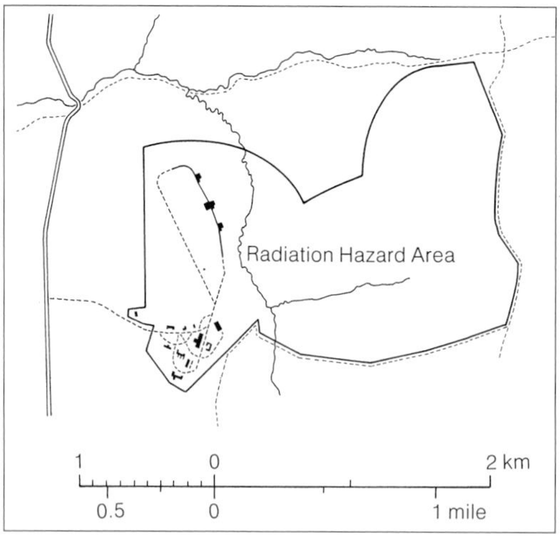

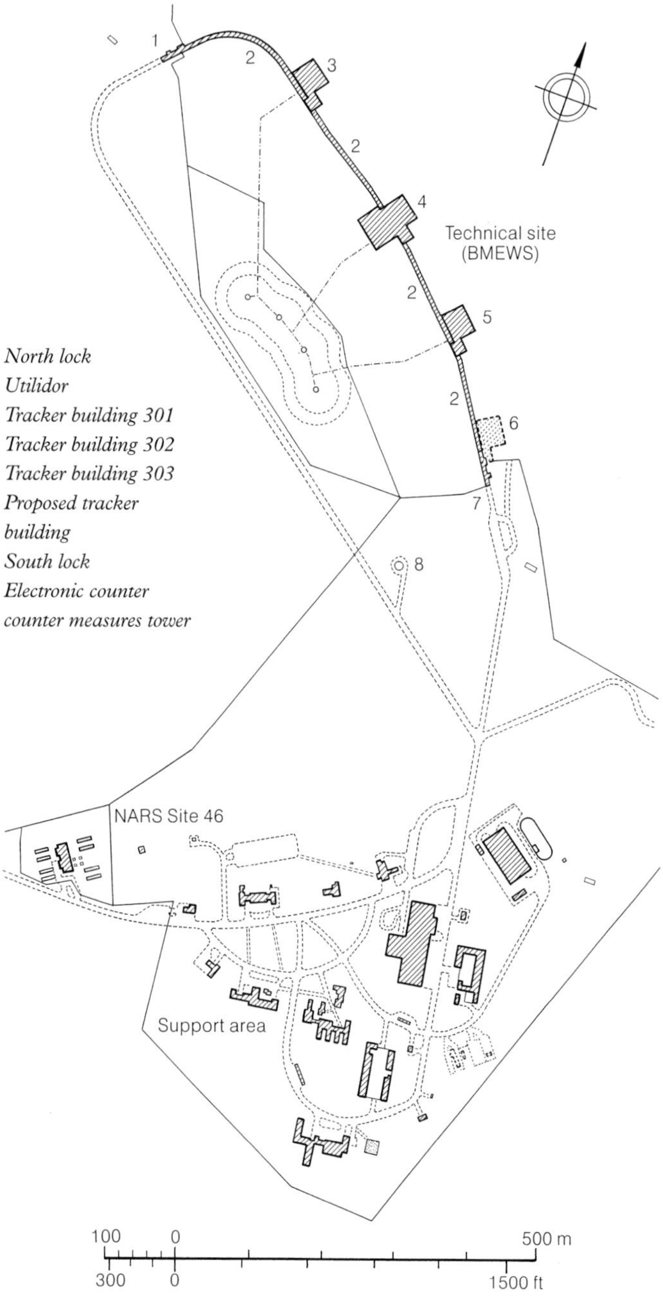

Figure 6.3
RAF Fylingdales, North Yorkshire.
a: (right)
Overall site plan showing the radiation hazard area

b: (below)
Plan dating from about 1964, showing both the BMEWS site and the NARS installation [original material Crown copyright MoD]

1 North lock
2 Utilidor
3 Tracker building 301
4 Tracker building 302
5 Tracker building 303
6 Proposed tracker building
7 South lock
8 Electronic counter counter measures tower

In 1968 RAF Fylingdales had already acquired a secondary role – that of space surveillance ('Spacetrack'). This has two purposes: it monitors the activity of military satellites and, by tracking their orbits, can determine which military bases in the world are being spied upon at any given time; and it enables disused space equipment and debris to be identified and its eventual re-entry into the earth's atmosphere to be predicted (a major consideration since, of the 7,548 man-made objects in orbit in April 1994, 5,356 were debris).

Systems and structures at RAF Fylingdales

In 1963 two discrete functional areas were built at RAF Fylingdales – a technical area and a support area. They lay on a fenced section of moorland called the radiation hazard area, which was 2,500 acres (1,011ha) in extent (Figs 6.3a and b) and was designed to protect people from the powerful microwave emissions of the system. The technical area contained the radar arrays, protected by golf-ball shaped radomes, and the facilities necessary to run them and interpret the information they received. In an attempt to overcome Soviet radar jamming, an electronic counter-counter-measures (ECCM) tower was added in 1964.

The support area occupied only a tenth of the site and contained buildings including a guardhouse, station headquarters, accommodation for the fire, maintenance and motor transport sections, messes, a canteen, stores and a powerhouse. Domestic accommodation was provided elsewhere, both at Whitby and at the domestic camp of RAF Goldsborough, near East Barnby. Next to the radiation hazard area was North Atlantic radio system (NARS) site 46, a tropospheric scatter communication complex (described below).

Within the technical area were three tracker radar arrays (four were planned), each mounted on the roof of a tracker building (Figs 6.4a and b). Each array consisted of a parabolic dish 84ft (25.6m) in diameter, which had a two-piece central hub carrying twenty-four radial lattice girders linked by braces that supported an aluminium mesh. The dish was held by a counterweight, pivoted on an axle and carried on a ball-bearing race mounted on top of a hollow conical pedestal 33ft (10m) high. The pedestal was formed from steel segments arranged in four

Figure 6.4
RAF Fylingdales, North Yorkshire.
a: (previous page)
General view of tracker buildings and radomes

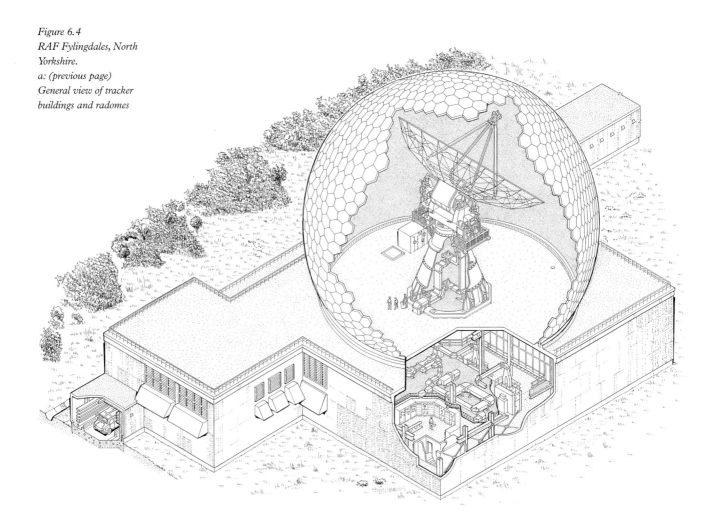

b: (above)
Cutaway, showing the antenna on top of the building, enclosed in a radome. Power generated on the ground floor was mixed on the top storey then passed through waveguides to the antenna; power generation was monitored on the intervening floor. The utilidor through the rear of the structure provided access for cable runs and motor vehicles.

superimposed rings, below the lowest of which was a series of hydraulic rams that enabled the aerial to be levelled. Microwave energy was supplied to the dish through four waveguides (air ducts capable of transmitting greater levels of energy than cables) which terminated at the hornfeed (which transmitted and received the radar pulses). Each array had a range of 3,000 miles (4,828km) and could scan an arc of 75 degrees. Under normal circumstances two of the arrays (TR1 and TR2) undertook surveillance (covering 135 degrees) while the third array (TR3) tracked selected targets. The functions of the trackers were interchangeable and they could be turned off for maintenance.

The arrays were enclosed by protective radomes to protect them from the weather while still enabling the efficient transmission of microwave signals (Fig 6.5a). Each radome consisted of 1,646 five- and six-sided panels, 6in (150mm) thick, made of

glazed fibrous-cardboard honeycomb, sandwiched between polyethylene-coated fibreglass (Fig 6.5b). The construction involved the use of 60,000 bolts. The outside was painted with pale blue Hypalon paint to reduce conspicuousness, while ropes and bosun's chair attachments permitted basic maintenance and the clearance of snow.

During the late 1970s a fire severely damaged one of the radomes at the BMEWS site at Thule (Greenland) and as a result the three radomes at RAF Fylingdales were replaced. Although the new design – an aluminium framework clad in a tensioned Kevlon plastic skin – provided the necessary degree of fire resistance, it was susceptible to damage by birds pecking holes in it and minor repairs were often necessary.

The dish, pedestal and protective radome stood on top of a three-storey tracker building, which was constructed using a frame of steel girders clad in $^3/_{16}$ in (4.7mm) thick, mild steel panels. These provided shielding

from microwave radiation. The structure enclosed a concrete radar tower set on eight concrete pillars 8ft (2.4m) in diameter, which extended down to the bedrock 50ft (15.23m) below ground. Two of the three tracker buildings (301 and 303) were built to the same plan (Fig 6.6a). Each building contained equipment for generating the high levels of power required for the radar (Fig 6.6b–f): on the ground floor (Level 0) were five Klystron generators, while on the second floor (Level 2) the energy from the generators was mixed and regulated before it was transmitted to the dish through the main waveguide. Also on Level 2 was an airlock that gave access onto a stairway up into the radome.

The third Fylingdales building (302) was similar, but also had a rear extension containing equipment for controlling the arrays and analysing the data they gathered. The original computer system, which was situated on the ground floor, was renewed in the

Figure 6.5
RAF Fylingdales, North Yorkshire.
a: (above)
The AN/FPS-49 array and the inside of the golf-ball shaped radome on tracker Building 302 [AA92/04492]

b: (left)
Detail of an original radome panel, which was constructed of condensed corrugated cardboard and fibreglass [AA92/04464]

129

Figure 6.6
RAF Fylingdales, North
Yorkshire.
a: Floor plans of tracker
building 301 [original
material Crown copyright
MoD]

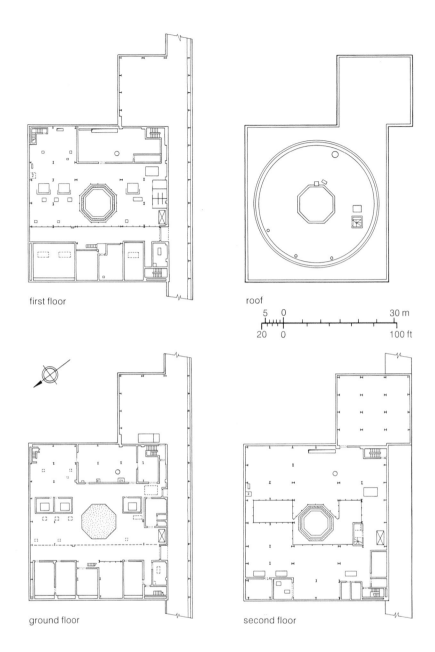

first floor

roof

ground floor

second floor

1980s though its function remained broadly similar. The radar provided analogue data that was converted into digital form before being analysed to determine whether any of the objects detected posed a threat. The analysis was carried out by two separate computers so that its accuracy could be verified. The operations room was permanently staffed so that the information, which was digitally displayed, could be continuously monitored. Also in the operations room was electronic counter-measures (ECM) and electronic counter counter-measures (ECCM) equipment, used to overcome enemy jamming of radar signals. Although the operations room was staffed by military personnel, the equipment was controlled (from a control room next door) by civilians. Many of the electronic systems were duplicated so that there was always a standby system in case of failure. In the twenty-nine years during which the original equipment was used there were only fourteen hours during which operations were suspended.

Access to the tracker buildings was by means of a one-way loop road from the north, the portion nearest the buildings being enclosed within a 1 mile (1.2km) long 'utilidor' (Fig 6.7a) – a tunnel laid along the ground surface rather than under it – giving protection from radiation. It ran between building 302 and the rear operations block,

b: (far left)
Power generation displays
on the first floor of tracker
building 302
[AA92/04455]

c: (left)
Klystron power generation
cabinet (tracker building
302) viewed from the
second floor, showing the
waveguide rising from it to
transmit power to the
mixing area
[AA92/04463]

d: Mixing area on the
second floor of tracker
building 302. Power from a
pair of Klystron generators
enters through a waveguide
at the right, is mixed
(centre) and transmitted to
a frequency modulator that
varied the transmitting
frequencies of the radar (off
picture, left) before being
conducted to the antenna
above. [AA92/04460]

Figure 6.6
e: Computer room on the
ground floor of the
operations annex of tracker
building 302, showing the
impact predictor display
(centre) that predicts the
location of impact
[AA92/04479]

f: Operations room on the
second floor of the
operations annex of tracker
building 302
[AA92/04466]

Figure 6.7
RAF Fylingdales, North
Yorkshire.
a: (far left)
Inside the utilidor, showing
the roadway, crash barrier
and cable runs (left and
right) [AA92/04489]

b: (left)
Police post and steel shutter
doors at the south lock of
the utilidor [AA92/04495]

behind tracker buildings 301 and 303. The ends of the tunnel were closed by north and south locks – double-doored, radiation-shielded chambers with police posts (Fig 6.7b). Cabling, ducting and pipework were carried on cable trays suspended from the walls. The road was large enough for maintenance vehicles and buses, and there were passing places at the unloading bays for each tracker building.

The advent of new types of weapon and of satellite technology from the late 1970s meant that, by the mid-1980s, BMEWS was no longer able to provide adequate warning of attack. After much debate the modernisation of BMEWS was sanctioned by US President Reagan in 1982 and in 1986 the British and United States governments announced the upgrading of Fylingdales. The result was that a new radar array (Fig 6.8), that can detect attack from any angle, was constructed between 1988 and 1992, after which the old arrays and buildings were demolished.

Over the horizon radar (OTHR)

Although BMEWS had a long range, its radar only operated in a straight line with the result that, like the human eye, it could not 'see' beyond the horizon (Fig 6.9). This meant that, although it could track a missile very accurately once it had entered the area covered, it could not detect a missile until some time after it had been launched. In order to overcome this, various kinds of over the horizon radar (OTHR) were developed. These were intended to complement BMEWS, as they could detect missiles at a range of 2,000 miles (3,218 km). In theory,

OTHR systems were less susceptible to jamming than BMEWS and could detect the actual launch of a missile as well as the incidence of nuclear tests. Hence, although they were less well suited to tracking and predicting the actual course of missiles, they could give greater warning of attack.

Figure 6.8
RAF Fylingdales, North
Yorkshire. AN/FPS-115
solid state phased array
radar (SSPAR), built
between 1988 and 1992
[AA94/03148]

Figure 6.9
Diagram showing the
inability of conventional
radar (including the
BMEWS) to detect objects
below the horizon

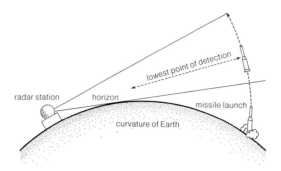

Figure 6.10
Diagram showing the
advantages of a
groundwave over the
horizon radar (OTHR)
compared to conventional
radar

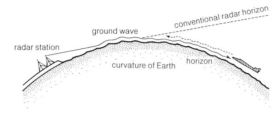

Figure 6.11
Diagram showing the
advantage of airborne
radar

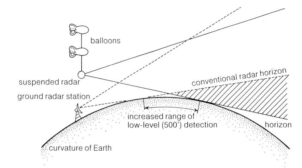

Figure 6.12
RAF Cardington,
Bedfordshire.
a: (right)
View showing the 'Blue
Joker' system during launch
and the layout of roads,
hauling and tethering
positions created for the
trials work. [© Crown
copyright. RAF Air
Defence Museum]

b: (far right)
Detail of 'Blue Joker'
during launch [© Crown
copyright. RAF Air
Defence Museum]

Development of 'over the horizon'

The first British OTHR system, named 'Orange Poodle', was developed from the late 1940s to detect low-flying aircraft. It used the movement of the sea to send high frequency signals over the horizon (ground-wave – Fig 6.10). Trials in 1953 were based at RAF Downderry radar station in Cornwall, where an array was constructed between two timber towers but, while they demonstrated that the system was workable, it was clear that it was too susceptible to jamming to be viable. Attention was therefore diverted to an alternative system, 'Blue Joker', in which a conventional radar array was suspended inside a pressurised radome, 30ft (9m) in diameter, which was hung from captive balloons flown 5,000ft (1,425m) above the ground (Figs 6.11 and 6.12a and b). Power was passed up the tethering cable, and information was relayed to the ground by a light-weight microwave transmitter. This system was developed at several locations, including RAF Cardington, Bedfordshire, and Drum, near Llanfairfechan in Gwynedd but, although it reached an advanced stage, it was abandoned by the British in 1960 as by then the main threat was perceived to be from Soviet ballistic missiles rather than aircraft. Despite this, the United States continued to work on related projects and, by bouncing radar signals off the ionosphere (sky-wave), were able significantly to increase the range at which aircraft could be detected. This eventually gave rise to two major systems that were partly deployed in Europe with some sites in England.

Project 440-L

Project 440-L involved transmitting a signal into the ionosphere and bouncing it down to a receiver thousands of miles away, recording any disturbance caused by the passing of a missile (a forward-scatter system – Fig 6.13a). There were three transmitters (two in the Far East) and ten receivers were distributed across Europe, one of them at the former Thor missile site at RAF Feltwell, Norfolk. Planning for the facility included the preparation of a cover story for the press that the site was to be used for 'long-range communications research'. The system began to be used in 1968 and became fully operational in the early 1970s. There are now no physical remains of this project, apart from a small, prefabricated breeze-block hut.

Project 441-L – 'Cobra Mist'

At the same time as Project 440-L was being developed, work proceeded on another system: Project 441-L, or 'Cobra Mist'. This involved transmitting and receiving signals from the same station; the returning signals being reflected back by the object(s) detected (a back-scatter system – Fig 6.13b). The main aim was to monitor aircraft movements over eastern Europe and missiles launched from the USSR's Northern Fleet base at Plesetsk. Although it was intended to establish Cobra Mist in Turkey, problems in negotiating a suitable site led to the selection, in 1964, of a former airfield and bombing range at Orfordness on the Suffolk coast.

Construction and commissioning were beset by problems. First, the area had to be

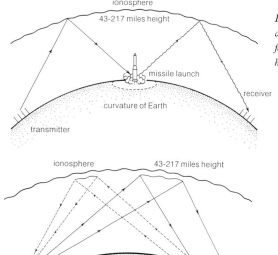

Figure 6.13
a: Diagram showing a forward-scatter over the horizon radar system

b: Diagram showing a back-scatter over the horizon radar system

cleared of bombs; this began in 1967. Then, although building was finished almost on schedule in July 1971, two of the masts collapsed on 23 September so that the site was only completed on 9 February 1972. Testing, which began at once, was further delayed by problems with the electricity supply caused by the coal miners' strike. When testing resumed, it was rapidly discovered that there were problems with background 'noise'. They eventually proved to be so severe and intractable that, despite the vast investment already made, the system was abandoned in June 1973.

By that time, the 705-acre (285ha) site near Orfordness lighthouse contained a

Figure 6.14
Orfordness, Suffolk.
a: 'Cobra Mist', back-scatter over the horizon radar system. Radar array field [15704/25]

Figure 6.14
b: General plan of the
'Cobra Mist' site
[reproduced from Ordnance
Survey mapping on behalf
of the Controller of Her
Majesty's Stationery Office
© Crown copyright. Licence
No. GD 03085G/02/01]

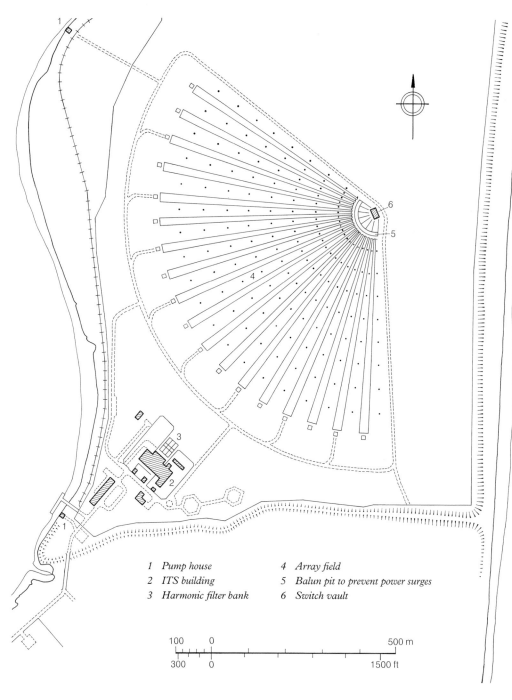

1 Pump house   4 Array field
2 ITS building   5 Balun pit to prevent power surges
3 Harmonic filter bank   6 Switch vault

c: Antenna string

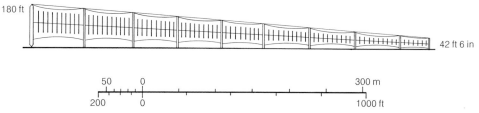

number of structures, the largest of which was the antenna fan area (Figs 6.14a–g), which was served by an operations centre (the ITS building), and structures including storm water pump houses, a helicopter pad and a jetty. From a distance the antenna looked like a spider's web of masts and cables. It consisted of eighteen radiating aeri-

136

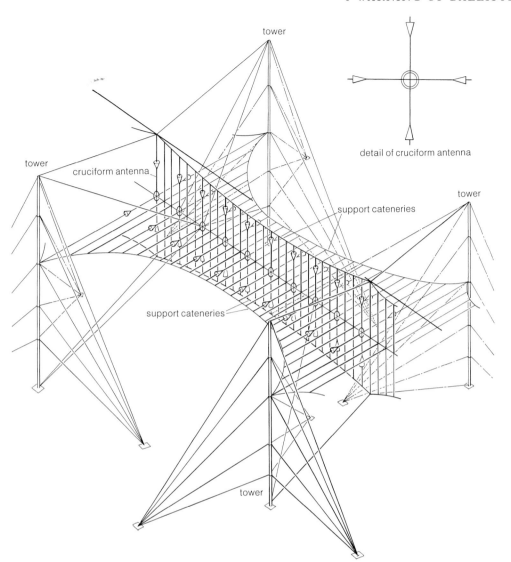

tower

tower

cruciform antenna

tower

support cateneries

support cateneries

tower

detail of cruciform antenna

d: Antenna string, showing its construction

e: (below)
Antenna string under construction [G14969/1]

als below which was a wire-mesh ground screen. Each aerial consisted of a horizontal and a vertical array and was 1,800ft (549m) long. The aerials rose from a height of 42ft 6in (13m) at one end to 180ft (55m) at the other and were suspended on a system of fibreglass rods, the whole being held in place by guy ropes attached to 152 asbestos cement or (at the upper end) steel towers. The array was built to exacting specifications so that it could survive extremes of weather.

The antennae were connected to a harmonic filter bank which was intended to filter out background 'noise' and sat on a platform at the north-east side of the operations centre (now used by the BBC World Service). The latter was a three-storey steel-framed building, the first and second floors of which were each divided into three sections. At the north and south ends of the

Figure 6.14
f: (above)
Harmonic filter bank which
removed unwanted
background 'noise'
[G/14341/15]

g: Installation of the line
feeds from the Balun tanks,
passing through the roof of
the switch vault. The Balun
tanks prevented in-
phase/out-phase surges of
energy in the antenna
string. [G14341/13]

138

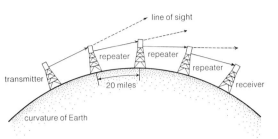

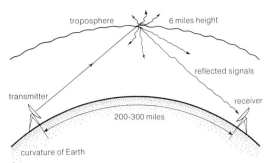

Figure 6.15
a: (far left)
Diagram showing limitations of conventional microwave transmission (line of sight)

b: (left)
Diagram showing the advantages of tropospheric scatter communication

first floor were various stores and offices, while the central area contained equipment for the running of the antennae. The north of the second floor contained more offices and the central area further equipment; at the south were the main computer area and operations rooms from which the antennae were controlled and in which the data received was analysed.

Tropospheric scatter communication systems

Once information had been gathered by a long-distance radar site (whether BMEWS or OTHR) it had to be passed to the command structure by a means that was speedy, reliable and secure. Super high frequency (microwave) radio could not be used since its waves travel in a straight line and cannot be transmitted over the horizon without repeater stations every 20 miles (32km) (Fig 6.15a). This is particularly inappropriate for communications that need to cross large areas of sea or inhospitable terrain such as the Arctic.

The solution to this involved transmitting a 'beam' of radio waves from an antenna into the troposphere – part of the atmosphere 6 miles (9.6km) above the Earth's surface (Fig 6.15b). From there the signal is scattered over the horizon in all directions, including forwards, where it can be picked up by a distant receiving antenna. Because the signal is scattered in all directions much of it is lost into space, and very considerable levels of power have to be applied for the signal returning to Earth to be strong enough to be picked up. By this means it is possible for the gap between the repeater stations to be increased from 20 miles (32km) to between 200 and 600 miles (between 322 and 966km), depending on precise topographical conditions.

This technology was so successful that, in the 1960s, it became the basis of the major long-distance communications networks of the United States and other NATO forces. Several systems were developed, two of which – the North Atlantic Radio System (NARS) and 'Ace High' – have particular relevance to sites in Britain.

North Atlantic Radio System (NARS)

The North Atlantic Radio System (NARS) was constructed in the early 1960s for communication between the BMEWS III site at Fylingdales and the North American continent, using a chain of five stations: Fylingdales, Mormond Hill near Fraserburgh (Aberdeenshire, Scotland), Tórshavn (Faeroe Islands) and Höfn and Keflavik (both in Iceland). This then linked into other systems that extended from Greenland to Canada and the United States (Fig 6.16).

With the exception of Fylingdales, each

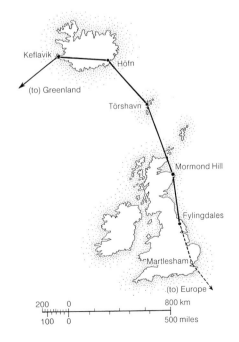

Figure 6.16
Map of NARS stations in the United Kingdom and Ireland

Figure 6.17
60ft billboard antenna,
NARS site 46

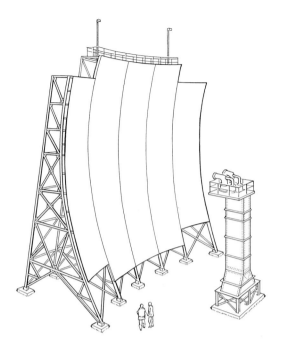

NARS site consisted of two pairs of concave 'billboard' antennae, a radio building and a building housing both electronic equipment and a generator. As originally designed, Fylingdales had only one pair of antennae, each 60ft (18m) across (Fig 6.17), since it lay at one end of the chain and therefore only needed to transmit and receive in one direction. In 1964, however, a second pair of antennae was added, enabling communication to the south and providing a link into the European network of the USAF which had a base at Martlesham Heath in Suffolk. Even then, Fylingdales was not quite the same as the other sites because it was able to draw its power from the neighbouring BMEWS site rather than requiring its own generators. During the late 1970s, the electronic equipment was replaced to enhance the capabilities of the system and reduce maintenance costs.

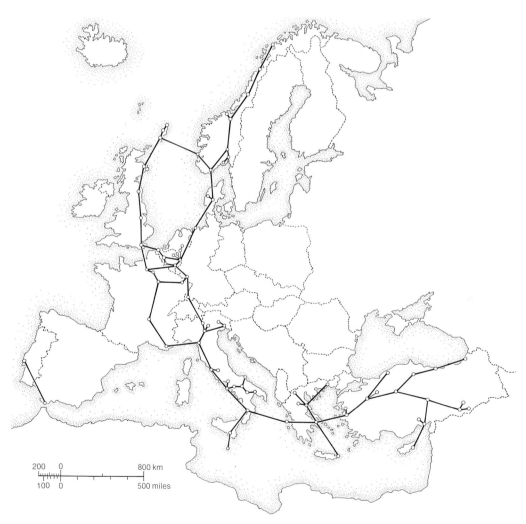

Figure 6.18
Map showing the main
elements of the Ace High
communication system

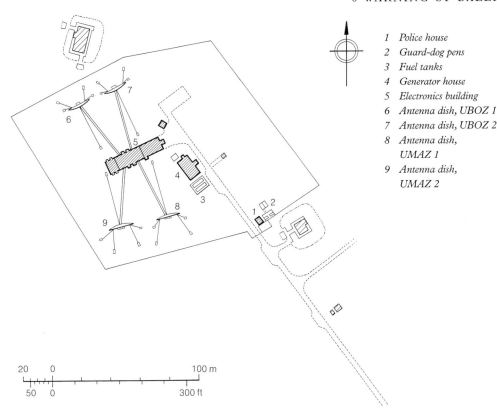

1 Police house
2 Guard-dog pens
3 Fuel tanks
4 Generator house
5 Electronics building
6 Antenna dish, UBOZ 1
7 Antenna dish, UBOZ 2
8 Antenna dish,
   UMAZ 1
9 Antenna dish,
   UMAZ 2

Figure 6.19
RAF Stenigot,
Lincolnshire. Plan of the
NATO forward scatter
station (NFSS) [reproduced
from Ordnance Survey
mapping on behalf of the
Controller of Her Majesty's
Stationery Office © Crown
copyright. Licence No. GD
03085G/02/01]

'Ace High'

Ace High was built for Allied Command Europe (ACE) and allowed the use of both speech and telegraph circuits. The contracts for the construction of the system were used in 1959 and construction work at the British sites was completed during 1960, with the system becoming operational the following year and remaining in service until the early 1990s. Even after abandonment, little of the equipment was removed from the British sites until 1996, with the result that more is known about them than about some of the other sites described in this chapter.

It is believed that a total of eighty-four sites, extending from Norway to Turkey, have, at one time or another, been equipped with Ace High troposcatter equipment (Fig 6.18). They included command centres and radar sites as well as the relay stations. There were five sites in Britain: one on the Shetland Islands, Mormond Hill near Fraserburgh (on the same site as the NARS station – *see above*), Brizlee Wood near Alnwick in Northumberland, Stenigot in Lincolnshire and Maidstone in Kent. There were also three spurs to satellite communication stations.

Local topographical conditions combined with technical features meant that no two tropospheric scatter communication sites were identical, but the NATO forward scatter station (NFSS) Stenigot (Fig 6.19) may be taken as typical. It was on the site of pre-war radar station some 10 miles (16km) south west of Louth, was 4.72 acres (2ha) in extent and was enclosed by a security fence illuminated from within by high intensity lighting. Access was provided by a single-track road that passed through a double gateway flanked by a two-storey police house.

The site was dominated by two pairs of parabolic dish antenna 60ft (18m) in diameter (Fig 6.20), now demolished. Each consisted of aluminium panels on a girder framework and was supported on seven lattice legs made of steel girders, anchored to large concrete blocks. Power was supplied from the National Grid, although there was an emergency generator, and energy was conveyed to the antennae through waveguides (air ducts through which energy was transmitted) that crossed the site supported on scaffolding poles and were protected from the weather by a timber and roofing-felt cover. The main building was a single-storey brick structure, thirteen bays long, placed between the pairs of antennae. It housed the transmitters, receivers and other equipment required for running the antennae as well as a range of offices and facilities for the staff.

*Figure 6.20
RAF Stenigot,
Lincolnshire, NATO
forward scatter station.
Sixty-foot dish antenna
(UBOZ 2) with the
electronics building in the
background*

The end of tropospheric scatter systems

During the 1980s new forms of communication technology were developed, and new systems evolved. The most important elements of those new systems relate to the use of microwaves and of space satellites. By the early 1990s tropospheric scatter systems had been superseded and both the United States and the rest of NATO rapidly abandoned them, with the result that the North Atlantic radio system and Ace High were decommissioned and the sites associated with them closed down.

7
The response – air defence

This chapter discusses the armed response that might have met any attack by manned aircraft. It can be divided into three main categories – interceptor aircraft, anti-aircraft guns and surface-to-air missiles (*see* Fig 5.1).

Airborne interceptors

It was not only radar defences that were reduced after the war. There was a similar rundown in the number of fighter airfields so that, by 1951, there were eighteen left to defend the United Kingdom. Towards the end of the war jet fighters began to enter service. Their operating needs, and the development of tactics to counter the changing Soviet threat and to embrace new technology, created new demands for airfield infrastructure and directly influenced the layout of Cold War airfields. All the fighter interceptor squadrons were stationed at existing airfields, where in most cases the domestic and technical buildings were less than twenty years old. The most noticeable changes were made to the runways and surrounding grassed areas – the flying field – to make them suitable for the new jet aircraft.

Some of the peculiarities of jet operation made a concrete runway essential. Jet aircraft usually had a nose-wheel tricycle undercarriage, which on landing tended to dig in on soft grass. Back blast from the engines was liable to scorch vegetation, exposing the bare earth, which wet weather could soon reduce to a quagmire. Aircraft were also getting heavier and required longer runways. Reconstruction work at Duxford, Cambridgeshire, begun in 1950, is typical of the modifications carried out to many fighter airfields (Fig 7.1). In place of the open grass flying field, perhaps strengthened with steel matting, or the typical wartime airfield plan with its runways laid out in the shape of a letter 'A', a single concrete runway became the dominant form. Faster aircraft reduced the warning time of attack and, in an attempt to cut the reaction times, operational readiness platforms were constructed, usually at both ends of the main runway.

During the early 1950s, under 'Operation Fabulous', aircraft were held on such platforms in constant readiness from dawn to dusk. In front of the hangars large concrete aircraft servicing platforms were constructed. In this position aircraft were very vulnerable to attack and, on some airfields such as North Weald, Essex, existing wartime fighter revetments were retained to protect parked aircraft from low-flying attackers, while at Duxford (Fig 7.1) Y-shaped dispersals with protective blast walls were built between 1953 and 1955. Around the same time at other airfields freestanding 16ft (4.88m) vertical walls were erected, between which aircraft could be parked: they were generally of reinforced-concrete and usually close to the end of the main runway. Examples survive at Coltishall, Norfolk, Wattisham, Suffolk, and Waterbeach, Cambridgeshire (Fig 7.2).

No standard type of control tower is associated with the post-war fighter airfields. At some, such as Duxford, the wartime tower was updated. Elsewhere, earlier towers were demolished to make way for new aprons and taxiways, or were resited to provide better visibility. Increased use of radios, electronic navigation aids and, later, local radar-guided

Figure 7.1
RAF Duxford, Cambridgeshire. This view of November 1955, shows the recently laid single concrete runway with operational readiness platforms at either end. Next to it is the earlier and still operational pieced steel plank runway. Also visible are the large aircraft servicing platforms in front of the hangars. At the four corners of the airfield are Y-shaped dispersal pads, to accommodate the Duxford Wing, of two squadrons of sixteen aircraft. [58/1924, V, 25 Nov 1955, frame 0061 © Crown copyright MoD]

Figure 7.2
RAF Waterbeach,
Cambridgeshire. Revetment
walls built to protect parked
aircraft from low-flying
attackers. The rear wall is
probably later [AA009782]

features introduced in the late 1950s to increase aircraft safety were arrester wires and nets, which were strung across the runway either to catch a special hook on the aircraft or to capture it in a nylon web.

Airfield infrastructure was also influenced by changes in aircraft armament. The Hawker Hunter, introduced in the early 1950s (Fig 7.3a), used a demountable 1,700lb (771kg) 'cannon pack' instead of permanently mounted guns, which enabled the weapons to be serviced and loaded without the aircraft being removed from operational duties. In response to this a new armoury was built at Duxford (Fig 7.3b), close to one of the new servicing aprons. It was chiefly used for the maintenance of the cannon packs but some space was also set aside for overhauling ejector seats; another innovative feature of post-war jet aircraft. No explosives were kept in the building apart from some small arms ammunition. Cannon shells for the gun packs were linked together and loaded in the remote ammunition storage area.

air traffic control systems demanded larger control towers. At North Weald, Essex, and Biggin Hill, Greater London, large Type 5222A/51 towers were built (see Fig 4.5), while many other airfields were equipped with Type 2548a/55 (see Fig 3.3). Less intensively used and reserve airfields were often given single-storey local control towers. Other

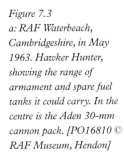

Figure 7.3
a: RAF Waterbeach,
Cambridgeshire, in May
1963. Hawker Hunter,
showing the range of
armament and spare fuel
tanks it could carry. In the
centre is the Aden 30-mm
cannon pack. [PO16810 ©
RAF Museum, Hendon]

b: RAF Duxford,
Cambridgeshire. Armoury,
now in use as a museum
cafe. To the left were offices,
stores and a small-arms
armoury. Cannon packs,
carried on trollies, were
brought along the curving
track to the servicing bay.
Other sections of the
building contained dipping
tanks for cleaning the guns,
and storage areas for spare
cannon packs and ejector
seats. [BB99/01542]

The most significant change in fighter armament was the introduction of guided air-to-air missiles, making it possible for aircraft to engage in combat at a much greater distance from each other than previously. In comparison to the simple belted ammunition, or even to the cordite-propelled rockets of the Second World War, missiles were vastly expensive and required controlled environmental conditions for storage and maintenance. The introduction of Firestreak missiles at Wattisham, Suffolk, and West Raynham, Norfolk (*see* Fig 7.4), for example, prompted the construction of new facilities.

At RAF Binbrook, Lincolnshire, one of the main interceptor airfields from the 1960s to the 1980s, a large new missile servicing facility was developed to the east of the Second World War bomb stores (Figs 7.5a and b). Other alterations there included the lengthening of the main runway to 7,500ft (2,286m) and the construction of operational readiness platforms and of a concrete apron in front of the hangars. For more than twenty years from 1966, Binbrook was associated with the Lightning, manufactured by English Electric, which, with its tremendous rate of climb, was designed to meet Britain's unique Cold War air defence need for a

fighter which could rapidly engage intruders over the North Sea. To support this task, a steel-framed quick reaction alert hangar was built just off the southern end of the main runway in about 1972 (Figs 7.5c and d). In it, a pair of fully armed and fuelled Lightnings were kept at constant readiness. Similar hangars were built at Wattisham and Leuchars in Fife, Scotland.

Figure 7.4
The Gloster Javelin was the first British purpose-built all-weather fighter. In the foreground is a Fairey Firestreak air-to-air missile, introduced in 1958. [PO19095 © RAF Museum, Hendon]

Figure 7.5
RAF Binbrook, Lincolnshire. a: Missile servicing facility. At the bottom left are the pre-Second World War bomb stores and, above, the far larger area developed during the early 1960s to hold guided weapons. [17020/09]

Figure 7.5
b: Plan of the missile
servicing facility [original
material Crown copyright
MoD]

1	Picket post and crew rooms
2	Components testing
3	Trolley stores
4	Garages
5	Ready use store
6	Magazine
7	Bomb stores
8	Systems testing, servicing, compressor house and plant room
9	Missile stores
10	Launcher servicing
11	Components stores
12	Tail unit stores
13	Incendiary bomb stores
14	Bomb stores
15	Components store
EWS	Emergency water supply

20 0   200 m

50 0   600 ft

c: (right)
Quick reaction alert
hangar, built on top of a
wartime dispersal pad. To
the front a new taxiway has
been laid to the runway.
[17020/24]

d: (far right)
Quick reaction shelter, with
armed Lightning interceptor
[Photo by Aldon P
Ferguson]

From a post-war peak of thirty-one air defence airfields in the mid-1950s the number dropped to nine in 1962, and was further reduced to four by the 1980s. By that time, the United Kingdom's air defence was fully integrated with that of the rest of NATO. During the late 1970s and 1980s this was reflected in a massive Europe-wide programme to provide hardened accommodation for key airfield buildings (*see* Chapter 4). Four airfields assigned to air defence were protected in this way – Wattisham, Coningsby (Lincolnshire), Leuchars, and Leeming (North Yorkshire). The late 1980s building programme at Leeming was the most extensive and, in addition to hardened facilities, included new domestic accommodation, an air traffic control building, a mission simulator and an engine test facility for the Tornado's RB-199 engine.

Heavy anti-aircraft defences

If the interceptors failed to destroy attacking aircraft the last line of defence was ground-based anti-aircraft guns and, later, missiles (*see* Fig 5.1). During the Second World War nearly 1,000 anti-aircraft gun sites were designated and at the end of the war it was proposed to retain 210, which

were to be known as the 'Nucleus Force' and would form the core of any future expansion. Under this scheme, guns and fire control equipment were maintained on half the sites while equipment for the remainder was stored (Fig 7.6). Even this plan proved to be too ambitious for the available manpower, and by 1950 it had been pared down under a new scheme known as 'Igloo'. This envisaged defences concentrated on three key areas – Forth/Clyde, Mersey/Midlands and London/South East – a total of seventy-eight sites, fifty-four of which were to have permanently mounted guns. With the outbreak of the Korean War in June 1950, and fears that it might be a prelude to an attack on western Europe, Britain's air defences were considerably strengthened. By April 1951 the mobilisation plan for Anti-Aircraft Command listed 684 positions for the full force, though it is unlikely that this total was ever achieved. Identified positions were a mixture of retained Nucleus and Igloo scheme sites, rehabilitated wartime sites and new builds. Field visits to some sites close to Manchester Airport revealed no gun positions, suggesting that they were for mobile guns or, more probably, that shortage of money prevented work from starting.

The army retained responsibility for anti-

Figure 7.6
Strensall, North Yorkshire.
Second World War anti-
aircraft ordnance depot.
Stores such as these
continued to hold guns and
radar equipment until the
1950s. [12800/05]

Table 7.1 Administrative organisation of anti-aircraft defences during the early 1950s

Gun defended area	AAOR	Group	Brigade	Group commander
Harwich	Mistley Heath	1	6	Bawburgh (Rotor SOC)
Norwich	Not known		16	
Thames North	Vange		9/11	
Thames South	Fort Bridgewoods		1/59	
London North	Lippetts Hill		7/63	
London South	Pendell Camp		15/64	
London West	RAF Uxbridge		67/82	
Dover	Dover Castle		99	
Portsmouth/Southampton	Fort Fareham	2	10	Box (Rotor SOC)
Bristol	Lansdown		14	
Brockworth	Ullenwood		106	
Plymouth	Crownhill Fort		81	
Portland	Ridgeway Hill			
Lock Ewe	Gairloch	3	78	Barnton Quarry (Rotor SOC)
Glasgow/Clyde	East Kilbride		68	
Clyde Anchorage	Inverkip		77	
Forth/Rosyth	Craigiehall		12	
Belfast	Lisburn		51	
Londonderry	Not known			
Birmingham	Wylde Green	4	74	Longley Lane (Rotor SOC)
Mersey	Frodsham		79	
Coventry/Rugby	Stoneleigh Park		13	
Cardiff	Wenallt		71	
Barrow	Abbeywood		93	
Swansea	West Cross		95	
Milford Haven	Llanion Barracks			
Manchester	Worsley		70	
Tyne	Gosforth	5	8	
Tees	Kirklevington Hall		83	
Hull	Wawne		17	
Leeds	Birkenshaw		69	
Sheffield	Conisborough		65	
Derby	Elvaston		58	

aircraft defences, which were divided into thirty-three gun defended areas (Table 7.1). Within each of these areas, guns were commanded from an anti-aircraft operations room (AAOR) staffed by army personnel. In a few instances, such as Dover Castle and Crownhill Fort, Plymouth, the AAOR were placed in existing fortifications, but in most cases they were in purpose-built monolithic reinforced-concrete bunkers costing between £20,000 and £35,000. The standard type is rectangular in plan and two-storeyed, one storey being sunk below ground level (Fig 7.7a). At Frodsham, Cheshire (Fig 7.7b), and nearby at Worsley, Manchester, they have been partly set into the surrounding hillside to gain extra protection, with one entrance to the lower level and another, at the opposite end, to the upper floor.

The role of AAOR staff was to filter information from the RAF sector operations cen-

tres to the individual gun sites. At the heart of the building was a double-storey plotting room overlooked by a viewing gallery and control cabins, surrounded by equipment and rest rooms (Figs 7.8a and b). The anti-aircraft operations rooms were usually some distance from their gun sites, but at Elvaston, Derbyshire, and Lippetts Hill and Vange (both in Essex), gun emplacements were located with them. At the latter two sites and at Ullenwood, Gloucestershire, blocks of wartime standard Ministry of Works timber hutting survive, suggesting troops were barracked at some anti-aircraft operations rooms.

After the war, heavy anti-aircraft guns were standardised at two calibres: 3.7-inch and 5.25-inch. Both were emplaced in batteries of between two and eight guns, although four was the norm. Associated with each calibre of gun is a distinctive emplace-

Figure 7.7
Anti-aircraft operations
rooms
a: Mistley Heath, Essex.
Semi-sunken type
[BB97/10570]

b: Frodsham, Cheshire.
[© Roger J C Thomas]

ment and site layout. Many of the sites were of wartime date and, together with those 5.25-inch sites constructed immediately after May 1945, reflect wartime needs rather than those of the Cold War. The site at Bowaters Farm, Essex, may be seen as typical of this category. First requisitioned in 1939, new 5.25-inch emplacements were built between 1945 and 1946 and further buildings, including a reinforced-concrete command post, were added in about 1950. This particular site, along with some other 5.25-inch sites, had a dual role, as it could be pressed into service for coastal defence.

The early post-war 5.25-inch sites follow late wartime designs, being square or dia-mond-shaped with a gun emplacement at each corner (Fig 7.9). On sites constructed during the early 1950s the gun emplacements are laid out in a shallow arc (Fig 7.10). The emplacements on these sites are substantial features, 43ft 4in (13.2m) in diameter, with a central gun pit 19ft (5.8m) across and 5ft 3in (1.6m) deep, to accommodate the traversing mechanism of the gun and the hydraulics which served the automatic loading system (Fig 7.11). Attached to each emplacement was an engine room which housed a diesel generator, hydraulic pumps, and an air compressor to power the recoil system.

Post-war examples of 3.7-inch sites, such

Figure 7.8
a: (right)
Plan of typical anti-aircraft operations room [redrawn from Cheshire County Council plan]

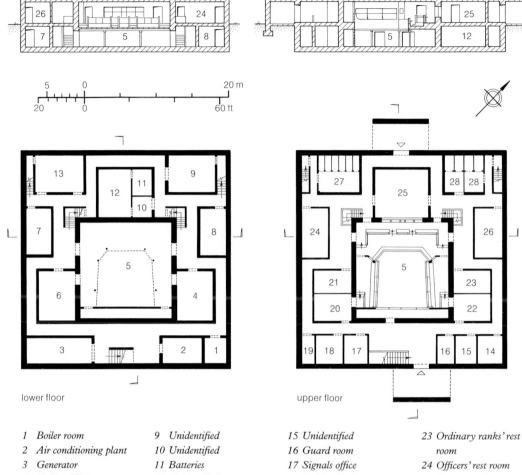

lower floor

upper floor

1 Boiler room	9 Unidentified	15 Unidentified	23 Ordinary ranks' rest room
2 Air conditioning plant	10 Unidentified	16 Guard room	24 Officers' rest room
3 Generator	11 Batteries	17 Signals office	25 Switchboards
4 Unidentified	12 Unidentified	18 Unidentified	26 WRAC rest room
5 Plotting room	13 Womens' Royal Army	19 Unidentified	27 WRAC lavatory
6 Unidentified	Corps (WRAC)	20 Civil servants	28 Officers' and OR's
7 ?Electrical switch room	rest room	21 WRAC officers	lavatories
8 Unidentified	14 Clerk's office	22 NAAFI	

b: (right)
Frodsham, Cheshire. Anti-aircraft operations room. Interior showing upper gallery of the central operations room [303X/7]

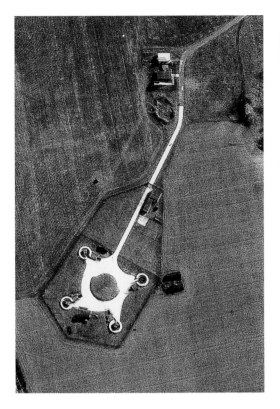

Figure 7.9 (far left)
Trimley Heath, Suffolk.
Characteristic late war or
early post-war square 5.25-
inch gun site [Sortie
F21.58/RAF/1672, 3 Mar
1955, 11527, frame 0366
© Crown copyright MoD]

Figure 7.10 (left)
MY 51 Lower Kinnerton,
Flintshire/Cheshire border.
5.25-inch gun site probably
built about 1950 [Sortie
F543/RAF/385, F22,
frame 0048 © Crown
copyright MoD]

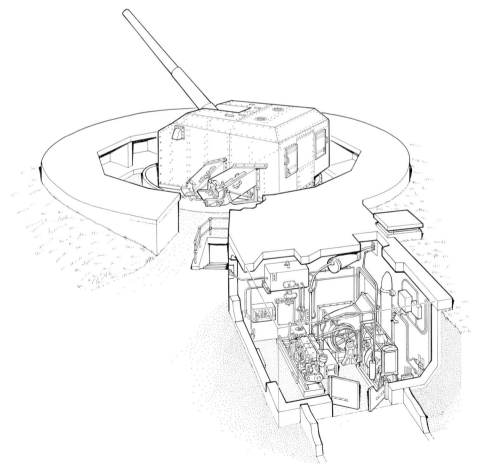

Figure 7.11
Cutaway showing a 5.25-
inch gun emplacement and
engine house

1 Holdfast for gun
2 Ammunition locker
3 Generator

Figure 7.12
a: (above)
Halls Green, Essex.
3.7-inch anti-aircraft gun
emplacement built on a
greenfield site about 1950.
The building to the bottom
right housed a standby
generator, and the building
to the top was the command
post. [18324/20]

b: (above right)
Beddlestead, Surrey. Plan
of a 3.7-inch gun
emplacement [original
material courtesy of
Michael Shackel]

c: (right)
3.7-inch anti-aircraft gun,
Mark VI, No. 5. Note the
metal grill platform and
automatic ammunition
loading system. [© Royal
Artillery Historical Trust]

as Halls Green, Essex (Fig 7.12a), and Broom Bank (near Biggin Hill), Greater London, have four emplacements arranged in a shallow arc. They are eight-sided in plan, constructed from reinforced-concrete, and measure 49ft (15m) across. At the centre are eight holdfast nuts to which the gun was fixed, and around them rings of sawn-off bolts which held the loading platform. On four of the walls there are lockers for ready-use ammunition, which contrasts with the six walls normally used in wartime examples (Figs 7.12b and c). At Kilnsea, Spurn Point, East Riding of Yorkshire, the wartime battery has been clearly adapted to accept the new version of the 3.7-inch gun by the insertion of a ring of nuts around the holdfast on which to mount its loading platform.

To counter the threat from ever-increasing aircraft speeds, emphasis was placed on developing automatic radar-guided gun-laying – positioning the gun for firing – to replace older and slower optical and manual methods. These objectives are clearly evident in the fabric of both the older wartime sites and newly built ones, key structures in this respect including buildings for the generators which supplied electrical and hydraulic power, which can either be free-standing or attached to a gun store (Fig 7.13a). Stand-

ings for the gun-laying radar depended on the local landscape.

At Trimley Heath, Suffolk, a tall brick tower and a ramp were built so that the radar could be raised above local ground clutter (Fig 7.13b), whereas elsewhere, such as at Lower Kinnerton, Flintshire/Cheshire, there was just a simple ramp.

After 1950 the introduction of newer and heavier fire-control radar required the rebuilding of radar positions at some sites. It was also proposed to develop a tactical control radar, codenamed 'Orange Yeoman', to feed data to sixteen remote gun sites. Trials

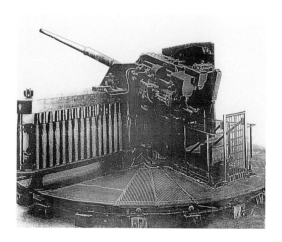

Figure 7.13
Trimley Heath, Suffolk.
a: 5.25-inch gun site.
Generator building with
attached gun shed [© Roger
J C Thomas]

b: (left)
5.25-inch gun site.
Command post with radar
tower in the foregound. The
ramp was used to haul the
mobile radar set up to the
platform. [© Roger J C
Thomas]

began at Frodsham, but no associated infrastructure has been identified. Command posts large enough to accommodate the new No. 11 Predictor, recognisable by the cable ducts in their floors, are also a feature of most post-war gun sites. Using data acquired by the radar, the Predictor was able to calculate target trajectories and to feed the information directly to the guns. Ultimately it was intended that all gun loading would be automatic, and that the gun crew's role would be reduced to one of feeding ammunition to the automatic loading trays from ready-use ammunition stores close to the emplacements. Surviving examples at Lower Kinnerton measure 8ft × 6ft (2.44m × 1.83m), the body of the shelters being formed from curved corrugated steel sheets with brick ends and door openings to either end: at Norley, Cheshire, only footings remain.

Most of the post-war buildings were of reinforced-concrete, with heavy steel-shuttered doors and windows. One way of identifying them as post-war buildings is by the distinctive heavy drip-moulds above openings (see Figs 7.13a and b). Although the buildings would offer some protection against the heat and blast effects of a nuclear explosion, no attempt was made to protect against radioactive fallout, a phenomenon

c: Early 1950s Mark VII,
No. 3, Yellow Fever mobile
fire control radar, of the
kind which would have
been used with the 40-mm
Bofors L70 LAA gun
[© Roger J C Thomas]

poorly understood in 1950. The sites were also probably thought to lie sufficiently distant from the main targets not to be at immediate risk from atomic attack.

A Conservative government, led by Win-

Figure 7.14
One way of countering fast jet aircraft is by using a rapid rate of fire. Green Mace, developed during the mid-1950s, could achieve a rate of fire equivalent to ninety-six rounds per minute. The gun was fed from two revolving drum magazines. Its development was ended in 1956. This gun can be seen at Firepower at the Royal Arsenal in Woolwich, south-east London.
[© Roger J C Thomas]

ston Churchill, was elected in October 1951. Although strongly committed to defence, the Government acknowledged that the economy was unable to maintain commitments at home and abroad, and modernisation of Anti-Aircraft Command assumed a lower priority. Some development work did continue on 'Green Mace', a new anti-aircraft gun with a very rapid rate of fire (Fig 7.14), mainly as insurance against the failure of the new missile systems still being developed (*see below*). By 1954, however, it was clear that a system designed to counter piston-engined aircraft carrying atomic bombs could no longer be regarded as an effective deterrent against high-altitude bombers and unstoppable missiles armed with hydrogen bombs. As a result, in March 1955 Anti-Aircraft Command was disbanded and the gun sites were dismantled and abandoned. Many of the anti-aircraft operations rooms, however, went on to have a further part to play, as local authority emergency control centres (*see* Chapter 9).

Light anti-aircraft defences

The 1951 anti-aircraft mobilisation plan lists 110 key locations, including master radar stations and airfields, which were to be defended by light anti-aircraft guns in the event of war. Normally the guns, 40-mm Bofors, were held in stores together with some searchlights but, in times of tension, between one and six guns would be sent to

predetermined positions. No infrastructure associated with them has been recorded. Light anti-aircraft guns remained in service with the Army and RAF into the 1970s when they were phased out. They did, however, make a brief reappearance during the 1980s when a Skyguard system, with 35-mm Oerlikon guns (captured from the Argentineans during the 1982 Falklands War), was deployed at RAF Waddington.

By the late 1960s portable ground-to-air

Figure 7.15 (right top)
a: RAF West Raynham, Norfolk. Rapier dome trainer [304P/15]

b: RAF Upper Heyford, Oxfordshire. Emplacement, originally prepared for a Rapier launcher [AA98/12362]

missiles such as Shorts Tigercat were becoming available for low level air defence. They had few, if any, infrastructure requirements. One of the most successful air defence missiles was, and still is, Rapier, introduced in the late 1960s. It is fully mobile, a unit usually comprising two Landrovers, a launcher with four missiles, an ET316 optical sight, and a trailer carrying reloads; in some instances an extra Landrover might be used to pull a Marconi DN181 Blindfire radar. Rapier was used to defend key installations at home and abroad. In the 1980s, thirty-two Rapier/Blindfire systems were ordered by the United States Air Force to defend its seven principal British airfields (*see* Table 4.2). In times of tension they were to be manned by the RAF Regiment Rapier squadrons based at Brize Norton, Oxfordshire, and at Honington, Suffolk and West Raynham, Norfolk, which would move out to pre-surveyed positions in times of tension. This highly sophisticated system has left very little archaeological trace, the most substantial items of infrastructure associated with it being training domes (Fig 7.15a) found at the squadron bases. When in use, Rapier might be set up in the open, in a sandbag revetment or a corrugated-steel and earth emplacement (Fig 7.15b). At Upper Heyford, Oxfordshire, its integration with the wider defence of the airfield was evident from the fact that the Rapier unit command was allotted a room within the hardened battle command centre.

Surface-to-air guided weapons

In post-war Britain the research and development of guided missiles, to destroy bombers potentially armed with nuclear weapons, was considered as important as atomic work and was often in competition for the same high-grade scientists and scarce resources. Britain's involvement in this field may be traced back to experimental wartime programmes including missiles such as 'Brakemine' and the subsequent 'Lopgap' (liquid oxygen and petrol guided anti-aircraft projectile), and early post-war successors known simply as 'research test vehicles'.

In 1947, contracts for the new weapons were placed with two lead companies, although with considerable practical support from government research establishments. The English Electric Company was to design a missile codenamed 'Red Shoes',

which was later developed as a mobile system for the army known as Thunderbird, and the Bristol Aeroplane Company began work on a system codenamed 'Red Duster', which became Bloodhound when it entered service with the RAF. Bloodhound may be seen as an archetypal Cold War weapon system; its development, deployment and eventual withdrawal, in 1991, covering the entire span of the Cold War.

Bloodhound

At first British defence planners proposed that the new weapons would be used to replace anti-aircraft guns in defence of key sites and regions, and they were initially designed with identical mountings to the guns so that they could be installed at existing anti-aircraft sites. The change in the nature of the threat, from that posed by low-flying aircraft to that from high-flying jet bombers armed with hydrogen bombs which could be launched at great distances from their targets, meant that the system of defence had to be altered.

The new defences had to destroy incoming missiles before they crossed the coast and provide a constant deterrent against surprise attack. In 1953, after the Air Ministry assumed responsibility for Britain's active air defence, it at first planned to create a number of very large sites down the east coast which were to be organised in fire units, each comprising sixteen missiles subdivided into

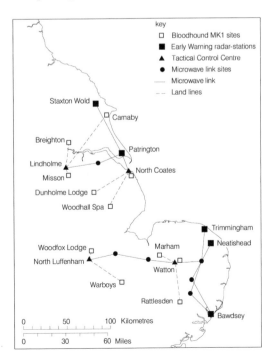

Figure 7.16
Map showing the location of Bloodhound Mark I sites and its main communications links. Up to 368 missiles were available, divided between 23 fire units on 11 sites.

Table 7.2 Deployment of Bloodhound Mark I missile squadrons

Site	Squadron	Arrived	Stood down
North Coates	264	1 Dec 1958	30 Nov 1962
Dunholme Lodge	141	1 Apr 1959	31 March 1964
Watton	263	1 Jun 1959	30 Jun 1963
Marham	242	1 Oct 1959	30 Sep 1964
Rattlesden	266	1 Dec 1959	30 Jun 1964
Woolfox Lodge	62	1 Feb 1960	Jan 1963
Woodhall Spa	222	1 May 1960	30 Jun 1964
Carnaby	247	1 Jul 1960	31 Dec 1963
Warboys	257	1 Jul 1960	31 Dec 1963
Breighton	112	7 Nov 1960	31 Mar 1964
Misson	94	1 Oct 1960	30 Jun 1963

Figure 7.17
RAF North Coates,
Lincolnshire. Here three fire
units, each with sixteen
missile pads, were laid out
over the wartime airfield. In
the foreground is the later
four-pad Bloodhound
Mark II trials area; to the
top right is the isolated
explosives handling area.
[17543/36]

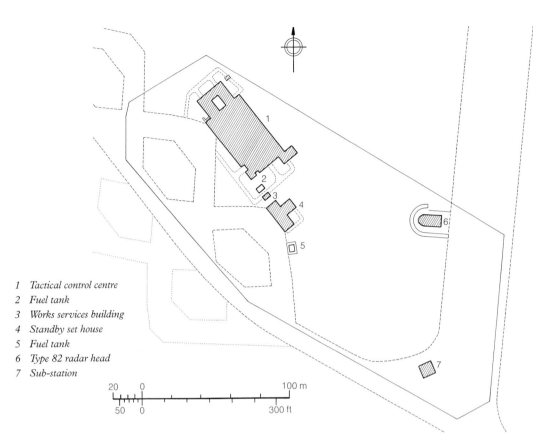

Figure 7.18
RAF North Luffenham.
Plan of tactical control
centre [redrawn from Drg
No. CLG/1. Original
material Crown copyright
MoD]

1 Tactical control centre
2 Fuel tank
3 Works services building
4 Standby set house
5 Fuel tank
6 Type 82 radar head
7 Sub-station

20   0   100 m

50   0   300 ft

Figure 7.19
a: (below)
RAF Lindholme, South
Yorkshire. View from the
entrance in 1971 showing,
in the foreground, the Type
82 'Orange Yeoman' radar.
The array comprises a 45ft
(13.72m) horizontal
transmitter aerial with a
receiver aerial above. To the
rear is the tactical control
centre. [Photo by Aldon P
Ferguson]

two flights of eight missiles. Early Air Ministry plans were to base six fire units on one site but this was later reduced to three, while the number of sites was increased to extend the geographic coverage. The final arrangement (Fig 7.16, Table 7.2) comprised ten sites with two units, plus the trials site at RAF North Coates, Lincolnshire (Fig 7.17), which had three units. The Chief of the Air Staff chose a pattern, known as Stage 1, to provide adequate defence for the bases holding the nuclear deterrent forces – the V-force and Thor intermediate-range ballistic missiles (*see* Chapter 3). Stage 1 also offered some incidental protection to the Midlands. We have compiled a simplified engagement sequence for the system (*see* pp 158–9).

Tactical control centres

b: Tactical control centre at
RAF Lindholme
[277K/25]

Diagram showing Bloodhound Mark I engagement sequence

Bloodhound Mark I

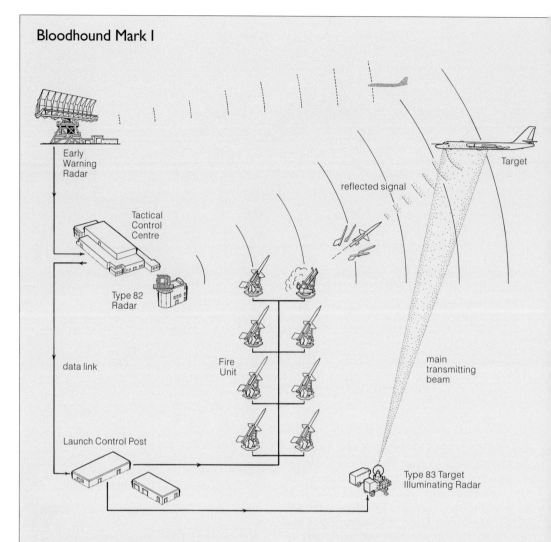

Bloodhound was designed to be an integral part of an overall air defence system, co-ordinated with the early warning radar and manned fighters. Warning of an incoming raid would be transmitted from one of the early warning radar to a tactical control centre (TCC). The weapons control team at the TCC, using the Type 82 'Orange Yeoman' tactical control radar (TCR), would then begin to track the hostile aircraft from a range of up to 140 miles (225km) and up to an altitude of 60,000ft (18,287m). Once the target selection officer had decided to engage a raid, he would transmit data to a fire unit and when it was in range of the Type 83 Yellow River target illuminating radar (TIR) (55 miles or 88.5km) it would then be tracked. After confirming with the TCC that they were tracking the same target, the missiles of the fire unit would be turned to the correct bearing. Target data would then be contin-

uously fed from the TIR through the launch control post (LCP) to the missiles and their launchers. Once the reflected radar signal from the target was of sufficient strength, the radar receiver dishes in the radome at the nose of the missile would be activated, and the decision taken to fire a volley or single missile. In flight, the missile was kept on course by a semi-active homing system that followed the radiation reflected from the target illuminated by the TIR. This fed information into its Ferranti control equipment, the interception point being calculated by an on-board computer.

Each missile was 25ft 3in (7.7m) long, with a launch weight of 44.101lb (2,000kg). On launch, four Gosling booster rocket motors propelled the missile from 0–760mph (0–1,200km/h), within its own length. Four seconds after launching, shortly after the boosters fell away, the two Thor ramjet engines ignited. These engines were capable of accelerating the missile up to Mach 2.2 – more than twice the speed of sound. The maximum range of the system was about 50 miles (80km). Detonation was by means of a proximity fuze that unleashed a hoop of metal rods to cut into any aircraft caught in its path. Ten seconds before the estimated time of detonation an automatic signal was sent back to the Target Selection Officer (TSO) to inform him that another target could be engaged by the missile unit.

At one stage it was proposed to arm Bloodhound with a small nuclear warhead. This would not only have increased its lethal range but would also have caused any nuclear weapons in the vicinity to detonate prematurely or to be 'poisoned' and their destructive power lessened (the so called R1 effect) (*see also* Fig 7.24).

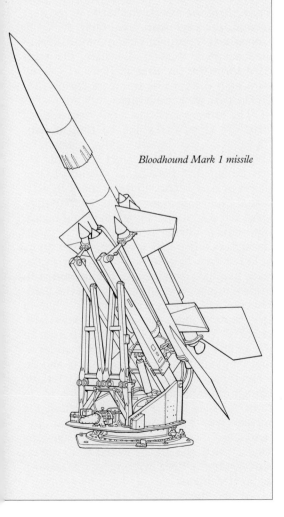

Bloodhound Mark 1 missile

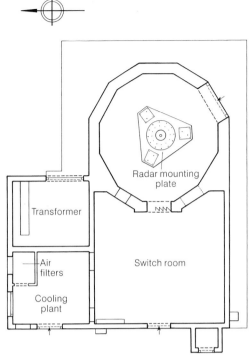

Figure 7.19
c: (left)
RAF North Coates, Lincolnshire. Plan of experimental Type 82 radar building

d: (below)
Type 82 radar at RAF North Coates. This was the first 3-D radar to enter RAF service and was capable of continuously tracking eighteen targets, providing data on range, bearing and elevation.
[© Crown copyright. RAF Air Defence Radar Museum]

Administratively, the Bloodhound units formed part of Fighter Command and were divided into four wings, based at tactical control centres (TCC) – No. 21 RAF Lindholme, South Yorkshire, No. 148 RAF North Coates, No. 51 RAF North Luffenham, Leicestershire and No. 24 RAF

Watton, Norfolk (Fig 7.16). At each of these there was a missile repair section, usually located in an existing hangar (often newly lined in fibreboard to improve insulation and prevent dirt getting in). A building was also provided for servicing the launcher assemblies. Where the wing headquarters were in the same place as the missile units, at North Coates and Watton, facilities normally associated with squadron servicing are also found.

In the event of attack, information would be fed from one of the main early warning radar (*see* Box) to the tactical control centres where targets would be allocated to individual missile sites. The TCC were all equipped with Type 82 Orange Yeoman tactical control radar, and all except North Coates, the trials site, had a standard range of structures (Fig 7.18). The radar was mounted on top of a twelve-sided concrete tower, joined to which was a three-storey rectangular structure (Fig 7.19a) housing transmitting and receiving equipment. Close by was a large steel-framed and brick clad TCC (Fig 7.19b) which housed the weapons control team whose task was to feed data on designated targets to the missile sites. At North Coates the radar was mounted on top of a single-storey twelve-sided building, with attached equipment rooms (Figs 7.19c and d). Data was fed from it to a TCC in a disused hangar, the only evidence for which today are the cable ducts cut into its floor.

Missile sites

With the exception of North Coates the missile sites were also built to a relatively standard form, with an identical set of about fourteen buildings. Despite their relatively recent date we have discovered hardly any detailed original site plans or building drawings, which shows how important archaeological recording and analysis can be in our understanding of the modern as well as the ancient world. The rate of loss of the physical fabric has also been high, and only four of the eleven sites retain their complete plan together with most associated structures. The site at Woolfox Lodge (Fig 7.20) may be regarded as typical, although the location of the support buildings could vary to fit into an existing road or runway pattern. Usually, the whole site was within a single secure perimeter, although at Woolfox Lodge two enclosures were formed. The structures within the site fall into three distinct groups. The first, close to the entrance, may be categorised as administrative and technical and

includes a picket post (No. 2 on Fig 7.20), a station headquarters (3), Air Ministry works directorate buildings (4) and an electricity intake sub-station (1): all were brick, with flat concrete roofs. The largest building on site was the missile servicing building (6): it had two bays with gable roofs, was clad in corrugated aluminium sheeting and was lit by large metal-framed windows and, inside, by standard sealed lighting units similar to those used in explosives stores. Along one side were plant rooms, in a flat-roofed brick annexe, while within the structure offices, workshops and stores were set along the outside walls.

In the missile servicing building people assembled and tested missiles, which arrived as separate components in wooden packing crates. After assembly a missile would be taken to the static running section (5) for testing, then loaded onto a trolley and taken to the remote drive-through refuelling building (9) – a light structure built from corrugated asbestos sheets set on low brick walls – where its fuel tank was filled with kerosene. From there the missile was taken to the next section, the explosives area. Only at North Coates was a purpose-built mounded magazine complex created; elsewhere, the standard form was an arming shed (22) served by a loop road. Close by was a latrine (21) and a static water tank (20).

The arming shed was a tall, single-storey structure (Figs 7.21a and b) clad in reinforced-concrete 'Hy-rib' walls, created by applying concrete to a steel mesh. Hy-rib was designed to prevent the scatter of large pieces of flying debris in the event of an accidental explosion, as even if the concrete shattered the steel frame and mesh would buckle but remain intact. The shed was a drive-through building with concertina-type doors at either end. In common with other explosives handling buildings it was floored with gritless asphalt and all structural metal components and fittings were earthed, while in the fitment bay the missiles were also attached to earthing plates. On the front of the building were two small brick annexes, one containing electrical switchgear and an air compressor and the other used for the storage of explosive components for up to three missiles. It was in this shed that the missile was fitted with its warhead and detonators, booster motors and igniters. Once armed, the missile would be towed on a trolley to the third and largest area, known as the fire units.

At all the stations, except for North

1 Electricity intake sub-
   station
2 Picket post
3 Station headquarters
4 Works directorate
   building
5 Static running section
6 Missile servicing
   building
7 Oil storage catchpit
8 Oil store
9 Refuelling building
10 Oil storage catchpit
11 Footings for hut
12 Hydrogen store and
   balloon-filling room
13 Site of Type 83 target
   illuminating radar
14 Works services building
15 Launch control post
16 Officers' and airmens'
   mess
17 Latrine
18 Missile hardstandings
19 Pyrotechnic store
20 Static water tank
21 Latrine
22 Arming shed

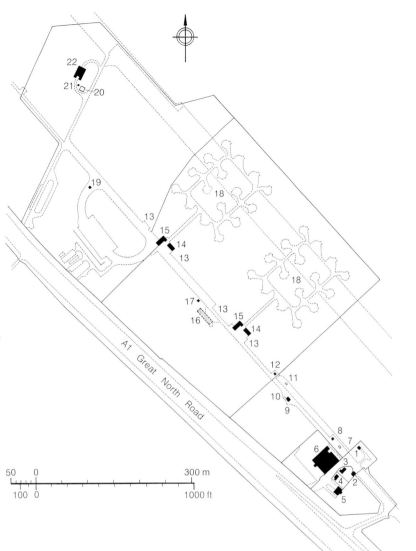

Figure 7.20
RAF Woolfox Lodge,
Rutland. Plan of
Bloodhound missile site
[reproduced from Ordnance
Survey mapping on behalf
of the Controller of Her
Majesty's Stationary Office
© Crown copyright. Licence
No. GD 03085G/02/01]

Figure 7.21
a: (below left)
Arming shed. The two
small brick projections on
the front of the building
housed generators and an
air compressor to the right
and an explosives handling
area to the left. The
building in the foreground is
a latrine. [305B/18]

b: (below)
Detail of Hy-rib wall
construction

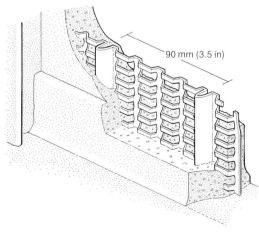

90 mm (3.5 in)

Figure 7.22

Type 83 'Yellow River', also known as Stingray. This target-tracking and illuminating radar was originally manufactured by British Thomson-Houston. It was able to produce a wide radar beam for target acquisition and a narrow pencil beam for tracking and illumination. Next to it are two mobile generators and the display vehicle.

[Flight December 1958, p5 © The Flight Collection]

attack (Figs 7.23a and b). Most of the launch control post was taken up with bulky metal-cased equipment to calculate and synchronise the target illuminating radar and the missiles, and by electrical and air conditioning plant (mainly to remove the heat generated by the electrical valves). It also housed the missile engagement controllers, who were able to view the missiles through an armoured window facing them. Also within the launch control post was a rest room, and next to it a latrine, often butted on to the building as if it had been an afterthought. The works services building housed two diesel generators, one for each missile section, and air compressors; next to it was an electrical transformer to step down electricity received from the national grid.

The missile pads were eight-sided, reinforced-concrete hardstandings or aprons (Fig 7.24) to each of which was bolted a cable termination pillar (for the electrical cables and control wires) and the launcher plant assembly. The latter consisted of steel blast-proof boxes which supplied the missiles with electrical, hydraulic and pneumatic power, and in later examples the cooled air (previously supplied from the works services building (No. 14 on Fig 7.20) needed to prevent the missiles overheating. Leading from the launcher plant assembly was a sunken service conduit covered by a galvanised metal tread, which led to the missile holdfast – a metal framework set in concrete, with a central 3ft (0.91m) square hole through which the services entered the base of the launcher.

During 1960 and 1961 tests were conducted at North Coates to design moveable missile shelters. The first type was a sliding

Coates, the missiles were divided into two fire units, with a launch control post (15) and, next to it, a detached works services building (14). On some sites a latrine is found. In front of these buildings were sixteen missile hardstandings (18), divided into two flights of eight (a 'missile section'), each served by its own Type 83 'Yellow River' target illuminating radar (Fig 7.22), positioned to either side of the launch control post on either gravel or concrete hardstandings (13). The launch control posts and works services buildings were identical, single-storey, breeze-block structures clad in brick with flat concrete roofs, which might offer protection against an errant missile but not sustained

Figure 7.23

RAF Woolfox Lodge, Rutland.

a: (right)

Launch control post. On the front of the building is the small armoured window that overlooked the missiles. Projecting from the side of the building, in slightly darker brick, is the added latrine. At the back is ornamental tree planting.

[305A/33A]

shelter (Fig 7.25) made at the Royal Arsenal, Woolwich, and similar to that used by Thor missiles (*see* Chapter 3). All that remains on the site are the rails. On another part of the site are small metal loops for securing an inflatable shelter manufactured by P B Cow Ltd. Both trials ceased in 1961. Apart from this field evidence and a brief mention in an official document, no other details of these experiments have been found.

Late in the programme many sites were furnished with a hydrogen store and balloon-filling building (No. 12 on Fig 7.20) for filling balloons which carried metal spheres used to calibrate and test the target illuminating radar.

Where missiles were placed on existing airfields accommodation for personnel was provided in existing housing. At remote sites personnel lived locally, either in nearby service accommodation or in private homes. A timber airmen's and officers' mess (No. 16 on Fig 7.20) was provided on each site, and could be used to house personnel in times of tension. Only at North Coates was additional housing built, to serve a Bloodhound deployment.

Bloodhound Mark II

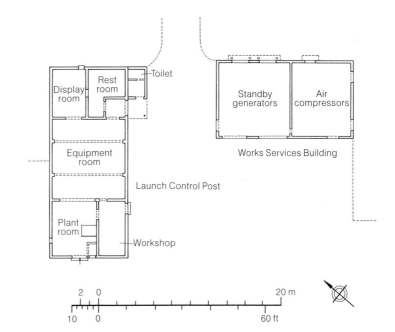

b: Plan of launch control post and works services building

Even before it entered service the limitations of Bloodhound Mark I were recognised. Its main shortcomings were the susceptibility of its Type 83 radar to jamming, and the fact that it was a static system, firmly rooted to its

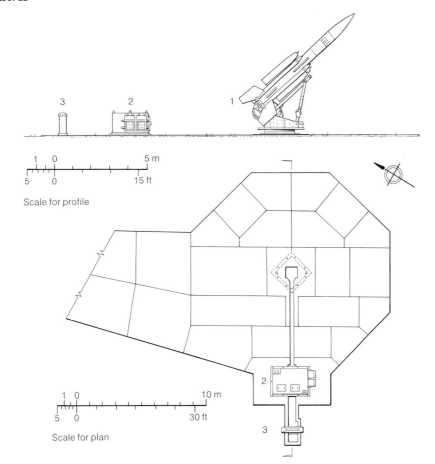

1 Missile
2 Launcher plant assembly
3 Cable termination pillar

Scale for profile

Scale for plan

*Figure 7.24
Bloodhound Mark I
launcher on its
hardstanding*

Figure 7.25
RAF North Coates,
Lincolnshire. Rails for
experimental sliding shelter
attached to one of the
missile pads [AA99/06119]

site and therefore lacking any flexibility in its deployment. Trials of its successor, Blood-hound Mark II, were started at North Coates in October 1963, probably on a detached group of four pads at the northern end of the site (*see* Fig 7.17). Slightly later, when Mark II missiles were positioned on the original pads, the old cable duct was filled with con-crete (Fig 7.26). In 1964 Mark II missiles were also deployed, for training purposes, at Woodhall Spa, Lincolnshire.

Although superficially both Marks looked similar, Mark II was a far more powerful sys-tem. The most significant improvement was to the target illuminating radar, in which the original pulsed radar was replaced with con-tinuous wave radar, which was far less vul-nerable to jamming. The capability of the missile was also increased: it was given a larger warhead, it could engage aircraft at higher and lower altitudes, and more power-ful Thor ramjet engines (not related to the Thor missile) gave it a greater range. Less visible were improvements to its many sub-assemblies, which resulted in greater effi-ciency and reliability and less time undergo-ing maintenance.

Outwardly, one of the most noticeable differences between the two systems was in

the design of the launcher mounting. In the earlier system, the need for electrical and hydraulic power, and for dehumidified air to maintain its internal temperature, were met from a metal box fixed to the pad – the launcher plant assembly. In Mark II, all this equipment was placed in modular units on the launcher, which could either be perma-nently mounted or operate as a mobile sys-tem with outriggers. To the rear was a tele-scopic aerial, which received command sig-nals from the target illuminating radar, to ensure both that the radar dish of the missile was tuned towards the correct target and that the launcher was facing in the proper direction. A schematic engagement sequence is shown in the Box opposite.

The first site to be developed solely for Bloodhound Mark II was at the eastern edge of the airfield at West Raynham, Norfolk. During the summer of 1964 an active mis-sile section was built, as well as a large ser-vicing area (Fig 7.27a) to be used for the entire Bloodhound force, at home and over-seas. The main buildings in the servicing section were a headquarters and instruction block, launcher and missile servicing build-ings and fuelling bays. All the servicing buildings were steel-framed and clad in dis-

Bloodhound Mark II

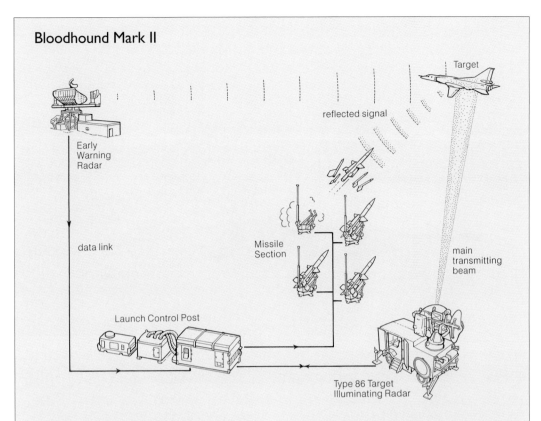

*Diagram showing
Bloodhound Mark II
simplified engagement
sequence*

Warning of an incoming raid would be obtained from the Southern Sector Operations Centre at RAF Neatishead, using information from its long-range Type 84 or Type 85 radar. A surface-to-air missile allocator would assign or 'put-on' a target to a missile flight operations room, where it was allocated to a missile section's engagement controller in one of the semi-mobile launch control posts (LCP). The engagement controller would then begin to track the target using Type 86 or Type 87 target illuminating radar (TIR) and the associated missiles would automatically move to face the target. Once the reflected signal from the target was strong enough the computer would flash the 'free to fire' message on a screen and the engagement controller would be authorised to fire.

The Bloodhound Mark II was longer than its predecessor at 27ft 9in (8.45m) and was a far more powerful weapon, capable of intercepting targets at heights of between 150ft and 65,000ft (45.72m and 19,812m). It had a maximum range of around 115 miles (185km), with a minimum impact range at low level of 6.9 miles (11km) and a maximum impact range at high level of 86.25 miles (131km). As in the earlier version, the missile was kept on track by a receiver dish in the nose cone that picked up a reflected signal from the target aircraft. But commands could also be issued from the LCP through the TIR during flight. Detonation was controlled by a proximity fuze. A high explosive charge could be fitted but a continuous metal rod head was usual.

tinctive asbestos sheeting (Fig 7.27b) and the internal walls were of rendered breezeblock to a height of 8ft or 10ft (2.4m or 3m), above which they were lined with fibreboard. Vehicle-sized doors provided for the movement of missiles and launchers, and there were compartmentalised workshops for specific tasks around the outside. The missile squadron at West Raynham remained until

September 1970 when it was moved to West Germany, but the servicing activities remained, becoming known as the Bloodhound Support Unit. In the meantime, the units at North Coates and Woodhall Spa were also moved overseas and the stations closed.

Redeployment in the 1970s and 1980s

*Figure 7.26
RAF North Coates,
Lincolnshire. Missile pad,
illustrating the three phases
of Bloodhound deployment.
To the left are the holdfast
sockets for Bloodhound
Mark I and, leading to
them, the channel that
carried its cabling. When
the first Bloodhound Mark
II unit was stationed here
in 1963 the channel was
filled with concrete. In its
final phase, starting in
1976, another Bloodhound
Mark II unit was stationed
at the site, a cable channel
was cut through the earlier
features and new holdfast
sockets installed. [© W D
Cocroft]*

*Figure 7.27
RAF West Raynham,
Norfolk.
a: Missile-servicing area
built on top of earlier
aircraft hardstandings
[15807/32]*

*b: Launcher servicing
building, with distinctive
asbestos cement sheeting,
c 1964 [302C/31]*

In 1975, 85 Squadron was redeployed from West Germany to West Raynham, which became the headquarters of the Bloodhound Force in the 1980s and accommodated support units as well as the existing Bloodhound Support Unit. Subsidiary flights were later based at North Coates and Bawdsey (Fig 7.28 and Table 7.3). The Bloodhound Missile System Maintenance School at RAF Newton, Nottinghamshire, was an outstation of the Bloodhound Force, but it had few distinctive facilities; it was closed in 1987. Although Bloodhound missiles defended United Kingdom air space, they were an integral part of the wider NATO air defence system. The layouts of the Mark II sites are more varied than those for Mark I, opportunistically making use of existing infrastructure. In addition, Mark II was designed to be a semi-mobile, air-transportable system, and so did not need so many purpose-built facilities as the previous system.

The facilities at West Raynham were a mixture of original 1960s features and modifications made during the 1970s and 1980s. When it was at its largest, the site had nine launcher sections, each made up of four launchers, following the pattern established by the trials unit at North Coates. By the late 1970s they were controlled by five target illuminating radar, with a mobile launcher control post cabin allotted to each section. Nine rectangular earthwork revetments were built to hold spare missiles and, in at least seven of them, ready-use missile stores were built – steel-framed buildings similar to Dutch barns (Fig 7.29). Later, one was clad in pressed-steel sheeting and used as a servicing

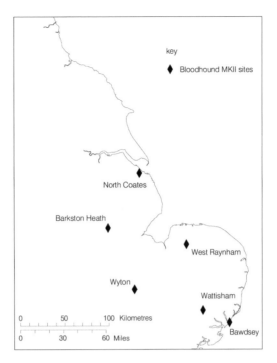

key
◆ Bloodhound MKII sites

North Coates

Barkston Heath

West Raynham

Wyton

Wattisham

Bawdsey

0   50   100 Kilometres
0   30   60   Miles

Figure 7.28
Deployment of Bloodhound Mark II missile squadrons during the 1970 and 1980s

workshop, and another was moved to Bawdsey, Suffolk. At other sites spare missiles were held in the open, on concrete floors surrounded by earthwork revetments (Fig 7.30b).

At North Coates the existing launcher emplacements were modified for a second time, this phase being distinguished by the addition of four sockets offset from the original holdfast (*see* Fig 7.26); at West Raynham, by contrast, the original 1960s hardstandings were simply reused. The former radar station at Bawdsey (Fig 7.30a) has a typical range of component features, all purpose-built. The hardstandings (Figs 7.31a and b) were laid

Table 7.3 Deployment of Bloodhound Mark II missile squadrons

Site	Squadron	Arrived	Stood down
North Coates	25	1 Oct 1963	1970
	85 B Flight	Mar 1976	30 Apr 1990
Woodhall Spa	112	2 Nov 1964	30 Sep 1967
West Raynham	41	1 Sept 1965	Sep 1970
	85 A Flight	July 1976	1 July 1991
Bawdsey	85 C Flight	July 1979	May 1990
Barkston Heath	25 A Flight		
	(*85 D Flight)	Mar 1983	June 1990
Wyton	25 B Flight		
	(*85 E Flight)	Mar 1983	July 1990
Wattisham	25 C Flight		
	(*85 F Flight)	Mar 1983	1 July 1991

* *from 1 October 1989*

Figure 7.29 (above)
RAF West Raynham,
Norfolk. Ready-use missile
stores in 1976. These
structures were used as
weather shelters for
assembled missiles ready for
reloading the launchers.
[303J/34]

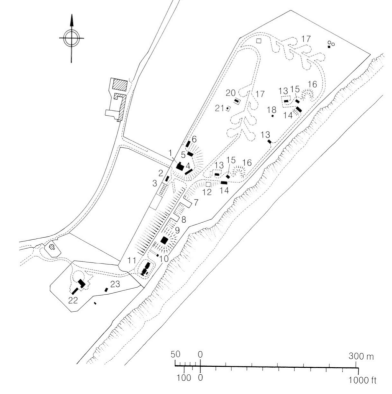

1   Guard house
2   Dog section
3   Dog pens
4   Store
5   Motor transport garage
6   Timber hut
7   Ready-use store
8   Ready-use store
9   Explosive fitment bay
10 Locker
11 Workshop
12 Emergency water supply
13 Generator house
14 Missile section office
15 Target illuminating
    radar
16 Launch control post
17 Missile section
18 Defence post
19 Sewage plant
20 R3 bunker exit
21 R3 bunker ventilator
22 Standby set house
23 Water tower

Figure 7.30
RAF Bawdsey, Suffolk
a: Plan of Bloodhound
missile site [based on Drg
No. CLG/S. Original
material Crown copyright
MoD]

b: Spare missiles held in a ready-use store (No. 7 on plan). The flexible pipes in the foreground blew dehumidified air into missiles to maintain the correct internal environment for their complex electrical systems. [144479-27 Reproduced by kind permission of the East Anglian Daily Times and Evening Star]

out in groups of six (No. 17 on Fig 7.30a) and are eight-sided in plan, with a low kerb around six sides. In the centre are four mounting sockets with a cable duct covered by steel plates leading out towards the launch control posts. Air transportable cabins were used in place of the brick launch control posts and works services buildings of the Mark I system, and were usually placed on a concrete hardstandings with recessed cable ducts (16). Otherwise, cables were simply run over the site to the missiles from metal drums which were set on a steel frame for ease of movement. Each missile section was provided with a Type 87 Scorpion target illuminating radar (15) placed on a substan-

tial semi-moveable plinth set on a hardstanding (Figs 7.32a and b).

In 1983, with the stationing of Rapier units in West Germany, the air defences of the United Kingdom were strengthened by the redeployment of 25 Squadron's Bloodhound Missiles (*see* Fig 7.28 and Table 7.3). The three RAF airfields to which they were allocated were chosen to ensure that the engagement zone of each missile station overlapped: they had no previous association with Bloodhound. In common with the existing Bloodhound stations no standarised layout was imposed, although there was a common range of facilities (Fig 7.33). Missiles were placed in groups of six, on eight-

c: Missiles were moved to and from the servicing areas by a specially designed Lancer Boss fork-lift transporter, seen here in the foreground. In line with the 1970s policy to dull down the appearance of installations, the missiles were painted dark green, in contrast to the anti-flash white of the 1960s. [143328-3 Reproduced by kind permission of the East Anglian Daily Times and Evening Star]

Figure 7.31
Bloodhound Mark II
launcher hardstanding

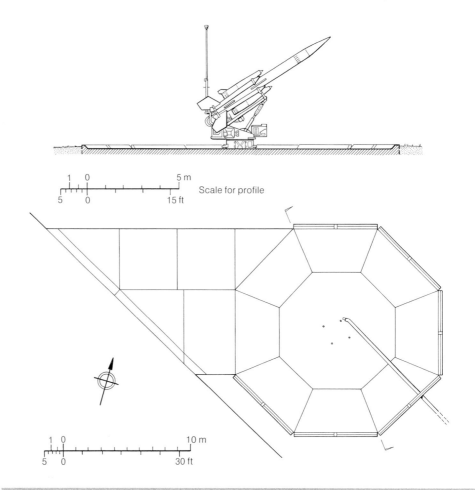

1 0   5 m

5 0   15 ft

Scale for profile

1 0   10 m

5 0   30 ft

Figure 7.32
a: Type 87 Scorpion radar,
manufactured by Marconi.
The main radar antenna is
13ft 8in (4.2m) in
diameter. It had a range of
up to 170 miles
(273.5km). This example
is preserved at the
Muckleborough Collection,
Norfolk. [303J/30]

b: RAF West Raynham, Norfolk. Type 87 Scorpion radar transmitter and receiver cabin, nicknamed the 'Dalek'. The whole set weighed about 50 tons (51 tonnes). Although it could be broken down for transport, it was usually installed on permanently occupied sites. The platform was added later to accept a Type 86 radar trailer. [3037/30]

Figure 7.33
RAF Wattisham, Suffolk. Launcher emplacements for two Bloodhound missile sections. To their rear are the offices of the flight, and generator buildings. In the foreground is the revetted arming shed. [18126/21]

Figure 7.34
RAF Wyton,
Cambridgeshire. 1980s
flight offices incorporating
an operation room to the
rear, behind which is a
Romney hut that was
brought back from the
unit's previous station in
Germany. [AA99/09787]

Figure 7.35
a: RAF Wyton,
Cambridgeshire. Tower for
a Type 86 radar. In the
foreground are a standby
generator building and the
foundations for a
transformer. To the rear is a
radar maintenance
workshop. [AA99/09789]

sided pads linked by servicing tracks, while the arming sheds were steel-framed, clad in corrugated sheeting and surrounded by earthwork revetments. Other buildings were brick, and included picket posts next to the entrances, flight headquarters buildings and generator buildings, often with large windows: all were built for ease of use rather than protection (Fig 7.34).

In place of the Type 87 Scorpion radar, 25 Squadron used mobile Ferranti Type 86 Indigo Corkscrew/Firelight radar sets which, to avoid ground clutter, were placed on top of 30ft (9.1m) steel towers (*see* Figs 7.35a and b). Elsewhere, Type 87s were replaced with Type 86 by September 1988, since the obsolescent electronic valves controlling the Type 87 were becoming increasingly difficult to maintain. Where this happened, rather than build new towers the Type 86 trackers were often set on a platform on the old Type 87 cabins (Fig 7.32b).

The constant upgrading of Bloodhound meant that even at the end of the 1980s it was still regarded as an effective air defence system. To prolong its life into the mid-1990s its missiles, support equipment and installations were once again modernised, though it was recognised that this would be the last change and permanent structures were therefore only built to last until its projected withdrawal. At North Coates, single-storey, brick crew rooms were erected, along with brick buildings to house the generators. Between 1989 and 1990 the computers in the mobile launch control posts were upgraded to a new digital Ferranti Argus 700 system, and fibre optic cables were laid to speed communications. During the 1980s flight operations rooms were established within existing buildings, although they offered little protection against blast or radiation: at North Coates a 1960s building was adapted, while at RAF Wyton, Cambridgeshire (Fig 7.34), the garage door of the relatively recent flight headquarters was blocked and the interior converted. In contrast, at RAF Bawdsey the flight had partly reoccupied the Rotor period radar bunker in the 1970s (*see* Chapter 5), affording it considerable protection. At Wyton small, brick radar-servicing buildings were built next to each missile section (Fig 7.35a) and at North Coates and West Raynham protective earthen banks were added around the launch control posts in 1989.

Events elsewhere quickly overtook the refurbishment programme. After the virtual evaporation of the Soviet threat the United

Kingdom's Bloodhound defences were quickly reduced: four sites were closed in 1990, though the intention was that Wattisham and West Raynham would survive until 1995. One of the few changes which resulted was the erection of temporary hutting at West Raynham to house the Missile System Maintenance School relocated from North Coates. But in early 1991 it was announced that the Bloodhound Force was to be stood down, and the squadron was disbanded on 1 July. Although most of the missiles and ground equipment were quickly scrapped, some have been preserved and at Cosford Aerospace Museum and the Imperial War Museum, Duxford, the mobile equipment attached to a missile section may also be seen. At the time of writing all the sites survive.

Overseas deployment

Despite the fact that the Bloodhound system did not live up to the expectations of the 1957 Defence White Paper, which intended that manned air defence fighters would be replaced by missiles by the late 1960s, it was one of the most successful, widely deployed and long-lived surface-to-air missiles of the Cold War. Britain's overseas commitments are evident in its global distribution in RAF service, with installations in Cyprus, former West Germany, Libya, Malta, Malaysia and Singapore, where there are remains similar to those described in this chapter. Bloodhound also saw service with the Royal Australian Air Force, while sales of both Marks of the system to the non-aligned countries of Sweden and Switzerland demonstrated Britain's ability to compete in the international market for technologically complex weapons.

b: Ferranti Type 86 Firelight radar mounted on trailer chassis. In the centre of the array is the main circular transmitter dish (6ft 10in (2.1m) in diameter). To its left is the receiver dish, and to the right the small circular jamming assessment aerial. The radar had a range of between 55 and 60 miles (88.5 to 96.5km). [304Z/33]

8
Observation and monitoring

The advent of the hydrogen bomb gave a fresh focus to the Royal Observer Corps (ROC) – to report nuclear attacks and their effects to a new Home Office body: the United Kingdom Warning and Monitoring Organisation (UKWMO). Initially the ROC had been an integral part of Britain's early warning systems (*see* Chapter 5), providing information especially on the passage of low-flying aircraft. But new threats, especially those posed by fast jet aircraft bombers and unstoppable missiles, could not be observed in the same way. More than 1,500 underground monitoring posts were built, making them the most numerous type of structure built during the Cold War. Equipped with relatively simple and robust instruments, they formed a vital part of the country's defences against nuclear attack.

Origins

During the First World War Britain began to develop defences to counter the new threat posed by air raids, which included setting up the Metropolitan Observation Service. By 1941 this had evolved into the Royal Observer Corps (ROC), whose role was to chart aircraft movements by audio and visual means, distinguishing between friendly and enemy machines. The information from each observation post was reported to a group control to be correlated with data from other posts and to be forwarded to the fighter squadrons. Infrastructure was modest, a post comprising a portable plotting table on a tripod, a telephone, telephone pole and, for protection from the weather, a canvas awning, replaced before the end of the decade by a wooden hut. Group controls were generally placed within a Post Office telephone exchange or in an adjacent building.

Despite the introduction of radar, the ROC performed a valuable function during the Second World War, filling gaps in radar cover, especially in relation to low-flying aircraft, and the system, which had concentrated on eastern England, was extended to cover the whole country except Northern Ireland. Monitoring posts were constructed in various ways, ranging from crude corrugated-iron, sandbag and earth installations to small two-storey structures of brick or concrete, with a crew shelter at ground level. From 1942 some group centres were provided with brick plotting-rooms (Fig 8.1), which provided proof against incendiary devices or close bomb blast. In 1941 women began to be employed both at control centres and individual posts, and this continued throughout the Cold War. With the end of the war and of the immediate threat of air attack, the Corps was quickly stood down on 12 May 1945.

Post-war revival

Post-war studies of Britain's air defence requirements (which included conducting mock raids by Allied planes on parts of the reactivated German air-raid detection and reporting system) recognised the importance of visual and audio reporting as a final defence against electronic jamming and low-flying aircraft. The ROC began to train again in January 1947, and a year later it could nominally operate from 1,420 posts and thirty-nine centres, though often with poorer infrastructure than just before the war. The problem of providing observers, most of

Figure 8.1
Second World War group headquarters, Bedford. At the centre is the two-storey operations room, which was surrounded by offices and dormitories. [BB98/27429]

whom were volunteers, with adequate protection against the weather was not tackled until 1951, when Messrs Orlit Ltd of Colnbrook, Buckinghamshire, were contracted to supply prefabricated shelters which were made in sections for ease of transport to often remote sites. The opportunity was also taken to move many posts to better positions.

Orlit posts

There were two types of Orlit post: Type A, where the structure was laid directly on the ground, and Type B, which was raised on four 6ft (1.83m) concrete legs. Not all Type A posts were built at ground level, some being placed on top of other structures as at Post 20/M2 at Tunstall, East Riding of Yorkshire (Fig 8.10). Records indicate that 413 Orlit posts were produced (207 of Type A and 206 of Type B), and that construction was complete by 1955 (Figs 8.2a–c).

The structure of the posts was determined by the role of ROC personnel in tracking and reporting aircraft movements. Each consisted of a 10ft (3.05m) x 6ft 8in (2.03m) box of bolted pre-cast concrete panels. It was entered at one end by a low hardwood door, which gave access to a 5ft high by 3ft 6in wide (1.52m by 1.06m) shelter/store area, or cubby-hole, with a flat concrete roof. A lower doorway, 4ft (1.21m) high, provided access from the sheltered part to the open observation area, which was fitted with a removable three-piece corrugated steel cover. In the centre of the observation area was a plywood pillar surmounted by the old wartime 'post instrument'. From 1955 the instrument was replaced by a removable circular graduated post chart, as the older equipment was deemed too slow to use for plotting low-flying jets. Not all posts built at this period were of an Orlit type: when the post at Ickleton near Elmdon, Essex, was moved in November 1953, for example, a new two-tier brick structure was built (Fig 8.2d).

Although not strictly part of the 'Rotor' programme to refurbish Britain's radar defences (see Chapter 5), the ROC evolved during the early 1950s in response to fundamental changes to the aircraft control and reporting system. The formation of NATO also demanded a standard military geographic grid system (Georef), which was adopted by the ROC in 1950. In 1953 the number of groups was reduced from thirty-nine to thirty-one, with corresponding

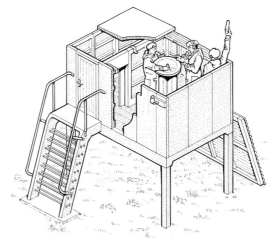

Figure 8.2
Orlit posts
a: Diagram showing the internal arrangements of an Orlit post. One observer is shown about to fire a flare from a Verey pistol to warn patrolling interceptors of a low flying intruder or 'Rat'.

b: Orlit post Type A. Post 18/S4 Elloughton, East Riding of Yorkshire [AA92/2602]

c: Orlit post Type B. Post 18/K1 Skirlaugh, East Riding of Yorkshire. All ROC posts were numbered in a standard manner. In these examples 18 refers to the Group, K and S to the clusters and 1 and 4 to the individual posts.

*Figure 8.2
d: Post 4/D1, Ickelton, near
Elmdon, Essex. Brick
observation post built after
1953 [BB016791]*

*Figure 8.2
d: Post 4/D1, Ickelton, near
Elmdon, Essex. Brick
observation post built after
1953 [BB016791]*

boundary changes, and coverage was extended to Northern Ireland. The posts were also rearranged into clusters of three or four, to simplify communications and the processing of information, and all were renumbered. This reorganisation also involved the massive, and largely unseen, task of rewiring most of the ROC's GPO circuits, and laying connections to the new RAF sector operations centres.

Despite all the improvements, however, exercises using the latest aircraft types, including the Hawker Hunter, confirmed that visual reporting methods and the time taken to disseminate information were both too slow for the jet age.

A new role for the nuclear age

In 1953 the Home Office began a series of studies to investigate how to record the fall of bombs on the country, the spread of fires, general conditions on the ground and the impact point of a nuclear weapon (ground zero). At first it was thought that the National Fire Service might perform this

function and that the ROC should be discontinued, since its network was largely rural and the main targets were thought to be the conurbations. One result of the Home Office's investigations was the creation of a national network of shadowgraphs, which were fitted to ROC posts. A shadowgraph, later known as a ground zero indicator (GZI), is an apparatus containing a piece of light-sensitive paper to register the point at which a nuclear device was detonated; it recorded the intense flash of light at the point of detonation (*see* Fig 8.8a). Earlier planning, mainly based on assessments of the devastation caused at Hiroshima and Nagasaki, had failed to appreciate the hazards that might be posed by fallout (the particles of radioactive dust thrown up by a nuclear explosion). Post-war atomic bomb tests began to reveal the threat, and it was recognised that many deaths and injuries would be avoided if people could be warned to take shelter before the arrival of a fallout plume, and remained under shelter until the radioactivity had decayed.

United Kingdom Warning and Monitoring Organisation

Partly in response to these concerns, in 1955 the Home Office created the United Kingdom Warning and Monitoring Organisation (UKWMO). It was formed by integrating the Air Raid Warning Organisation with the ROC, and its main responsibilities were to warn of air attack, to confirm nuclear strikes, to set off public warnings both of air attack and of approaching fallout, and to provide an emergency meteorological service to help predict fallout paths (Table 8.1). The information was to be disseminated to a variety of emergency centres (*see* Fig 9.11) at national and regional level, the armed forces and neighbouring countries. Not so readily acknowledged was the vital role of UKWMO

Table 8.1 The dissemination of information about an attack on the United Kingdom – UKWMO warning codes

	Signal	*Means*
Attack warning – red	Siren – rising and falling note	Imminent danger of attack from the air
Fallout warning – black	Maroon, whistle or gong – three loud bangs, blasts or strikes	Imminent danger of fallout
All-clear – white	Siren – steady note	No further danger

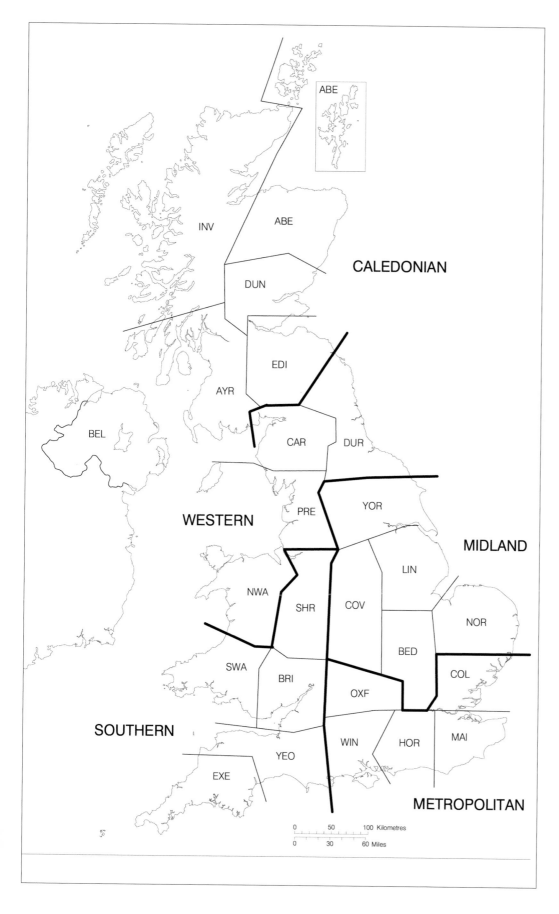

Figure 8.3
Map showing UKWMO
sector and group
boundaries during the
1980s

Figure 8.4
Preston, Longley Lane.
Western Sector Control.
Originally a wartime RAF
fighter command group
HQ, the building was
remodelled to form the
UKWMO sector
headquarters and local
ROC group headquarters.
[AA98/12225]

in Britain's nuclear deterrent strategy – confirmation of a nuclear attack would have led to the immediate scrambling of the V-force (*see* Chapter 3) and information concerning the targets attacked would have determined Britain's response.

UKWMO had little infrastructure of its own besides some communications equipment and radio masts. Instead it shared the ROC's facilities and the ROC acted as its 'field force'. From 1973 UKWMO was divided into five sectors, each covering five ROC groups (Fig 8.3). Sector headquarters were on the same site as the ROC groups at Dundee, Preston (Fig 8.4), Lincoln, Bristol and Horsham but, apart from minor changes to the configuration of the operations room, there was no impact on the appearance of the centres, though staffing levels would have been higher at around eighty.

Information about potential air attacks on the United Kingdom reached UKWMO from a number of sources, including the North American Air Defense System (NORAD) and the NATO Air Defence Ground Environment (NADGE), which took in the British sector operation centres (SOCs) and their associated air defence radar. Following the completion of the ballistic missile early warning system (BMEWS) at RAF Fylingdales in 1963, it was also possible to gain warning of attack by ballistic missiles (*see* Chapter 6).

Having confirmed that a threat was real, the principal warning officer based at the United Kingdom Regional Air Operations Centre (UKRAOC) at High Wycombe, Buckinghamshire, would have initiated the sounding of 'attack warning red' using the national warning system. If the UKRAOC was itself destroyed, selected sector controllers would have received the early warning messages; BBC central control would also have been alerted to broadcast the attack warning on radio and, later, on television.

At the same time, the turning of a key in the control position at UKRAOC or the selected sector controls would automatically have alerted the 250 carrier control points sited at main police stations. In turn, their operators would have initiated some 7,000 power-operated sirens in towns and villages and have broadcast verbal warning messages to 750 warning districts via some 19,000 rural warning points equipped with carrier receiver units (Fig 8.8e). Although many sirens were removed just after the war, the network was reinstated in the late 1940s, with sirens often placed on poles outside police stations; most were removed in the early 1990s except in a few areas prone to flooding.

The Royal Observer Corps reorganised

By 1955 the Home Office had realised that, in addition to the national network of shadowgraphs, a system was required to monitor the passage of radioactive fallout. In May that year the ROC, with its countrywide distribution of posts and communications, was identified as the best organisation to undertake the task. In order to do this it was reorganised: the national system of groups and posts was retained, but a completely new physical infrastructure was required to pro-

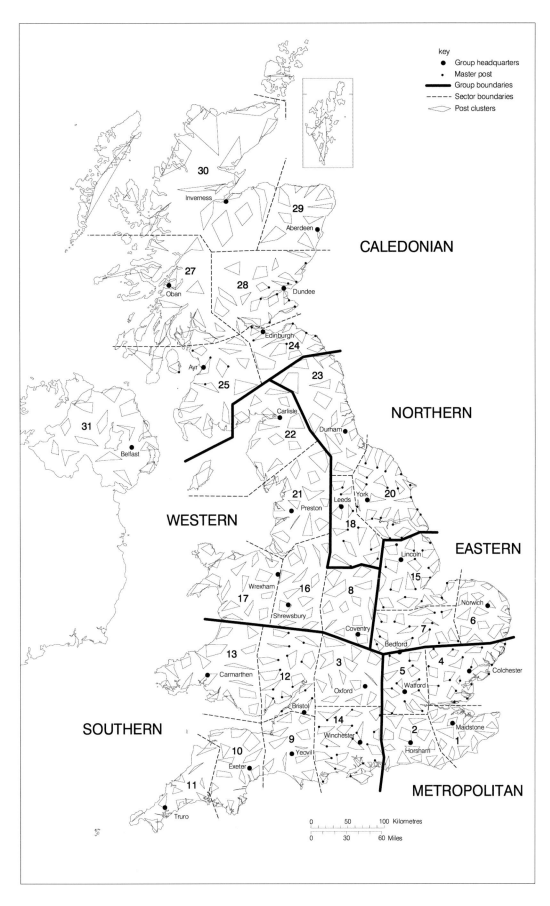

key
● Group headquarters
• Master post
━━ Group boundaries
- - - Sector boundaries
◇ Post clusters

Figure 8.5
ROC posts, clusters, groups
and sectors, at the height of
the Corps' extent during the
mid-1960s

CALEDONIAN

30
Inverness

29
Aberdeen

27
Oban

28
Dundee

Edinburgh
24

23
NORTHERN

25
Ayr

22
Carlisle

Durham

31
Belfast

21
Preston
Leeds
York
20

18

EASTERN

WESTERN

Wrexham
16
8
Lincoln
15

17
Shrewsbury
Norwich
6

Coventry
7
Bedford

13
3
4
Colchester

Carmarthen
12
5
Watford

Oxford

14
2
Maidstone

SOUTHERN

9
Winchester
Bristol

10
Yeovil
Horsham
1

Exeter

11
METROPOLITAN

Truro

0   50   100 Kilometres
0   30   60 Miles

vide its volunteer personnel with protection from the effects of nuclear weapons. Henceforth, monitoring posts would be placed underground and, in most cases, new protected accommodation was also built for the group headquarters.

Where possible, the monitoring posts were placed on the sites of the old visual reporting posts, partly to avoid delays in acquiring land and establishing communications links. They were fairly evenly distributed across the country, and were in prominent positions at intervals of 7–10miles (11.25–16km). All had to be readily accessible, so that most are next to lanes or tracks, some with a parking lay-by, or close to a public footpath. A simple post and wire fence surrounded most rural posts, while those close to urban areas were provided with more substantial barriers.

Construction work began in 1957 and 1,518 were in use by the time the programme was complete in 1965, making them the most common variety of Cold War monument (Fig 8.5). The number actually built was slightly greater than that, as some, such as that at Fulford, York, had to be resited when a new road was built, and the one at March, Cambridgeshire, was relocated because of flooding.

A mere three years later, in 1968, drastic reductions were made to the system, partly because of an easing of tension with the Soviet Union, but also in response to a major budget crisis which resulted in widespread defence cutbacks. In all, 686 posts and two protected group headquarters (No. 5 Watford and No. 18 Leeds) were closed, and the nominal strength of the Corps was reduced from 25,000 to 12,500. Further restructuring in 1973 resulted in the loss of two more group headquarters (No. 11 Truro and No. 27 Oban), although both were kept as nuclear reporting cells. Following that reorganisation, the ROC was divided into five areas, twenty-five groups, 272 clusters and about 870 posts.

Underground monitoring posts

By May 1956 the Home Office had decided on its requirements for underground monitoring posts, which were to be protected and able to accommodate four people (Fig 8.6). The prototype, now demolished, was constructed at Farnham, Surrey, and in September 1956 a number of trials took place to test it under sealed conditions.

The monitoring posts were monolithic reinforced-concrete structures, cast on site, and covered in earth to increase protection from radiation. Those we found in the field all displayed a standard arrangement of surface features, the only noticeable variation being the aerial attachments which were different on the master posts (see Fig 8.10). The form of the installations directly reflects the task of their personnel: confirming that a nuclear detonation had taken place; recording its location, strength and type (air or ground burst); monitoring the passage of any radioactive fallout cloud; and reporting all relevant information to the appropriate group headquarters for up to fourteen days following an attack (Figs 8.7 and 8.8).

Each post consisted of an entrance shaft sealed with a steel hatch, two ventilators with wooden or steel louvres, a small bore pipe to which the circular steel plates of the bomb power indicator were attached, and a larger pipe which carried the probe for the fixed survey meter. Next to the entry hatch was a mushroom-shaped casting with three holes, which carried the ground zero indicator (GZI). The functions of the principal instruments are described in the box on pages 182–3.

Such was the urgency to get the system up and running that at a number of posts the Corps began its new task from its existing positions. Examples have been recorded by fieldwork at Out Newton, East Riding of Yorkshire (Fig.8.9), where the GZI was placed on top of a brick pillar, and at Tunstall where it was attached to an Orlit post which was itself placed on top of a wartime pillbox (Fig 8.10). At West Raynham, Norfolk, the monitoring post was situated in the wartime airfield battle headquarters, which was provided with a bomb power indicator and a fixed survey meter probe.

By the 1980s the underground posts usually had a crew of three, sometimes of mixed sex, and living conditions were rudimentary (Fig 8.11). The post consisted of an underground chamber – a reinforced-concrete box 19ft × 8ft 6in × 7ft 6in (5.8m × 2.6m × 2.3m). Access was via a 15ft (4.5m) deep, 2ft (0.6m) square, vertical shaft in one corner of the structure. In the Farnham prototype a pair of hinged, outward-opening steel hatches closed the shaft. A concrete drainage sump let into the floor at the base of the shaft could catch water and be emptied as necessary by a rotary hand pump on the wall. Also at the foot of the shaft were two doorways, one giving access to the main chamber and the other, with a louvred tim-

Figure 8.6
Post 6H.2 Soham,
Cambridgeshire. Showing
the surface features typical
of all underground
monitoring posts
[BB98/27500]

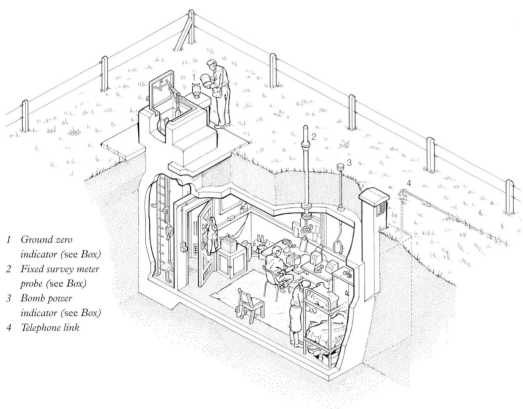

1 Ground zero
   indicator (see *Box*)
2 Fixed survey meter
   probe (see *Box*)
3 Bomb power
   indicator (see *Box*)
4 Telephone link

Figure 8.7
Underground monitoring
post, cutaway

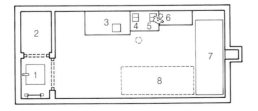

1 Drainage sump
2 Elsan toilet
3 Carrier receiver (see *Box*)
4 Loudspeaker telephone
5 Fixed survey meter (see *Box*)
6 Bomb Power Indicator (see *Box*)
7 Bunk bed
8 Optional additional bed

Figure 8.8
Underground monitoring
post, plan

Principal monitoring post instruments

Above: Ground zero indicator (No. 1 on Fig 8.7) also known as a shadowgraph. A cylindrical pinhole camera (left) has four $^3/_{16}$-in (5-mm) holes each facing a cardinal compass point. Internally (right), it was divided into four quadrants, each of which had a transparent plastic pocket, known as a cassette, which was marked off by a gridded screen graduated in degrees of bearing and elevation. A piece of low-sensitivity photographic paper was placed behind it. If there were a nuclear explosion the image of the burst would be burnt into the paper as a 'spot'. No. 3 Observer was tasked with retrieving the paper. From the bearing and height of the explosion indicated by papers from several posts, the group headquarters could use triangulation to determine the position of the detonation. The GZI had a range of about 7 miles (11.25km). [BB98/ 20007]

Left: Probe unit of the FSM was housed in a domed ionising chamber of extremely strong rubberised plastic, that was bolted to a flanged plate on top of a pipe which passed down to the monitoring room (No. 2 on Fig 8.7). A co-axial cable descended to the meter in the post. [AA99/04573]

Right: Bomb power indicator (BPI). On the surface (No. 3 on Fig 8.7) the BPI had a pair of circular steel plates attached to a galvanised steel pipe that passed through the roof of the post to the indicator unit below. The latter had an $8^1/_2$-in (210-mm) face graduated from 0–50 kilopascals (units of pressure). If a nuclear device were detonated, metal bellows in the casing would be expanded by the blast, forcing a rod against a spindle which in turn rotated the indicator needle. As it was not attached to the bellows,

it would not return to zero when the bellows deflated, thus recording the maximum or peak blast (over pressure). After ten seconds it would be reset to record any further explosions. [AA92/2516]

Below: Fixed survey meter (FSM) – Plessey Dose Rate Meter (PDRM) 82F (No. 6 on Fig 8.8). This was the final version of FSM issued to the ROC in the 1980s, and allowed post staff to record external gamma radiation levels without venturing outside. The PDRM 82F was contained in an orange polycarbonate waterproof case. Radiation levels would have been shown on the liquid crystal display. The meter could also be used for mobile monitoring [BB98/20005]

Above: Carrier receiver unit (No. 3 on Fig 8.8). All ROC posts were fitted with a unit of this kind, at the end of a unidirectional line. Its function was to receive warning of an imminent attack 'attack warning red'. Similar units were installed at 19,000 rural warning points. [BB98/20002]

Above, right: Individual dosimeter. When operating outside the post all personnel would have worn this device, similar in size and shape to a fountain pen, which measured the accumulated gamma or X-radiation exposure over a period of time. A magnifying window in the top of the dosimeter allowed the wearer to view a quartz fibre

electroscope scale calibrated 0–150 roentgen (r) or, later, 0–500 centigrays (units of ionising radiation). It was zeroed using a dosimeter charging unit. A larger radiac meter was used for the mobile monitoring of radiation levels. [BB98/20004]

Below: Maroon training kit. Maroons were explosive devices issued to the posts for them to use to warn of the imminent approach of a fallout cloud, 'fallout warning black'. The signal was three loud bangs or three sharp blasts on a whistle or blows to a gong. Many posts were also equipped with hand-cranked sirens to warn of an air attack or to issue the all-clear signal. [BB98/ 20006]

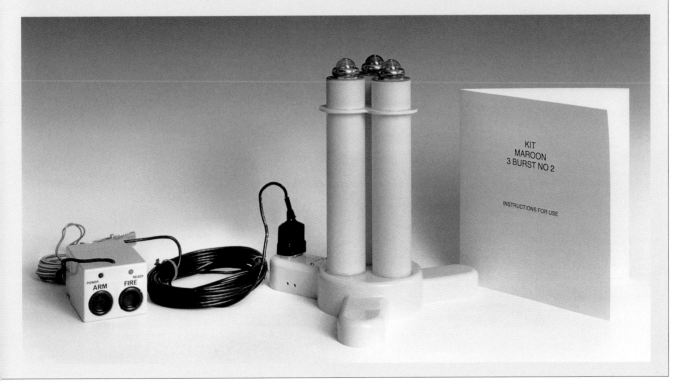

Figure 8.9
Out Newton, East Riding
of Yorkshire. Ground zero
indicator mounting on a
brick pillar on top of a
wartime pillbox
[MF98/00251/3]

Figure 8.10 (below)
Post 20/M2, Tunstall, East
Riding of Yorkshire. This
key site on the Holderness
coast illustrates three
successive phases of defence
activity. Originally a
wartime pillbox, an Orlit
post, was placed on top of it
in the early 1950s; later, a
ground zero indicator
mounting and access steps
were added. In its final
phase an underground
monitoring post was built,
on the nearest vent of which
is the fitting for a post radio
indicating that it was a
master post. [AA92/2561]

ber door, to a store cupboard which also housed an Elsan latrine.

Furnishing in the main chamber generally consisted of a two-tier steel-frame bunk bed, canvas chairs, a folding table and a store cupboard; a rubberised floor was later installed at many sites to help insulate the chamber from cold. Lighting was provided by a single bulb or fluorescent tube, powered by a 12-volt car battery which was periodically recharged using a petrol-driven charger, though in the late 1980s a few posts were issued with portable generators. In an emergency, food would be issued in standard military ration packs but, because of the risks of both fire and carbon dioxide poisoning, warming food was difficult, even using self-heating tins. The prototype post was ventilated by louvres in the split hatch doors and by a shuttered flue in the end wall, which rose to a ventilator on the surface. One of the few modifications found in actual posts was the addition of an extra shuttered ventilation flue in one side of the entrance shaft. More robust, single 'Broad's Pattern' chequered steel hatch covers were also adopted, but they were not strong enough to resist a determined attempt to break in (such as was often mounted by anti-nuclear protesters during the 1980s), and a number of

Figure 8.11
Leek, Staffordshire. A
typical ROC post interior
[AA99/04554]

vulnerable posts were fitted with more secure 'Torlift' hatches.

The main method of communication within the ROC was by landline, and a line of telephone poles terminating in the middle of a field may be one indication of an underground monitoring post (Fig 8.12). Each post in a cluster was interconnected, with a single link from the designated master post to the group headquarters and the nominated post plotter. In case the landline failed, the master posts were also equipped with VHF radio sets.

All posts also provided emergencyweather information, but eighty-seven were specially equipped to provide information on atmospheric pressure and temperature. These posts also had an aneroid barometer fixed to the monitoring room wall – all other measurements were made with hand-held instruments.

Visual reporting continued at 280 posts in the part of eastern England where the nuclear deterrent was based (*see* Fig 3.1) – an area roughly bounded by a line from the Thames at London, through Bedford and York, and from there northwards to the coast at the Tees. At many of these sites the old wartime

Figure 8.12
Post 6/E2 Watton, Norfolk.
The telephone line
terminates at the ROC
post. [BB98/30038]

or Orlit post continued in service, but at others there was a simple, newly-built structure comprising three concrete steps, a frame of galvanised scaffold pipe (to which an awning could be fixed) and a truncated telephone pole (Fig 8.13). Even though the RAF

decided in 1965 that it no longer required the ROC to perform its visual reporting role, aircraft recognition remained part of the activities of the Corps, and there were periodic debates about its possible reinstatement.

Figure 8.13
Post 6/H2 Soham,
Cambridgeshire. Visual
reporting post
[BB98/27501]

Group headquarters

The duty of the staff of the group headquarters was to establish the exact position, height and power of all nuclear explosions within their area, by collating information from the monitoring posts in their group (*see* Fig 8.5). They would also receive data from the posts on the time of arrival of fallout, and subsequent dose-rate readings. All this information would be passed to adjacent ROC group headquarters and to the local Home Office sector control, while at the same time the fallout warning would begin.

At first the planners thought that 31 groups would be required but, before building began, the number was reduced to 30 and eventually fell to 29 (Table 8.2). Initial design drawings produced in 1956 show group headquarters designed to offer protection against radiation. It seems that building work did not start until 1959 so that, at first, the monitoring posts continued to report to the existing group centres. Two basic types of protected headquarters were designed: semi-sunken, of which there were twelve, and surface, of which there were thirteen; the remaining six were placed in existing structures. The decision on which type to use appears to have been influenced by an assessment of vulnerability.

Although the two types differed in external appearance and internal layout, they contained a standard suite of rooms arranged either side of a main corridor, reflecting their identical purpose (Figs 8.14a–c). The surface type has a standard rectangular plan and is a single storey

Table 8.2   Summary of ROC group headquarters

Location	Group	Area	Type	Operational years	AWDREY*
Maidstone	1	Metropolitan	Semi-sunken	1960–1991	
Horsham	2	Metropolitan	Surface	1962–1991	Yes
Oxford	3	Metropolitan	Semi-sunken	1965–1991	Yes
Colchester	4	Metropolitan	Surface	1961–1991	Yes
Watford	5	Metropolitan	Semi-sunken	1961–1973	
Norwich	6	Midland	Semi-sunken	1961–1991	
Bedford	7	Midland	Semi-sunken	1962–1991	
Rugby	8	Midland	Semi-sunken	1963–1991	Yes
Yeovil	9	Southern	Semi-sunken	1961–1991	
Exeter	10	Southern	Surface	1961–1991	Yes
Truro	11	Southern	Surface	1963–1973	
Bristol/Bath	12	Southern	AAOR	1959–1991	Yes
Carmarthen	13	Southern	Surface	1961–1991	Yes
Winchester	14	Metropolitan	Surface	1961–1991	
Lincoln	15	Midland	Semi-sunken	1960–1991	
Shrewsbury	16	Southern	Surface	1962–1991	
Wrexham	17	Northern	Surface	1962–1991	
Leeds	18	Northern	Semi-sunken	1964–1968	
Manchester	19	Northern	Unprotected	1955–1961	
York	20	Midland	Semi-sunken	1961–1991	Yes
Preston	21	Western	RAF Grp HQ	1962–1991	
Carlisle	22	Carlisle	Surface	1962–1991	
Durham	23	Northern	Surface	1961–1991	
Edinburgh	24	Caledonian	Semi-sunken	1964–1991	
Ayr	25	Caledonian	Surface	1962–1991	
Glasgow	26	Caledonian	Unprotected	1955–1962	
Oban	27	Caledonian	Surface	1962–1973	Yes
Dundee	28	Caledonian	Semi-sunken	1961–1991	Yes
Aberdeen	29	Caledonian	Surface	1961–1991	
Inverness	30	Caledonian	RAF Grp HQ	1961–1991	Yes
Belfast	31	Western	AAOR	1963–1991	Yes

* *atomic weapon recognition and examination of yield (see p 191)*

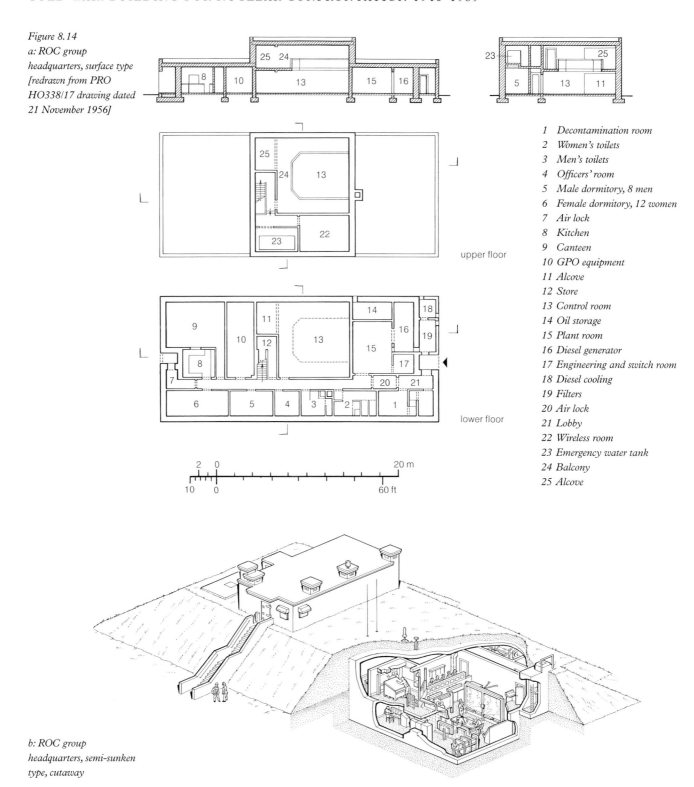

Figure 8.14
a: ROC group
headquarters, surface type
[redrawn from PRO
HO338/17 drawing dated
21 November 1956]

upper floor

lower floor

1 Decontamination room
2 Women's toilets
3 Men's toilets
4 Officers' room
5 Male dormitory, 8 men
6 Female dormitory, 12 women
7 Air lock
8 Kitchen
9 Canteen
10 GPO equipment
11 Alcove
12 Store
13 Control room
14 Oil storage
15 Plant room
16 Diesel generator
17 Engineering and switch room
18 Diesel cooling
19 Filters
20 Air lock
21 Lobby
22 Wireless room
23 Emergency water tank
24 Balcony
25 Alcove

b: ROC group
headquarters, semi-sunken
type, cutaway

building except for the central two-storey operations room. Features on the roof include vents and an emergency water tank. There are, however, differences between the outsides of these buildings. At Wrexham, Flintshire, the walls are of plain brick, while at Horsham, Sussex, and Shrewsbury, Shropshire, the brick walls also have decorative stepped brick door cases or surrounds (Fig 8.15). By contrast Poltimore, near Exeter, has walls which are either concrete or cement rendered, though it has a similar

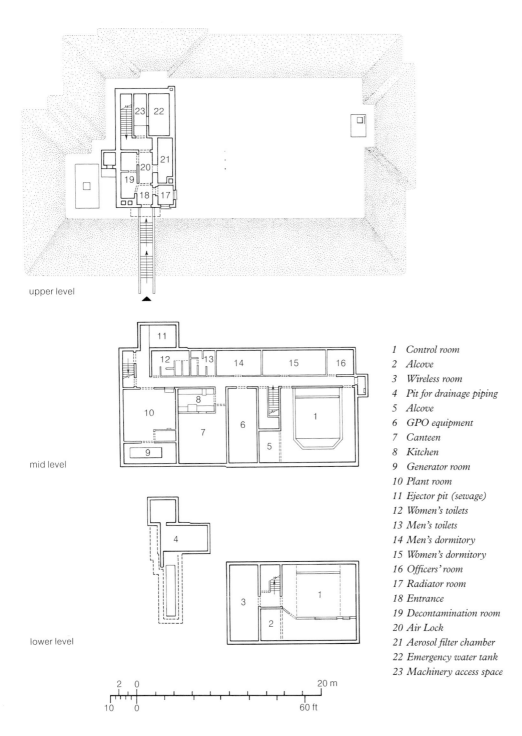

*c: ROC group
headquarters, semi-sunken
type*

upper level

mid level

lower level

2 0   20 m

10   0   60 ft

1   Control room
2   Alcove
3   Wireless room
4   Pit for drainage piping
5   Alcove
6   GPO equipment
7   Canteen
8   Kitchen
9   Generator room
10 Plant room
11 Ejector pit (sewage)
12 Women's toilets
13 Men's toilets
14 Men's dormitory
15 Women's dormitory
16 Officers' room
17 Radiator room
18 Entrance
19 Decontamination room
20 Air Lock
21 Aerosol filter chamber
22 Emergency water tank
23 Machinery access space

stepped brick door surround and its corners are embellished in brick. At Truro the door case and corners are finished in local stone, as is the administration building next door.

The semi-sunken type (Fig 8.16) appears on the surface as a rectangular earth mound with a projecting two-storey blockhouse. Steps lead to the entrance on the upper level and there is a small protruding emergency exit, but the main structure is encased in a protective covering of earth. When built, all the exposed concrete surfaces were painted

Figure 8.15
Horsham, Sussex, No. 2
Group Headquarters. Front
elevation [BB99/00495]

which was used to protect the bunker's electrical systems against the effects of the electromagnetic pulse released by a nuclear explosion. Originally the headquarters were fitted with fixed radio aerials, but from the late 1960s many were furnished with less vulnerable telescopic lattice girder masts which, for example at Bedford (Fig 8.16) and York, involved the removal of part of the earth banking.

At the heart of both kinds of structure was the operations room (*see* Fig 8.14a–c), close to which were the wireless, teleprinter, and General Post Office (GPO, later BT) equipment rooms. The operations room was roughly square and could be entered directly off the main corridor at gallery level, or from a flight of steps which descended to the well (lower level). In the centre of the well was the command table at which the duty controller and senior warning officers would sit. From there they could view the nuclear burst tote board, the dose log charts, Display E (European situation map), Display T (United Kingdom situation map), Display B (cumulative situation map, updated at two-hourly intervals), and Display A (current situation map) (Figs 8.17a–d). The plotters and tellers were situated on the gallery on opposite sides of the well. The post display plotters sat in a row behind rotating Perspex-covered post display and first fallout early warning boards, upon which they wrote (in waxy chinagraph pencils) the data which was received (and updated at five-minute intervals) from the monitoring posts and then passed to other

white to reflect the heat from nuclear flashes, but by the 1980s, along with the underground monitoring posts, most had been changed to a less conspicuous green. Other external features include the mounting for a ground zero indicator, usually on top of the air intake vent, and pipes for the bomb power indicator and the fixed surge monitor,

Figure 8.16
Bedford, No. 7 Group
Headquarters. The
operations room in this
semi-sunken type was on
the right. [BB98/27432]

adjacent sections. The bomb power indicator, its map, and the group triangulation table were in an alcove on the same side of the gallery as the post display plotters. Information derived from the triangulation table would have been transferred to a slatted burst display positioned on the gallery between the plotters and the tellers. The teleprinters, transmitting heads and tape reperforators were all in a sound-proofed room under one side of the gallery.

To complement the manually operated detection instruments at the individual posts, twelve group headquarters (*see* Table 8.2) were, by the 1960s, equipped with an automatic 'atomic weapon detection recognition and estimation of yield' or AWDREY unit. It was usually contained in a grey steel cabinet placed on the upper gallery close to the triangulation table (*see* Fig 8.17d), and was designed to detect both the optical and electromagnetic signatures of a nuclear explosion and set off an automatic alarm signal. A detection head above the diesel exhaust duct marked out headquarters fitted with such units (Fig 8.18). From 1974, AWDREY units were used together with a device called the 'direction indicator of atomic detonation by electronic means' –

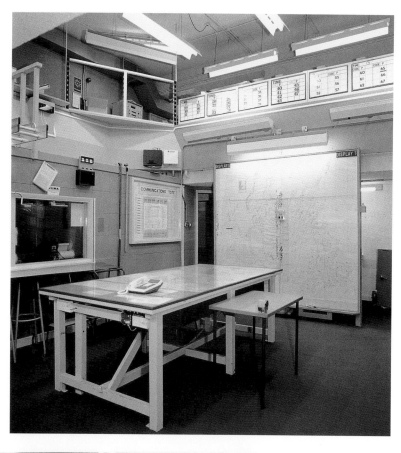

Figure 8.17
York, No. 20 Group Headquarters.
a: (above)
Operations room showing the central operations table, the display E and T maps. Above are the plotting boards on which information from the individual posts would have been recorded. [AA92/04297]

b: Operations room showing display screens A and B on which the track of fallout plumes would have been plotted [AA92/04296]

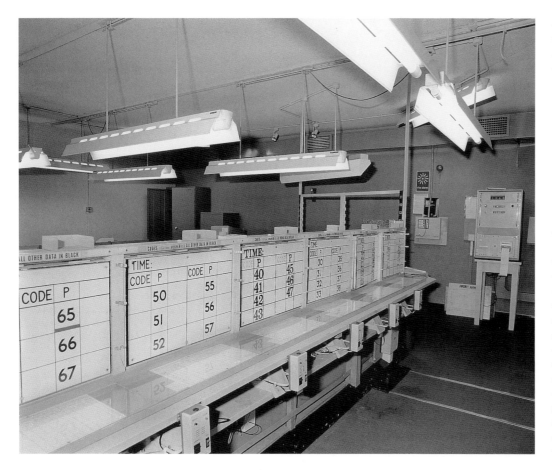

Figure 8.17
c: (opposite)
Plotting fallout plumes on
display A [AA92/02674]

d: (left)
Upper gallery showing the
rotating boards (see Fig
8.17a) on which post
details were written. To the
rear is the AWDREY
display unit, which was
capable of measuring the
time gap in milliseconds
between the two pulses of
light generated by a nuclear
burst, and could produce a
printout giving the precise
time of detonation and the
estimated yield of a
weapon. [AA92/02676]

DIADEM – which, as its name suggests, gave bearing information so that the location of a burst could be plotted by triangulation.

Each headquarters needed around fifty people to staff it, made up of around forty ROC members and ten Home Office warning and scientific officers, split into three watches – duty, standby and rest. Accommodation was in two dormitories with associated toilet and shower facilities. The larger dormitory was usually for women and was lined with six two-tier bunks, while the smaller, men's dormitory had provision for four such bunks, giving a total of twenty beds. All were occupied on a 'hot bed' system; that is, people did not have their own beds but used whichever was available. A small kitchen and a canteen were also provided.

Under normal circumstances the headquarters were connected to the mains services, but they were also designed to be self-sufficient for up to thirty days. Each had a standby generator (Fig 8.19), air conditioning plant, emergency water tank, bulk fuel storage tank and, in the case of the semi-sunken design, a sewage ejection system. The air conditioning unit (life support system)

Figure 8.18
York, No. 20 Group
Headquarters. Photo-
sensitive cells within the
AWDREY detection head
were able to identify a
nuclear explosion by
recording the intense flash
of light produced by the
detonation of the initiator of
a weapon and, milliseconds
later, the second intense
flash of the main explosion.
Measurement of the short
gap between the two events
enabled an estimate of the
bomb's power to be made.
The instrument could also
indicate the bearing of the
explosion. It had a range of
up to 150 miles (240km)
in good visibility, though
poor weather could halve
that, but even then the
twelve units provided
coverage of the whole
country. [AA92/02640]

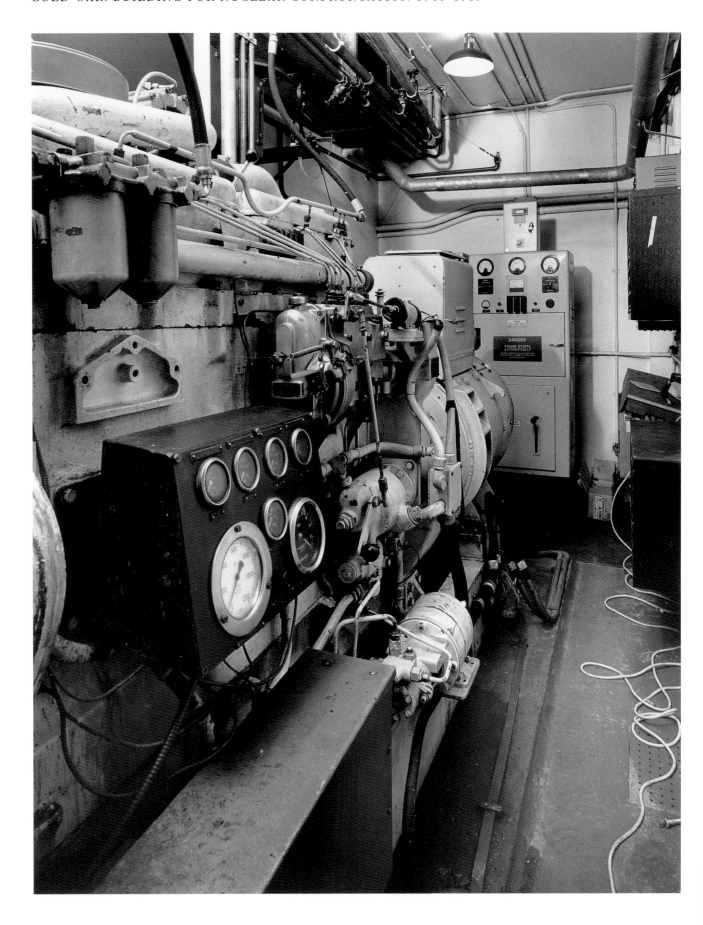

could operate in one of four modes – normal, modified normal, recirculation, and filtration. In closed up conditions the air would be recirculated around the building for as along as possible; once the air became foul, a 'gulp' of fresh air would have been drawn from outside through the aerosol/particulate filters. Most staff were to remain sealed in the bunker, but there was provision for rudimentary decontamination in a room near the main entrance, which was fitted with a couple of wash basins and a locker, or 'hot box', for contaminated items (Fig 8.20).

For most of the Cold War, data was carried between groups and sectors by teleprinters, supplemented by voice messages. During the late 1980s the way in which information was received, analysed and distributed was enhanced by the installation at some headquarters of new information technology, including the SX 2000 digital private automatic branch exchange and visual display units (Fig 8.21). The replacement of the manual plotting boards by desk-top systems was reflected in the buildings: by the flooring over of some operation room wells, as at Bedford, Horsham and Preston.

Throughout its history the ROC and its predecessors were voluntary organisations supported by a small number of permanent administrative and headquarters staff. The latter, along with a group training centre, were housed in a wide variety of buildings.

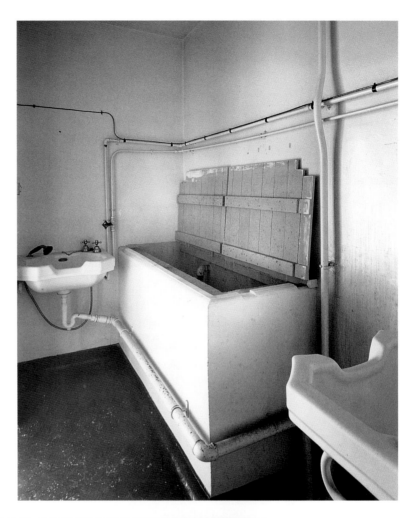

Figure 8.19 (opposite) Bedford, No. 7 Group Headquarters. Standby generator room [AA98/07879]

Figure 8.20 (above) Bedford, No. 2 Group Headquarters. Decontamination room [AA98/07876]

Figure 8.21 York, No. 20 Group Headquarters. SX 2000 communication equipment [AA92/02672]

Figure 8.22
York, No. 20 Group
Headquarters. Isotope store
[304P/13]

Since many of the new protected headquarters were on the same sites as their wartime predecessors, the older buildings often became administration and training blocks, as at Bedford (*see* Fig 8.1), Watford and Winchester, while at Maidstone a large Victorian villa was retained. Where a new site was chosen, for instance at Lincoln, Wrexham, and York, purpose-built single-storey brick or prefabricated structures were built. A final, distinctive, feature of group headquarters were the small detached brick isotope stores (hutches), used in the testing and calibration of instruments (Fig 8.22).

Secondary operations rooms

Although most of the old non-protected group headquarters were abandoned once the new protected headquarters were available, ten were retained as secondary operations rooms. This was thought necessary in case the relative remoteness of many of the newer headquarters had an adverse effect on training, manning and recruitment. Their purpose was solely to accommodate the training staff who worked at the operational headquarters, and no wartime role was envisaged for them. During the 1960s their numbers were gradually reduced, and by 1976 all were closed.

Stand down

In May 1991 the Home Office informed the Commandant of the ROC that the UKWMO was to be disbanded and that the ROC was to be stood down in view of the reduction of the perceived nuclear threat to the country. Training ceased in July and the ROC's operational role ceased in September, though the full-time staff continued the run down until 31 March 1992. After that a small number of observers were retained by the armed services in their nuclear reporting cells. More recently almost two-thirds of the underground posts have been cleared in some counties, though in others most still survive. Of those that remain, the majority lie abandoned, but a number have been purchased by individuals and maintained as monuments, often complete with their fittings. Most group headquarters remain intact and a few have found new uses, including two that have been converted into veterinary surgeries.

9
The home front

If the warning and air defence systems described in the preceding chapters had failed to destroy attacking aircraft – and any assault by missiles would, of course, have been unstoppable – an elaborate and largely voluntary network of 'civil defence' organisations would have been activated. Emergency government headquarters would have co-ordinated this activity, supported by an infrastructure of emergency communications and foodstores. The structures built to house the officials designated to govern the country after a nuclear attack, along with its supporting infrastructure, are the focus of this chapter.

Emergency regional government

The post-war provision of emergency central government was based on that of the 1920s, when Stanley Baldwin's 1924–1929 Government was concerned about the threat to internal stability posed by revolutions on the Continent and industrial strikes at home. In the late 1930s, the spectre of air attacks led to a redefinition of the system, under which the country was divided into twelve regions each headed by a regional commissioner. Originally, the commissioner's role following an incident such as a devastating air raid was to co-ordinate all local civil defence activities. This was soon extended to include, in an extreme emergency, the assumption of full state power.

The wartime regional commissioners' offices were usually regional civil defence centres; often large Victorian houses below which, in hardened basements, were war rooms containing map, operations, message, switch, teleprinter and typing rooms. The system, never fully activated, was put into abeyance at the end of the war.

War rooms: early 1950s

In the uncertain world of the early 1950s, the Government not only renewed its commitment to civil defence but also began to restructure its plans for internal administration, around a series of protected regional commissioners' offices or war rooms. Apart from London, each of the twelve early post-war mainland 'home defence regions' was provided with a war room, as was Northern Ireland. London Region was provided with four, making sixteen in all (Fig 9.1). All but one, at Newcastle upon Tyne, were located in purpose-built structures. The war rooms were placed in the same cities as their wartime predecessors but were usually moved to government estates which housed a variety of ministries, from whose ranks commissioners were to draw their staff. Many of the estates, such as those at Bristol, Cambridge, Nottingham, Reading, and Tunbridge Wells, were wartime dispersal estates made up of prefabricated temporary office buildings. Dates on drawings show that design work for the war rooms had begun by October 1951, and aerial photographs of the Cambridge bunker show that construction was well advanced by 1953; a date confirmed by manufacturers' plates seen on machinery elsewhere (Fig 9.2).

The system of the early 1950s, uniquely, provided the regional commissioners with an architecturally coherent group of structures. We found three standard types of war rooms: surface single-storey (found in the London region, only one of which survives in its original form at Mill Hill, Barnet); surface two-storey; and semi-sunken two-storey (Figs 9.3a–c). The functions of the war rooms were reflected in the internal arrangements of all three types and may be divided into three categories: physical protection of the commissioner and his staff; receipt and filtering of information about the condition of the region after an attack; and the dissemination of decisions.

The design of the war rooms, with their central map and information filtering room, was derived from that of Second World War RAF and Royal Observer Corps filter and operations rooms, but was enhanced to meet the devastating new threats posed by atomic warfare and to provide a 'protective factor' of

Designing a nuclear bunker

> Anachronistic in normal periods, in peacetime, the bunker appears as a survival machine, as a shipwrecked submarine on a beach. It speaks to us of other elements, of terrific atmospheric pressure, of an unusual world in which science and technology have developed the possibility of final disintegration.
>
> (Virilio, 1994 *Bunker Archeology*)

Before considering the architecture of structures designed to withstand, and operate after, a nuclear attack, the effects of a nuclear explosion must be understood. The severity of an explosion varies according to many factors including the type and power of the weapon, height of detonation, local topography and weather conditions.

The four main effects of a nuclear explosion are blast, heat, radiation (subdivided into initial radiation, secondary radiation from fission products, and radioactive fallout), and electromagnetic pulse. Up to 50 per cent of the energy released by a nuclear explosion forms blast and shock waves; 35 per cent is dissipated in heat radiation and 15 per cent as nuclear radiation (5 per cent in initial ionising radiation, and the remaining 10 per cent as residual radiation). Blast and heat are devastating within an area (varying with the size of the bomb) around the ground zero. Some of the initial radiation is quickly absorbed and lost with its passage through the atmosphere, though neutrons and gamma rays can travel considerable distances through all materials.

Secondary emissions, including gamma radiation, are produced by the decay of fission products. Radioactive contamination is spread further through fallout created by the uptake of particles of debris created by the force of the explosion. These fall as radioactive dust over a wide area, varying with local weather conditions. Within ten days most radiation decays sufficiently for people to emerge from shelters, although many of the decay products will create long-term environmental hazards.

The final immediate effect of a nuclear detonation is electromagnetic. The most devastating part is the electromagnetic pulse (EMP) – a powerful pulse of radio frequency energy created by the interaction of gamma rays with the atmosphere. When electronic equipment relied on valves this posed little threat but, as solid state semi-conductors were introduced from the early 1960s, EMP had the power to destroy or damage unshielded electronic equipment over thousands of kilometres. Related to this is the ionisation of the atmosphere, which may affect the transmission of radio signals for hours after an attack.

It is impossible to design a structure that will survive within a couple of kilometres of the point of detonation of a nuclear explosion. Beyond this range, depending on the size of the bomb, some types of structure can survive. The strategies for designing such buildings are similar to those adopted to withstand powerful conventional bombs. Since the building of massive reinforced-concrete bomb-proof structures was relatively unusual in Britain during the Second World War, they represent a new type of architecture, perhaps inspired by German designs of the 1930s and 1940s. If a bomb was detonated on the ground (a ground burst) bunkers were subject to ground shock – similar to a small earthquake. To counter this, most are of monolithic form and stand on a gravel raft, allowing them to move without the integrity of the whole being affected. The blast, which travels as a wave of peaks and troughs of pressure, also exerts stress on buildings as the pressure inside differs from that outside.

The most penetrating kinds of radiation are gamma radiation and neutrons, and shielding against their effects offers protection against all other forms. The effectiveness of the barrier depends on the density of the materials used, with 2.2in (56mm) of concrete affording the same protection as 3.3in (84mm) of earth or 0.7in (18mm) of steel, all of which halve the amount of radiation received (the dose rate). The protection provided (the protective factor or PF) is derived by comparing the dose rate of an unprotected person standing in the open with that received by a person in a building. For example, a person in a structure with a PF of 100 receives a hundredth of the dose of a person outside. The further danger from radioactive fallout is reduced by the provision of thick walls and by the installation of filters to absorb dust particles.

Shielding against electromagnetic effects may be achieved by placing all electronic equipment within a 'global shield' or 'Faraday Cage', which ensures all elements are electrically continuous, and this protection can be enhanced by the provision of surge arrestors.

The design of most civil facilities was based on the assumption that any attack would either be by conventional high explosives or nuclear weapons, and the possibility that the civil population would be attacked with biological or chemical weapons was largely discounted. This was in sharp contrast to planning for military sites, especially during the 1980s when many military facilities were protected against this kind of attack. It also flew in the face of evidence that the Warsaw Pact had a lethal arsenal of such weapons. Despite that, in bunkers where both civilians and members of the armed forces were stationed only military personnel were issued with nuclear biological and chemical warfare suits.

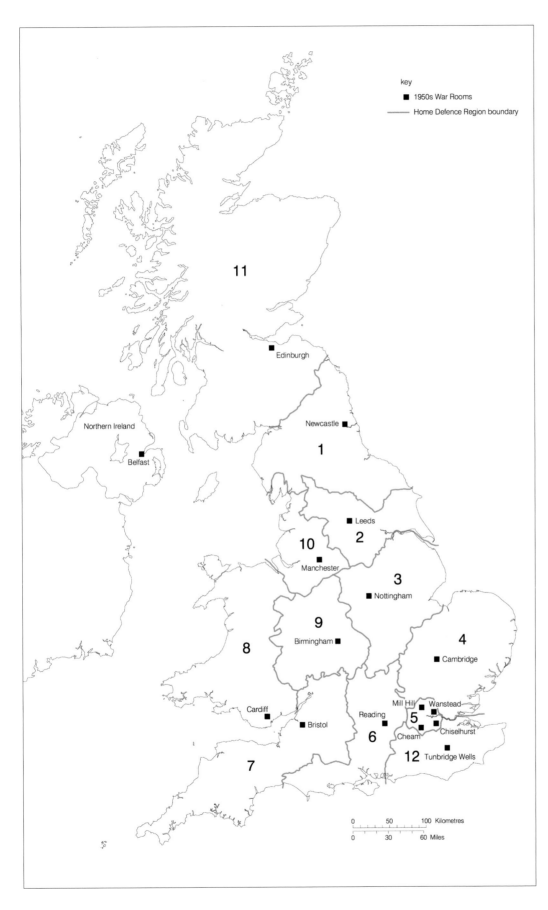

Figure 9.1
Map of England and Wales showing Civil Defence Regional boundaries and locations of 1950s war rooms

key
■ 1950s War Rooms
— Home Defence Region boundary

Figure 9.2
Brooklands Avenue,
Cambridge, is a typical
government wartime estate
comprising gabled
temporary office buildings,
and late 1940s flat-roofed
office buildings. The 1950s
war room and early 1960s
regional seat of government
(RSG) is in the bottom left
corner. Next to it was the
regional Civil Defence
headquarters. [18026/08]

Figure 9.3
a: (below)
Cambridge, war room,
surface double-storey type.
Visible in this photograph is
one of the entrances and the
ventilation openings over
the plant room. To the left is
the attached early 1960s
regional seat of
government. [BB98/01033]

*b: (above)
Reading, Berkshire, war
room, semi-sunken
double-storey type. Here,
horizontal lines clearly
mark the layers in which
the bunker was cast; also
evident is the crude finish of
this structure and later
modifications to the
ventilation openings.
[AA98/02649]*

*c: Chislehurst, war room.
London region surface
single-storey type
[AA008678]*

Figure 9.4
Cambridge, war room.
Electrically driven fans
drew air into the bunker
through banks of filters, just
visible through the open
entry hatch, of this
otherwise sealed-in
compartment.
[BB98/01035]

400 (*see* p 198). Accordingly, the war rooms were constructed of reinforced-concrete walls 4ft 10in (1.45m) thick, capped with a 5ft (1.50m) thick roof. Apart from the partitions in the toilets (which are built of hollow bricks), the internal walls were also reinforced-concrete, while the internal doors were wooden with Bakelite fittings. Protection against dust-carried fallout was provided by an elaborate air filtration system using filters made of glass fibre or metal wool cells which also filtered out gas (Fig 9.4). Ventilation was supplied by rectangular section ducting suspended from the ceilings.

Although no original 1950s list of functions for a war room has been found, the allocation of space for the various activities may be inferred (Figs 9.5a–c). The crucial importance of the map room at the heart of the decision-making process is reflected in its position at the hub of the bunker. In the two-storey bunkers it occupied the full height of

the building and was overlooked by control cabins with curved Perspex windows. The staff consisted of around fifty people, including the commissioner, a scientific adviser and members of fire and hospital control, as well as police and military liaison officers. Other rooms were occupied by telephonists, telex operators and secretaries, who fed information to the map room and relayed the commissioner's decisions back to the outside world.

Regional seats of government: 1950s/early 1960s

In August 1953, almost before the concrete of the war rooms was dry, the detonation of the Soviet H-bomb required a reappraisal of Home Office plans. The Soviet Union now had the power not only to destroy whole cities but also their surrounding transport and communications infrastructure. It was

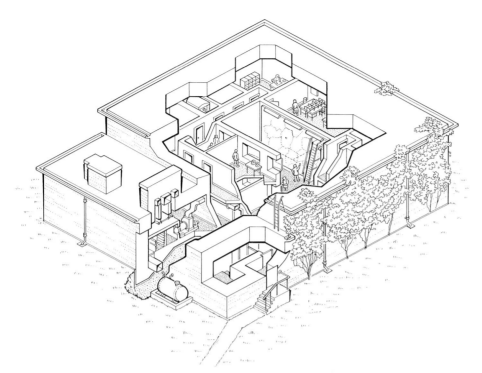

Figure 9.5
Suggested arrangement of a
1950s war room: cutaway
and plan

necessary not only to extend the post-explosion recovery period but also for each region to be autonomous for longer. To support the commissioners in their extended roles a new system of regional seats of government (RSGs) was planned, providing for a greater number of officials (Fig 9.6). (Despite some common usage, RSG is an administrative term, not a description of a particular type of bunker.)

The structure of emergency government continued to be based around 'home defence' regions, though they were reorganised. Pessimistic projections about the effect of an H-bomb attack on London led to the abolition of Region 5: in future London would be administered from the surrounding regions, and all the English regional centres (or 'citadels') were relocated, apart from those at Cambridge and Nottingham. In some places existing buildings were reused but elsewhere new building was required – a mixture that was to be repeated in later reorganisations.

In 1956 a system of sub-regional controls (SRCs) was planned in order to co-ordinate rescue in the immediate aftermath of an attack. Much of this system does not appear to have progressed beyond the paper plan. London was to be split into five sub-regions administered by centres outside the region. In 1961, the former Rotor-period R4 at Kelvedon Hatch, Essex, (see Chapter 5) was designated SRC 5.5, while other centres included the former anti-aircraft operations

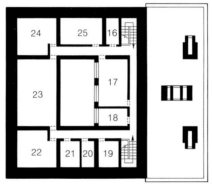

upper floor

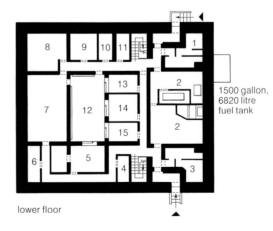

lower floor

1500 gallon, 6820 litre fuel tank

1 Female toilets
2 Plant Room
3 Male toilets
4 Messenger and entry control
5 Control cabin
6 Male dormitory
7 Canteen and welfare
8 Female dormitory
9 Telephone exchange
10 Telephone exchange
11 Messenger and entry control
12 Map room
13 Control cabin
14 Control cabin
15 Control cabin
16 Water tank
17 Control cabin
18 Control cabin
19 Office
20 Water tank
21 Office
22 Office
23 Office
24 Office
25 Office

5 0   20 m
20 0   60 ft

Figure 9.6
Map of early 1960s
regional seats of
government

room (AAOR) at Fort Bridgewoods, an unidentified control in Stoughton Barracks, Guildford, and the old war room at Tunbridge Wells.

In a rare display of openness about emergency government a 1963 statement in the House of Commons revealed that eleven RSGs were to be built: nine in England and Wales and one each for Scotland and Northern Ireland. It was also stated that the primary purpose of the RSG buildings was,

> not of protecting the occupants, but enabling succour and relief to be brought to the public after an attack to be carried out to the best advantage and to marshal services and supplies essential for survival.
>
> (*Hansard*, 27 June 1963, Volume 679 column 1842)

The staff in the RSG were split into five main functional groups: units from various ministries; public information distribution services (including the BBC); the police and fire services; civil defence control sections; and a communications section. The survival of door signs in the Cambridge building reflects the allocation of space during the late 1960s (Fig 9.7), including the newly designated rooms for army, navy and air force liaison officers. The BBC staff were responsible for a small studio which could be used to broadcast both live bulletins from the commissioner and recorded messages. Notices dated January 1966 indicate that the Cambridge RSG could accommodate about 400 people; 120 of these places were allocated in the female dormitories.

The location and design of the buildings implied an acknowledgement that there could be no protection against the blast and heat effects of the H-bomb, and emphasis was now placed on protection from fallout. This can be seen in the architecture of the purpose-built RSGs – at Cambridge, Nottingham and Kirknewton, Scotland. They all have thinner walls than the war rooms, while at Nottingham the cantilevered upper storey, supported by rectangular pillars, was particularly vulnerable to blast damage. At all three sites the existing war rooms were reused, a large two-storey surface bunker was butted onto the sides of those at Cambridge and Kirknewton (*see* Fig 9.8a), and most departments were accommodated on the ground floor of the new building with dormitories and dining facilities above (in the part of the bunker most susceptible to fallout

dust). The regional commissioner and his immediate staff occupied most of the old building, with access to the central area controlled by doors with combination locks. The main structural alteration to the old building was the insertion of a floor into the two-storey map room to create a new upper room.

At Nottingham the alterations were different, and the two-level, semi-sunken war room was virtually enveloped by the new RSG (*see* Fig 9.8b). The Cambridge, Kirknewton and Nottingham buildings are unusual in the degree of architectural embellishment in the contemporary Brutalist style. At Cambridge and Kirknewton the air intakes and outlets and their canopies are carefully formed geometric shapes, while some of the exterior walls are decorated with slightly raised, cast-concrete panels with alternating exposed aggregate and smooth finishes. On the plainer walls the surface is patterned by stripes made with rough formwork finishing boards of differing thicknesses. A similar method of decoration is evident on the upper storey of the Nottingham bunker.

Elsewhere other kinds of structures were adapted. At Drakelow, Kidderminster, and Warren Row near Maidenhead, RSGs were placed in Second World War underground aircraft factories. That at Drakelow was burrowed directly into Bunter sandstone and the complex was laid out on a grid pattern, with four main entry tunnels giving access to side passages and chambers hewn out to house workshops. In all, there was about 250,000 square feet (23,225 square metres) of underground space, of which the later RSG occupied a little under a quarter. Two other RSGs were sited in RAF Rotor-period bunkers at Bolt Head, Devon, and Barnton Quarry, Edinburgh (*see* Chapter 5), and conversion work was carried out on sections of the extensive tunnel system (parts dating from Napoleonic times) in the chalk beneath Dover Castle. There, the communications and operations rooms, as well as the government departments, were placed on the lowest floor (known as 'dumpy level'), which had been excavated during the Second World War. The higher levels were used as dormitories, stores and a canteen that is now used by visitors to the castle. One of the few visible surface traces of this work is a building beneath the officers' mess where the lift shaft emerged: it is stone-faced so as to blend with the rest of the castle. Air inlets and outlets were placed in the cliff face and existing

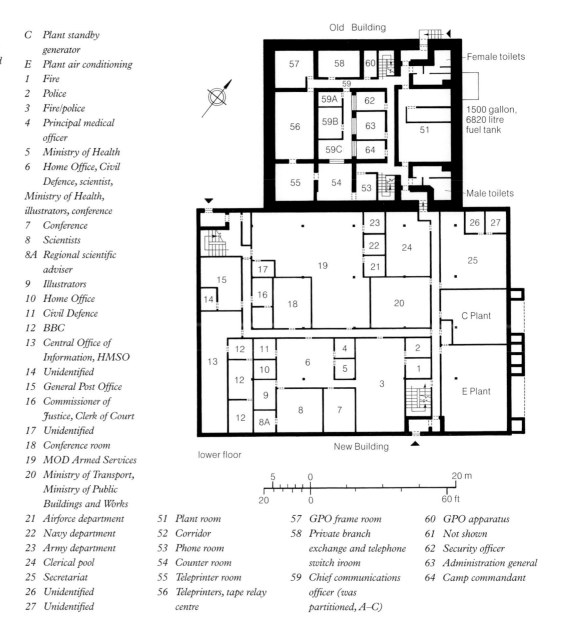

Figure 9.7
Cambridge, Regional Seat
of Government 4, allocated
room functions during the
1960s

Lower floor
(opposite) Upper floor

C   *Plant standby*
     generator
E   *Plant air conditioning*
1   *Fire*
2   *Police*
3   *Fire/police*
4   *Principal medical*
     officer
5   *Ministry of Health*
6   *Home Office, Civil*
     Defence, scientist,
Ministry of Health,
illustrators, conference
7   *Conference*
8   *Scientists*
8A *Regional scientific*
     adviser
9   *Illustrators*
10 *Home Office*
11 *Civil Defence*
12 *BBC*
13 *Central Office of*
     Information, HMSO
14 *Unidentified*
15 *General Post Office*
16 *Commissioner of*
     Justice, Clerk of Court
17 *Unidentified*
18 *Conference room*
19 *MOD Armed Services*
20 *Ministry of Transport,*
     Ministry of Public
     Buildings and Works
21 *Airforce department*
22 *Navy department*
23 *Army department*
24 *Clerical pool*
25 *Secretariat*
26 *Unidentified*
27 *Unidentified*

51 *Plant room*
52 *Corridor*
53 *Phone room*
54 *Counter room*
55 *Teleprinter room*
56 *Teleprinters, tape relay*
     centre

57 *GPO frame room*
58 *Private branch*
     exchange and telephone
     switch iroom
59 *Chief communications*
     officer (was
     partitioned, A–C)

60 *GPO apparatus*
61 *Not shown*
62 *Security officer*
63 *Administration general*
64 *Camp commandant*

openings were sealed – with nothing more than two-brick thick walls.

Little is known about the buildings of the remaining five RSGs, as they were on the same sites as local military headquarters and remain in Army control.

Sub-regional headquarters: 1960s/1970s

Before the new RSG buildings were complete the system was again altered, this time by the creation of sub-regional headquarters (SRHQ). A document of 1963 reveals that twenty-five were to be created, each to accommodate 200 people, but it appears that, although locations were chosen, construction or conversion work was not begun at all of them because of uncertainties surrounding civil defence planning during the 1960s.

The plan for the citadels from the RSG scheme was retained though those on the same sites as Army headquarters – at Catterick and York, both in North Yorkshire, Preston, Lancashire, Brecon, Wales and Armagh, Northern Ireland – were to be repositioned. The absence of a list of the new SRHQs in a top secret 1967 assessment of nuclear targets suggests the new arrange-

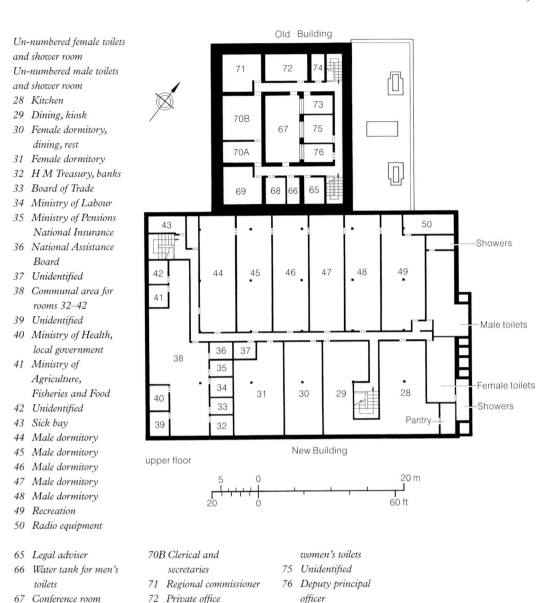

Un-numbered female toilets
and shower room
Un-numbered male toilets
and shower room
28 Kitchen
29 Dining, kiosk
30 Female dormitory,
   dining, rest
31 Female dormitory
32 H M Treasury, banks
33 Board of Trade
34 Ministry of Labour
35 Ministry of Pensions
   National Insurance
36 National Assistance
   Board
37 Unidentified
38 Communal area for
   rooms 32–42
39 Unidentified
40 Ministry of Health,
   local government
41 Ministry of
   Agriculture,
   Fisheries and Food
42 Unidentified
43 Sick bay
44 Male dormitory
45 Male dormitory
46 Male dormitory
47 Male dormitory
48 Male dormitory
49 Recreation
50 Radio equipment

65 Legal adviser
66 Water tank for men's
   toilets
67 Conference room
68 Finance officer
69 Typists
70A Duplicating

70B Clerical and
   secretaries
71 Regional commissioner
72 Private office
73 Deputy regional
   commissioner
74 Water tank for

women's toilets
75 Unidentified
76 Deputy principal
   officer

Regional government headquarters: 1980s

ments were not in place by then; nevertheless, at the end of the decade new SRHQs were constructed below the multi-storey Civil Service Commission headquarters in Basingstoke and beneath a government office block in Hertford (Fig 9.9). The system was reorganised once again in 1972 with fewer SRHQs, the sites of which are better known and involved adaptation of significant numbers of Rotor-period sector operations centres (see pp 103–4). It is, however, uncertain how many SRHQs were operational during the 1970s, and actual conversion work did not always follow designation of sites.

The infrastructure of civil defence inherited by the Conservative Government in 1979 was essentially unchanged from that of the early 1970s, and in the early 1980s received what was to prove a final overhaul. England and Wales were divided into ten home defence regions (see Fig 9.10), while the number of Scottish 'zones' (equivalent to regions) was reduced from four to two. Control within each region was given to the lead RGHQ. Under the previous system each of the sub-region and zonal headquarters had

Figure 9.8
a: (above)
Cambridge, Regional Seat
of Government 4, 1963
[BB98/01034]

b: Nottingham, Regional
Seat of Government 3,
1963. To the bottom right is
the 1950s war room
encased by the later bunker.
[AA98/03196]

Figure 9.9
Hertford, Sub-Regional
Control Centre
[AA99/09865]

been intended to exercise equal control in the immediate recovery phase. In the new dispensation, the secondary headquarters would only come into operation if the principal headquarters was destroyed.

The diagram illustrating the emergency communications network (Fig 9.11) reveals the organisation of a region. All communication was routed through the RGHQ so that, for example, counties could only communicate with neighbouring areas through their RGHQ. Within this circuit, however, other networks were intertwined, as United Kingdom Warning and Monitoring Organisation (UKWMO) and Armed Forces Headquarters were also linked to other national networks, and the unidirectional warning broadcast circuit was connected to all locations.

As with earlier schemes, most of the existing bunkers were retained, although a few were abandoned and some new ones were built, and it is also probable that some sub-regions were left without headquarters for a number of years. In northern England a new RGHQ was provided at Hexham, Northumberland, by the conversion of a wartime cold store, as had happened at Loughborough a few years before. Other schemes to improve the effectiveness of the bunkers (such as the installation of better filtration systems or plant renewal) had relatively little impact on their fabric.

Change to information technology is more difficult to document. A major programme to replace old-fashioned teleprinters with a computerised message switching system in the mid-1980s has left few physical traces, as much was stripped out in the early

1990s (although examples can be seen in some Cold War museums).

One of the most expensive projects of the early 1980s, at a reputed cost of £20 million, was the conversion of the Rotor-period R6 bunker at Hack Green, Cheshire, into an RGHQ (see Fig 9.12a). Although designated RGHQ 10.2, it would have taken the lead role in its region, as 10.1, at Southport, was abandoned because of flooding. Plans for Hack Green had been drawn up as early as 1976, but building work does not appear to have started before 1980. Externally the most noticeable alterations were modifications to the entrance and the addition of a plant room (housing air filters and two diesel generators). The internal plan followed the layout of the R6, retaining the slightly off-centre corridor and a plant room in the basement (see Fig 9.12b). The most significant change was the removal of a suspended basement floor (below which cables originally ran) and the insertion of a mezzanine. Partitions of this period are breeze-block rather than concrete. The upper level was mainly given over to domestic functions, only the uniformed services having some operational space there (see Fig 9.12c), and the main activities were carried out on the lower floor. The arrangement of the rooms and circulation pattern there reveals something of the segmentation of responsibilities and the functions of the staff.

Personnel in the north-eastern corner were concerned with receiving and analysing information from the outside world and maintaining communications with other surviving centres. Officials in the opposite

Figure 9.10
Map showing home defence
regions and regional
government headquarters in
the late 1980s and early
1990s

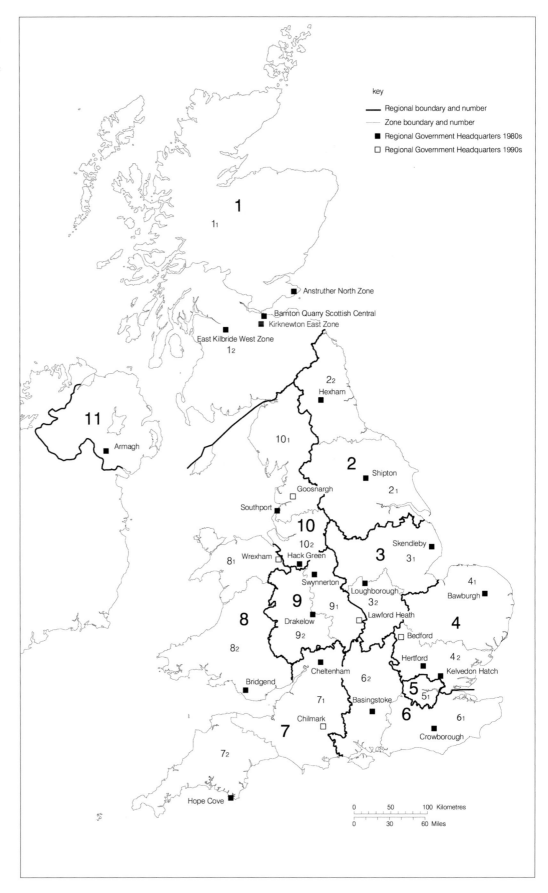

key

— Regional boundary and number
— Zone boundary and number
■ Regional Government Headquarters 1980s
□ Regional Government Headquarters 1990s

1

1_1

■ Anstruther North Zone

■ Barnton Quarry Scottish Central
■ Kirknewton East Zone

East Kilbride West Zone
1_2

2_2
■ Hexham

11

■ Armagh

10_1

2
■ Shipton
2_1

□ Goosnargh
■ Southport

10
10_2
Skendleby ■
3
3_1

8_1 □ Wrexham ■ Hack Green

■ Swynnerton   Loughborough ■
4_1
Bawburgh ■

9   9_1 3_2

8   ■ Drakelow   □ Lawford Heath
8_2 9_2
4
□ Bedford
4_2

Hertford ■
■ Cheltenham 6_2 Kelvedon Hatch ■

■ Bridgend
7_1 Basingstoke   5   6 6_1
Chilmark   ■ 5_1
□
7   6   Crowborough ■

7_2

■ Hope Cove

0   50   100 Kilometres
0   30   60 Miles

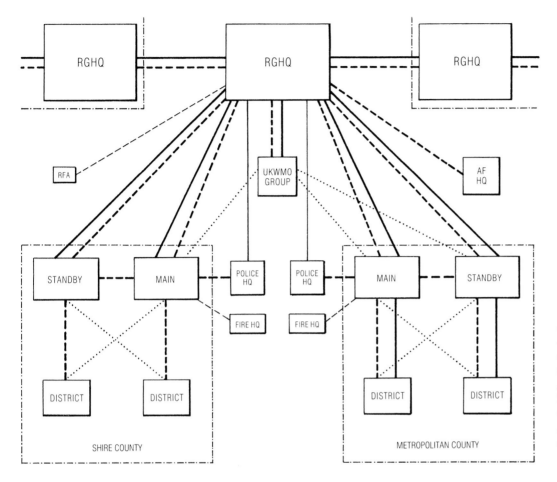

Figure 9.11
Diagram showing the
emergency communications
network in the mid-1980s
[from Home Office 1989
EPG Handbook 4
Communications, Annex
B to section 2(i) © Crown
copyright]

Key to symbols   S: Speech
                  T: Text

- - - - -   Line S & T
- - - - -   Line S only
···········   Line T only
━━━━━   Radio S & T
─────   Radio S only

corner were representatives of government departments, as were those on the new mezzanine floor. At the centre, co-ordinating all activity, was the commissioner, next to whom were the principal officer, the secretariat and typists.

There were between 150 and 200 staff allocated to Hack Green. The regional commissioner would have been a junior cabinet minister, perhaps assisted by a permanent secretary as principal officer. Government departments would have been represented by nominated officials, while the majority of the remainder of the staff would have been administrators, secretaries and technicians (to maintain the communications links) and a few scientific advisers and kitchen staff. The allocation of dormitory space indicates that there would have been twice as many men as women. Work patterns were organised on a three-shift system, with 'hot-beds' rather than individual

Figure 9.12
Hack Green, Cheshire,
Regional Government
Headquarters 10.2.
a: This photograph, taken
soon after the refurbishment
of the bunker during the
early 1980s, shows the fresh
concrete of the newly built
generator room and
modified entrance. It is now
open to the public as a Cold
War museum. [G28599/8]

allocation of bunks (except for the commissioner and principal officer). Most walls within the bunker were painted 'magnolia', but around the stairwell they were yellow – supposedly a 'happy' colour to counter any thoughts of suicide.

At Shipton, North Yorkshire, and Bawburgh, Norfolk, extensive conversion work was carried out in the late 1970s and early 1980s to Rotor-period R4 bunkers, with new vents supplied and an extra storey added, mainly to provide dormitory accommodation. Other fitting out work and the renewal of equipment had little impact on the layout of the bunker, as its central well had probably been floored over some years earlier. It was also in the early 1980s that an

extra storey and four new vents were added to RGHQ 3.1 at Skendleby, Lincolnshire; a former Rotor-period R3 bunker.

In Region 9 a new bunker at Swynnerton, Staffordshire, (RGHQ 9.1) took over the lead role from Drakelow. It consisted of two single-level bunkers linked by a 230ft (70m) underground corridor, placed on the site of two wartime explosives magazines (Fig 9.13). One half was largely devoted to domestic activities, while operations were carried out in the other; a pattern also adopted in Wales, at Bridgend (RGHQ 8.2). At Swynnerton, landscape murals were painted on the walls and artificial plants were provided in an attempt to brighten the depressing interior.

Lower floor

1 Store room
2 Telecom equipment room
3 Communications centre
4 Private branch exchange
5 Radio room
6 Scientists' room
7 Communications centre registry
8 BBC studio
9 BBC office
10 Communications centre services
11 Conference room
12 Commissioner
13 Principal's office
14 Secretariat and typists
15 Government departments
16 Store room
17 Store room
18 Military radio room
19 Plant room
20 Tank room
21 Information room
22 Senior telecommunications officer
23 Drivers and maintenance

upper floor

b: Functional layout during the 1980s (mezzanine level not shown) [original material courtesy of Hack Green Secret Nuclear Bunker]

Upper floor

24 Store room
25 Male dormitory
26 NAAFI canteen
27 Kitchen
28 Store room
29 Common room
30 Administration
31 Uniformed services
32 Filter rooms
33 Decontamination room
34 Decontamination room
35 Control room
36 Switch room
37 Standby generators
38 Filter room
39 Showers
40 Female toilets
41 Showers
42 Male toilets
43 Sick bay
44 Store room
45 Female dormitory
46 Male dormitory

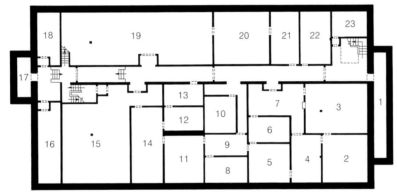

lower floor

c: Mezzanine level. Government departments room furnished in contemporary civil service style, 1984 [G28028(7)]

Emergency central government

Although it is possible to build up a fairly clear picture of the intended shape of home government in the event of war, little information is available on where the Cabinet was to be housed. In 1937 work began on a Cabinet citadel at Dollis Hill, in north-west London. Throughout the Second World War, however, the Cabinet preferred to work in the hardened accommodation of the Cabinet War Rooms below the New Public Offices in Great George Street, close to the Houses of Parliament, chosen because it was one of the few steel-framed buildings in the area. As the war progressed other ministries constructed shelters beneath the capital, linked together by deep telephone lines. Among them was the Admiralty citadel next to Horse Guards Parade – a sinister-looking surface bunker of massive proportions, protected by pillboxes on the roof. During the late 1930s when the building in Marsham Street was constructed, later occupied by the Department of the Environment, the bases of two large gas storage tanks were incorporated into its foundations and transformed into a protected operations area known as The Rotundas (Fig 9.14). They may perhaps be equated with the 1950s Central Government War Room: they were last used during the Gulf war in 1991. The main Cabinet citadel, variously codenamed 'Stockwell', 'Burlington' and 'Turnstile', was far from London, though relatively accessible by rail and road, in the former stone quarries and wartime ammunition storage vaults at Corsham, Wiltshire.

It was not only the British government that sought protection in underground complexes. During the 1950s and early 1960s the United States government established centres excavated deep into mountainsides to set up centres. This strategy was later abandoned in favour of airborne command centres, which presented far more difficult targets. In Moscow the well-developed underground railway system was designed to afford fallout protection, and perhaps access to other shelters, for the selected few. Both East and West Germany constructed heavily protected refuges, expecting to be the most likely battleground in any Cold War conflict. In the 1960s the West German government converted a disused railway tunnel into an emergency centre at Marienthal in the Ahr valley near Bonn, and during the 1980s the East Germans built a two-level bunker (codenamed 'Filigran') close to Berlin to house the government and up to 500 personnel.

The last phase of Cold War plans

The skeleton of emergency government was kept in place until the early 1990s. In about 1990 the RGHQ at Ullenwood, near Cheltenham, (decommissioned in 1985) was replaced by a new two-storey bunker at Chilmark in Wiltshire. At Crowborough, Sussex, the wartime underground BBC 'Black Broadcasting' station, known as 'Aspidistra', was substantially remodelled to replace the vulnerable and inefficiently organised labyrinth beneath Dover Castle. Other refurbishment work during the 1980s, for example at Warren Row and Cambridge, was perhaps undertaken to provide the armed forces with protected command and control centres. The unexpected opportunity from 1991, of adapting former Royal Observer Corps (ROC) Group Headquarters as RGHQs, was also exploited: Lawford Heath, Warwickshire, was to become RGHQ 9.2 to replace Drakelow, and Bedford was to become RGHQ 4.2. Similarly, in Wales it was planned to put a secondary control in the vacated ROC headquarters at Wrexham.

Provisions stores

The experience of the attempted U-boat blockades during the two World Wars, and of potential disruption to internal communications caused by heavy bombing, highlighted the need to maintain stocks of food and raw materials within the country. In the post-war period the greater threat posed by atomic weapons added a new dimension to the stockpiling of food, as whole areas of the country could be devastated and transit through them impossible. It was also

Figure 9.14
Marsham Street, London, South Rotunda. In this part of the complex the base of a large gas storage tank was initially used to create an air-raid shelter, and later a protected operations room.
[BB96/10048]

Figure 9.15
Cold store, Peasmarsh,
Surrey. Typically, this store
is situated next to a railway
line with road access to the
rear. [BB98/10426]

probable that it would take many months for the country to be resupplied from overseas.

During the Second World War a system of buffer depots had been established, supplemented by four inland sorting depots. They held a strategic stockpile of food and were large enough to permit the rapid removal of valuable imported goods from high-risk port areas, thereby not only ensuring their safety but also facilitating the speedy turn-around of shipping. One of the main factors in the choice of sites for buffer depots was the availability of good transport links: all depots were served by road, but most were also next to rail or waterways.

In 1951 there were 260 storage depots but by the middle of the decade there were only about half that number, administered by 60 firms. The stockpile held by the Ministry of Food in 1954 amounted to 745,000 tons (756,920 tonnes) and included oils and fats, flour, yeast, sugar, canned corned meat, tinned milk and special biscuits. Stocks of feeding, bakery and milling equipment were also maintained.

During the war commercial premises had been supplemented with a series of purpose-built stores. The government funded their construction and they were built to Ministry of Works drawing types, but were managed on behalf of the Ministry of Food by commercial wharf owners and storage companies. Five categories of store may be defined – cold stores, grain silos, fuel stores, general purpose stores and miscellaneous depots.

The government built forty-seven standard cold stores during the war, all but six of which were in England (Fig 9.15). There were two 1,000,000 cubic foot (28,300 cubic metre), five 500,000 cubic foot (14,150 cubic metre), and forty 250,000 cubic foot (7,075 cubic metre) stores dispersed across the country. They are very solid three-storey structures, with an internal steel frame, a two-brick thick external wall, a layer of insulation, and an inner skin one brick thick. A distinctive feature of their form was the provision of two plant rooms (one at each end of the building) in case one should fail through enemy action or malfunction.

Sixteen government grain silos, each with a capacity of 5,000 tons (5,080 tonnes), were erected during the war. They are steel-framed with a central tower 80ft (24.4m) high and 30ft (9.1m) square, which houses machinery and drying plant. There are two wings on the site, each housing six pairs of 62ft (18.9m) high reinforced-concrete silos, above which a conveyor delivers the grain from the intake elevators or dryers. Good surviving examples remain at Fulbourn in Cambridgeshire, Newport in Shropshire, and Whitley Bridge in North Yorkshire; another serves the docks at Boston, Lincolnshire. Construction continued after the war, including the one at Haughley Junction, Stowmarket, Suffolk (Fig 9.16) and a similar one next to the wartime cold store at Ely,

Figure 9.16
Grain silo, built in 1954 at
Haughley Junction,
Stowmarket, Suffolk
[G4223/2]

Cambridgeshire. Both were built under the direction of the chief architect at the Ministry of Works, Eric Bedford.

A secure fuel supply is vital to the prosecution of mechanised warfare and it was imperative that in emergencies the country's fuel stock was moved rapidly away from the vulnerable port areas where the bulk storage facilities and refineries are. The basic infrastructure of pipelines, linking terminals, refineries and inland buried storage facilities, remained from the war. The system was operated by commercial companies, the activities of which would be co-ordinated by the oil mobilisation control in time of war. Some of the aviation fuel depots were controlled directly by the RAF, but they were progressively relinquished to the Ministry of Power during the late 1950s and early 1960s. There are good examples at Sandy, Bedfordshire, Beeston and near Chelford in Cheshire, Saffron Walden, Essex, and Thetford, Norfolk. During the post-war period the network was maintained and extended so that most, if not all, the main airfields were linked to the system.

The general purpose stores were the most flexible of all the depots, and could be used for storing food or other emergency equipment. They are also the most structurally varied. During the war any suitable building or store was requisitioned, and thereafter sections of disused airfields were commonly used as stores. On the site of RAF Tilstock,

Shropshire, one B1 hanger and four T2 hangars were maintained in this way. At Rattlesden airfield in Suffolk one hangar was used and additional space created by the construction of seven curved asbestos huts. Elsewhere, as at Peasmarsh, Surrey, prefabricated huts (such as Romney huts) were used to increase capacity and some new depots only had buildings of this kind. All kinds of government property could be pressed into service, one of the most unusual conversions being the former mustard gas factory at Rhydymwyn, Flintshire.

Most of the 160 general purpose stores were built in 1941 or 1942. Their standard form is 214ft × 120ft (65.22m × 36.58m) and provides about 25,000 square feet (2,300 square metres) of space (Fig 9.17a). The buildings are steel-framed and have brick panel walls; the roofs and upper parts of the gables are of asbestos sheet. Asbestos was also used for gutter and rainwater pipes (which usually have vermin traps fixed to them), probably to economise on the use of metals. The stores were generally entered through sliding doors in one side wall and usually incorporated an office, sometimes hardened to serve as a refuge during air-raids. A water pool, for fire fighting, is typically found close by.

Seven pre-1974 stores have been identified in Cheshire. Aerial photographs show that all were built during the war, except the one at Tarporley which, although similar in

Figure 9.17
General purpose stores
a: Sale, Cheshire. During
the Second World War
canals remained important
routes for war materials;
here a store was sited next
to the Bridgwater Canal.
[303W/15]

b: Mickle Trafford,
Cheshire. One variation in
the design of this type of
store is the addition of a
clerestory, with windows in
the roof. [303W/10]

design to the wartime examples, was erected in the early 1950s. The only minor variant in the form is that two stores have a clerestory roof, with windows in a raised section at gable level (Fig 9.17b).

The Ministry of Supply was one of the largest of the government departments which maintained emergency stockpiles. It held around 700,000 tons (711,200 tonnes) of strategic stores, including explosives, chemicals, textiles, metal goods, machine components and tools. In addition to purpose-built depots, this Ministry used buildings which had formerly been Royal Ordnance Factories, such as those at Ruddington, Nottinghamshire, and Elstow, Bedfordshire, both of which had good rail access.

This kind of reuse also meant the factories were maintained in case of future need. Finally, the Home Office stored large stocks of civil defence equipment, including Green Goddess fire engines, in a variety of purpose-built and adapted stores.

Telecommunications

After a nuclear attack the effectiveness of any form of government relied on the survival of at least a skeletal telecommunications system. A conventional attack would wreak havoc by severing landlines or destroying essential communication intersections. In a nuclear attack not only would a far larger area be destroyed, but the electromagnetic effects of the detonation would also damage unshielded electronic equipment. It was also possible that an attack might include a nuclear burst beyond the atmosphere, specifically designed to disrupt communications, although the widespread nature of its effect would have rendered it damaging to friend and foe alike.

Part of the solution was to bury cables deep underground. The first deep tunnel below London for Post Office cables was dug in 1925; the system was considerably extended during the war, and in the early 1950s more tunnels were bored to provide protection against the destructive power of atomic weapons. Those tunnels were generally 100ft (30.5m) down and, by the early

Figure 9.18
The underground telephone exchanges were equipped to be self-sufficient for many weeks and included ventilation plant, kitchens, dining rooms, dormitories, a welfare room and even a bar. High Holborn, Kingsway underground exchange, London

a: (left)
Bar [BB96/00603]

1970s, the network was 14 miles (22.5km) in extent. One of the largest projects, started in 1951, was the construction of the Kingsway exchange beneath High Holborn. This took advantage of two partly finished tube tunnels, at right angles to which four further tunnels were added to house the switching unit. The complex had steel blast doors and was supplied with sufficient fuel for four diesel generators to operate for six weeks. Water for the staff of 200 and for cooling purposes was supplied from an artesian well, which supplied water by natural pressure, with little or no pumping required. The complex was also equipped with a kitchen, air-conditioning plant, a dining room, sleeping accommodation, a welfare room and a bar (Figs 9.18a–d).

Communications to the north were carried on the main trunk line which passed through underground exchanges beneath Birmingham (codenamed 'Anchor') and

b: (left)
Kitchen [BB96/00597]

c: (far left)
Restaurant [BB96/00598]

d: (left)
Ventilation plant [BB96/00619]

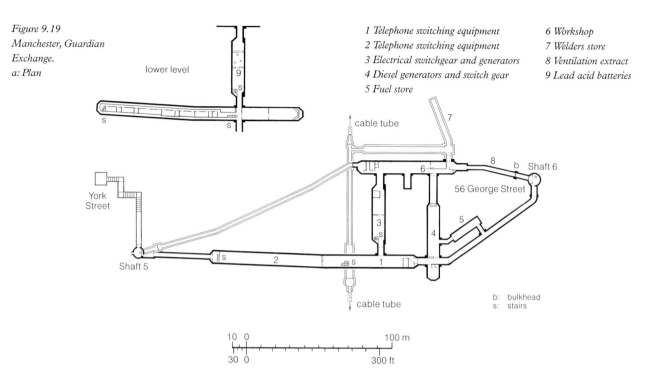

Figure 9.19
Manchester, Guardian
Exchange.
a: Plan

1 Telephone switching equipment
2 Telephone switching equipment
3 Electrical switchgear and generators
4 Diesel generators and switch gear
5 Fuel store

6 Workshop
7 Welders store
8 Ventilation extract
9 Lead acid batteries

b: (right)
Upper level test switchboard
[AA98/02416]

c: (below)
Blast doors at base of lift
shaft G [AA98/02423]

Manchester (codenamed 'Guardian'). The latter was equipped with a similar range of facilities to that at Kingsway (Figs 9.19a–c) but also had a room for the Civil Defence Corps.

At a local level the basements of most large telephone exchanges were protected 'Q rooms', provided with a stock of E-shaped bricks with which they could be sealed from the inside. These rooms were equipped with a manual plug-and-socket switchboard, an auxiliary power source (either batteries or a standby generator), a food supply and sanitary provision for one or two operators who were to maintain a very limited service after an attack.

In the event of an attack the familiar telephone speaking clock network, officially known as 'Handel', had a vital role in relaying the warning message. The turn of a key at the United Kingdom Regional Air Operations Centre would simultaneously alert 250 carrier control points in major police stations, via the speaking clock telephone circuits. The press of a button at any of these control points would activate 7,000 power sirens, 11,000 receiver points and 5,000 carrier broadcast receiver points (Fig 9.20) in a variety of police, fire, ambulance and coastguard stations, military establishments, emergency seats of government and planning centres. In remote rural areas they were even located in public houses or private premises.

*Figure 9.20 (above)
Warning broadcast speaker
1400, Cambridge Regional
Seat of Government. In the
event of an air attack
receiver points such as this
would emit a rising and
falling note. [BB98/01039]*

*Figure 9.21 (left)
RGHQ Kelvedon Hatch,
Essex, Home Office
communications mast. The
small building is an air
intake and emergency exit
for the bunker below.
[AA98/12613]*

221

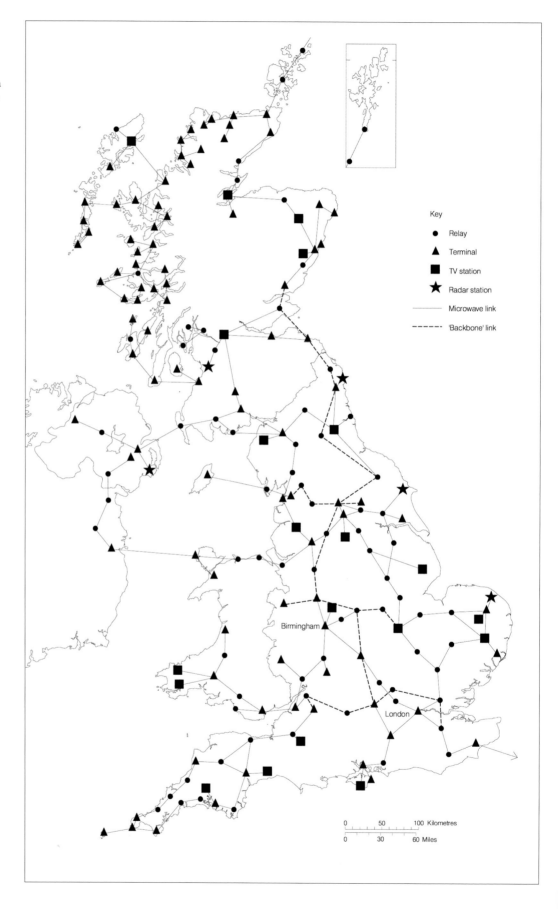

Figure 9.22
a: Map showing line-of-sight microwave network [redrawn from D Campbell, 1983 War Plan UK, *by permission of The Random House Group Ltd]*

Key
● Relay
▲ Terminal
■ TV station
★ Radar station
— Microwave link
--- 'Backbone' link

Birmingham

London

0   50   100 Kilometres
0   30   60 Miles

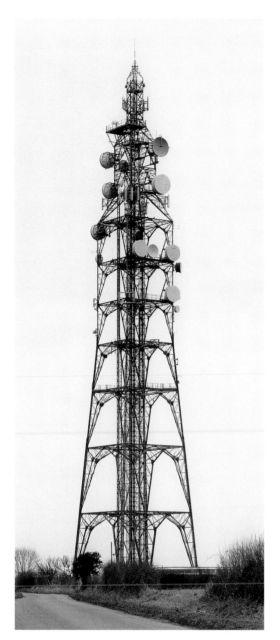

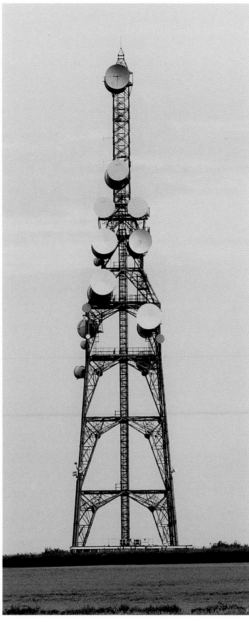

Figure 9.22
b: (far left)
Swaffham, Norfolk, stepped
tower, microwave relay
station [BB98/10087]

c: (left)
Over, Cambridgeshire,
microwave relay station
[BB98/10428]

As the main trunk lines were very vulnerable to attack, an emergency communications network based on microwave transmissions was developed from the 1950s, all or part of the network generally being known as 'Backbone' (further systems were established by the Home Office (Fig. 9.21), utilities and other organisations). From a notional origin at Stokenchurch, Buckinghamshire, its route may be followed up the spine of the country (Fig 9.22a), carefully avoiding major conurbations, to Sutton Common, Staffordshire, where the line cuts across to the east and thence to Scotland. Subsidiary routes provided links to the east and west, and the network was completed by a web of links between the relay and terminal stations, with both civil emergency centres and military establishments being connected.

Since microwaves travel in straight lines and are easily absorbed by obstructions, transmitter and receiver towers must be intervisible; being tall and, preferably, in prominent positions such as hilltops, they become well-known landmarks. Most are associated with single-storey buildings housing switch rooms and standby generators or batteries. The earliest steel towers, prefabricated from angle sections, were similar to pylons. However, the horn-shaped aerial (*see* Fig 9.22f) introduced in the 1960s was difficult to mount on them

and rendered them unsightly. One solution was the development of a stepped tower, with the horns mounted on the steps: the components were standard, but the overall form varied with location and the precise number of aerials required (Figs 9.22b and c). Another solution was provided by the 'daffodil' tower on which the horns were held by stalk-like supports. Both this and the stepped tower were, however, relatively short-lived because the demise of horn aerials rendered them obsolete, and only a few have survived.

Later designs included modular rectangular towers, which had a larger area for mounting aerials and could easily be extended upwards or laterally (Fig 9.22d). Smaller modular towers were also developed for highland areas, but pylons or guyed masts continued to be used for the tallest ones (Fig 9.22e). At Whinfell Common, to the north of Kendal, is a tubular steel structure, chosen mainly on the grounds of cost, but also to resist wind speeds up to 100mph (160kmph). Elsewhere, plain cylindrical reinforced-concrete towers were favoured (Fig 9.22f), partly as they offered low wind resistance, which was both desirable in peacetime and also enhanced the prospect of surviving the blast from a nuclear explosion.

These towers were considered more aesthetically pleasing than the others. The best known structure of this kind is the Post Office Tower in central London (Fig 9.22g), which became an icon of the new 1960s London rising from the Blitz. It has a central reinforced-concrete shaft 500ft (152m) tall, the lowest section of which is linked to the Museum Exchange building. The next level comprises seventeen cantilevered floors for plant and microwave equipment rooms, above which are platforms for aerials (including some original horn antennae) and, at the top, a kitchen, restaurant and observation floors. The design of the 1970

tower at Purdown, Bristol, was approved by the Royal Fine Art Commission (Fig 9.22h).

Although during the 1990s defence communications increasingly came to rely on satellite systems, the growth in demand for commercial and personal microwave communications has ensured a future for these sentinels of Cold War communications.

The utilities

The utilities (electricity, gas and water suppliers, as well as the rail network) were required to undertake contingency planning for the maintenance of 'due functioning' in

Figure 9.22
f: (above left)
Pye Green, Staffordshire,
terminal station. Visible on
top of this tower are
original 1960s horn-shaped
aerials. [BB98/08165]

g: (above)
London, Post Office Tower,
1961, designed by Eric
Bedford, Chief Architect at
the Ministry of Works
[BB99/09146]

*h: Purdown, Bristol, 1970.
The newly completed
platform tower, which won
the approval of the Royal
Fine Art Commission, is to
the right. [G14518/2]*

the event of attack: any necessary capital works were eligible for government grants. As major employers, the utilities were also encouraged, through the Industrial Civil Defence Service, to organise civil defence sections in their larger establishments.

During the Second World War the railway was the main mover of goods and people. After large scale closures of stations and branch lines in the early 1960s, the reach of rail transport to outlying depots and airfields was reduced, and the ability of the network to handle potential evacuees became limited. During the war hardened structures, such as signal boxes and control centres, had been

built at vulnerable locations, but subsequent policy was to site the centres at least ten miles (16km) from likely targets. The remoteness of some of the locations (such as Iridgehay, Derbyshire) suggests they were placed to assist in the movement of evacuation trains, and it is known that millions of railway warrants were held in case evacuation was necessary.

In the mid-1950s there were thirty-five control centres, some housed in bunkers while others were probably mobile and connected to auxiliary cabling. The design drawing for the early 1950s L-type (Fig 9.23) control building shows a long rectangular

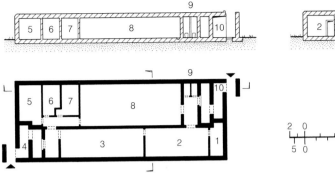
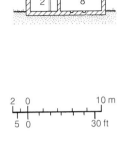

1 Battery room
2 Apparatus and telephones
3 Generator and ventilation
4 Entrance
5 District operating superintendent and assistant
6 Assistants
7 District engineer, signal and telegraph
8 Control rooms
9 Elsans
10 Entrance

reinforced bunker, 94ft 6in × 35ft 6in (28.8m × 10.8m), with a staggered double entrance cell, perhaps designed to act as a decontamination area. Curiously, no provision was made for sleeping accommodation. Auxiliary telephone exchanges, mobile control centres and dimming colour light signals were also provided. Later, the emphasis switched from permanent locations to mobile emergency controls in specially equipped trains, some of which were stored in sheds such as the bricked-up store at Craven Arms, Shropshire, while others sat in sidings with specially installed telephone lines. All the trains were sold in about 1980.

The other major investment in transport was aimed at ensuring supplies could reach Britain from abroad. For this emergency ports were prepared, and stocks of mobile cranes and floating grain elevators maintained.

Other public utilities were likewise prepared for war. The Central Electricity Generating Board maintained a central war room at Becker Hall near Leeds, and a related series of secondary war rooms. In addition to engineers, scientific intelligence officers were attached to these facilities, so that information received from local radiological officers could be acted upon. Many power stations constructed from the late 1930s were equipped with auxiliary control rooms, and Home Office advice in the 1960s suggested that small refuges should be incorporated to protect key personnel. Small equipment and spares stores were also dotted around the country.

Emergency local government

During the Cold War local authorities, from district councils upwards, had to maintain an emergency headquarters which could be brought into operation within a couple of hours. Despite their common function no standard building type emerged, although there is a generic similarity. The main centres, referred to as 'county mains' (of which there were forty-seven in England and Wales during the 1980s), were usually in the

Figure 9.23
Standard district railway control building, Type L, 1953 [redrawn from PRO HO 338/17]

Figure 9.24
Maidstone, Kent, County Council County Main Emergency Centre (since demolished)
a: Diagramatic floor plan

1 Spare room
2 Co-ordinator's office
3 Main store
4 Hallway
5 Main entrance
6 Larder
7 Kitchen
8 Male toilet
9 Female toilet
10 Administration and reception
11 Information room
12 Operations room
13 Water storage and air
   handling unit
14 Back entrance
15 Corridor
16 Annex
17 Liaison room
18 Fuses
19 Standby alternator 1
20 Diesel fuel tank
21 Engineer's control room
22 Research booths
23 Resource maps
24 Switchboard
25 Diesel fuel alternator 2
26 Radio/fax
   communications room

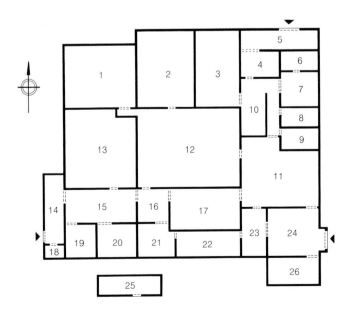

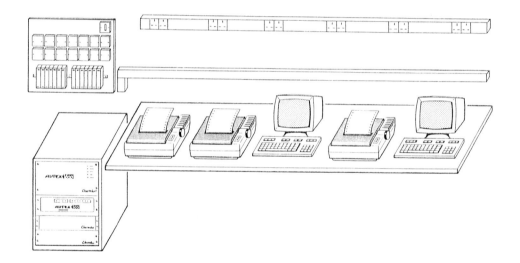

basements of county halls. Depending on when the county hall was built, they could be purpose-built structures or insertions into existing spaces.

At Maidstone, Kent, the control was moved to a self-contained bunker built in 1964 (Figs 9.24a and b). It is a single-storey reinforced-concrete structure above which is a light, steel-framed meeting room of lofty proportions, the collapse of which would cause minimal damage to the bunker below. The facilities are typical of those at county controls. At the centre of the bunker is the operations room where officials would co-ordinate activity in response to intelligence supplied from the information room, which had its own telephone lines to the outside world, and from the liaison room, research booths and the communications and radio rooms (Fig 9.24c). County council employees staffed the facilities and communications were to be supplemented by networks of radio amateurs. Instructions based on assessments made by the county controller and his staff were to be passed from the operations room to the emergency services or other officials. To shield the occupants the bunker was designed with a protective factor of 100 (*see* p 198), but owing to a design fault this could only be achieved by stacking sandbags on the floor above. The bunker was designed to be self-supporting for a number of weeks and was equipped with a standby generator and air filtration plant (modernised during the 1980s), a kitchen, toilets, and a store room which could double as dormitory.

If the county main were put out of action, control would pass to a reserve site. In Cheshire and Essex redundant anti-aircraft operations rooms at Frodsham and Mistley were adapted. There were also 333 smaller, district controls, which were similarly accommodated in a mixture of adapted basements and purpose-built bunkers. These continued to be built into the 1980s, for example for South Cambridgeshire District Council at Cambridge, and for Uttlesford District Council at Saffron Walden, Essex.

Emergency planning in London was devolved to borough level, where provision again followed a pattern of purpose-built and adapted structures. In Croydon, a control centre was placed beneath the Victorian town hall. Despite Home Office advice not to construct control centres beneath buildings, the basement at Wood Green (now Haringey) Civic Centre, built 1956–8, was built as a refuge against atomic attack. It has reinforced-concrete walls 2ft (0.61m) thick, below a ground floor of similar thickness, with escape exits to the surrounding gardens. A large room was earmarked for a 'future public shelter', but was later used as the emergency planning centre. Elsewhere, at Hackney, Hampstead and Dagenham (Figs 9.26a and b), control centres were placed next to buildings, sometimes beneath car parks.

Civil defence

The legal framework for wartime civil defence measures ended in 1945. By 1948 the new threat posed by the Soviet Union led a reluctant House of Commons to discuss new civil defence measures. By the time the King announced a new Civil Defence Bill in October, the escalating Berlin crisis had caused the international situation to deteriorate. The legislation gave the Home Secretary powers to make provision for civil defence and to require local and police authorities to prepare civil defence measures. Actual provision of civil defence was devolved to local authorities, with most if not all expenditure reimbursed by the Home Office.

Administrative structure of civil defence

The ethos of civil defence in Britain was summed up by Sir John Anderson (instigator of the wartime back garden shelter) who believed it was a 'citizen service based on the principle of self-help'. The Civil Defence Corps (CDC), formed in April 1949, was a voluntary organisation complemented by a few full-time staff (Fig 9.25). Responsibility for its recruitment, training and control generally lay with county councils, with the most appropriate official taking responsibility for one of the sections. There were initially six sections – headquarters, welfare, rescue, pioneers, ambulance and the wardens – but this was later reduced to five by amalgamating the pioneer and rescue sections (Table 9.1, Fig 9.27). In addition to the CDC, members of the Auxiliary Fire Service, Women's Voluntary Service, National Hospital Service Reserve, and the St John's and St Andrew's Ambulance Brigades could be called upon to undertake civil defence duties.

Late in 1952 the Industrial Civil Defence Service (ICDS), administered through the Home Office, was formed, and it was proposed that all companies employing more than 200 people should establish their own civil defence sections. This organisation operated in parallel to the CDC, on the principle of mutual aid when required. Units

Figure 9.25
Civil Defence Corps, from The Hydrogen Bomb, *Home Office 1957 [BB017254 © Crown copyright]*

Table 9.1
Administrative structure of civil defence

Region
Group
County main control
Sub-control
Sub-division
Sector
Warden post (parent)
Warden posts (3–6)

Figure 9.26
Dagenham, county message
switch (CMX)
a: Installation in a London
borough control centre,
equivalent to the equipment
used at district level
elsewhere in the country
[BB98/13129]

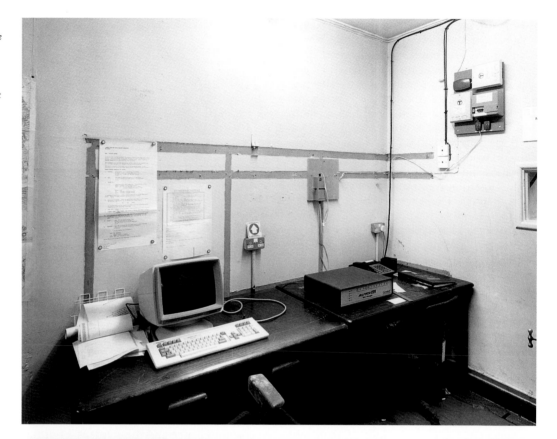

b: The motley collection of
obsolescent furniture is
typical of many local
centres, and symptomatic of
the low priority given to
civil defence planning.
[BB98/13131]

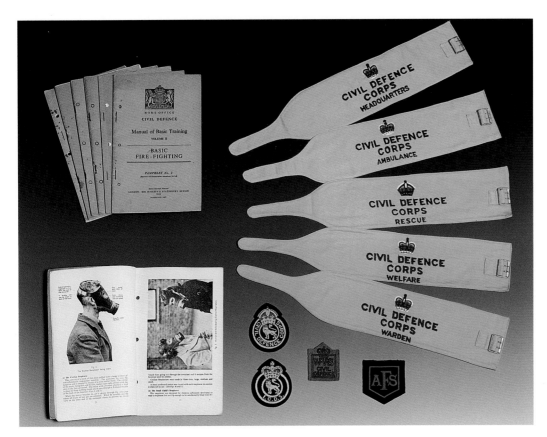

Figure 9.27
1950s Civil Defence
armbands and training
manuals for the five main
sections [BB013793]

were usually based in individual factories or on trading estates. The noticeable effect on the structure of a factory was slight, as many of the facilities, such as first aid posts and stores for fire-fighting equipment, were the same as those the factory required in peacetime.

Training at a national level was carried out at civil defence schools at Eastwood Park, Gloucestershire, at Easingwold, Yorkshire, and at Taymouth Castle, Perthshire. The Civil Defence Staff College was housed in the large country mansion at Sunningdale, Berkshire. All apart from Easingwold were later closed.

At first there were reports of difficulty in recruiting volunteers: as the minutes of Cambridgeshire County Council's civil defence committee noted in 1953 that 'many people believed there was no answer to the "A" bomb'. In 1954 the average establishment stood at only 65 per cent of the approved strength, and in West Bromwich it only reached 25 per cent. By the early 1960s, however, more than 600,000 people could be called upon to undertake civil defence duties – a greater degree of success than a poorly received 1951 scheme to resurrect the Home Guard of wartime 'Dad's Army' fame.

Civil defence premises

The basic requirement of any local civil defence organisation was a headquarters providing offices, facilities for training and for storing equipment, and garages. To keep costs down, buildings selected were usually already in local authority control, often large Victorian houses. In the more community-minded society of the 1950s, the Civil Defence Corps formed an important focus for the social lives of its members. Most training centres had rooms set aside for games and rest rooms; hot pot suppers, dinner dances, coach trips, and annual rallies were organised. All these activities helped to foster camaraderie amongst members, especially the home-based wardens whose roles would otherwise have left them isolated in the community.

The headquarters for civil defence in South Cambridgeshire, at Abberley House, Great Shelford, provides a good example of the facilities required. The large Victorian house, formerly a local authority children's home, was taken over for civil defence activities in 1958 (Fig 9.28). Twelve garages were built in the grounds at the back, as was a ramshackle store. In 1959 £4,000 spending was approved for a rescue training centre, which in 1965 was judged to be 'the best

training centre in East Anglia'. Although the building had been demolished by 1969, after the disbandment of the CDC, an earlier aerial photograph shows a roofless single-storey structure attached to a roofed two-storey building with a concrete apron outside. Elsewhere, facilities were similar or more elaborate (Fig 9.29). Closely allied organisations were given space in the grounds of Abberley House – the Women's Voluntary Service formerly occupied a surviving large timber hut, while another hut (now replaced) was used by the Red Cross.

The use of existing premises was widespread. Elsewhere in Cambridge a large

Victorian house close to the fire station was adapted: Warkworth Lodge. At Soham, Cambridgeshire, the old fire station itself was reused, and in Shrewsbury a three-storey town house in Quarry Place was taken over.

Purpose-built protected structures associated with civil defence in post-war Britain are rare. One is the civil defence control centre at Gravesend, built in 1954 (Figs 9.30 and 9.31). It stands at the entrance to a municipal park – a large open space which could be used to gather people together – and on a major route into Gravesend (probably an 'essential service route', which would be kept clear for official traffic). The building

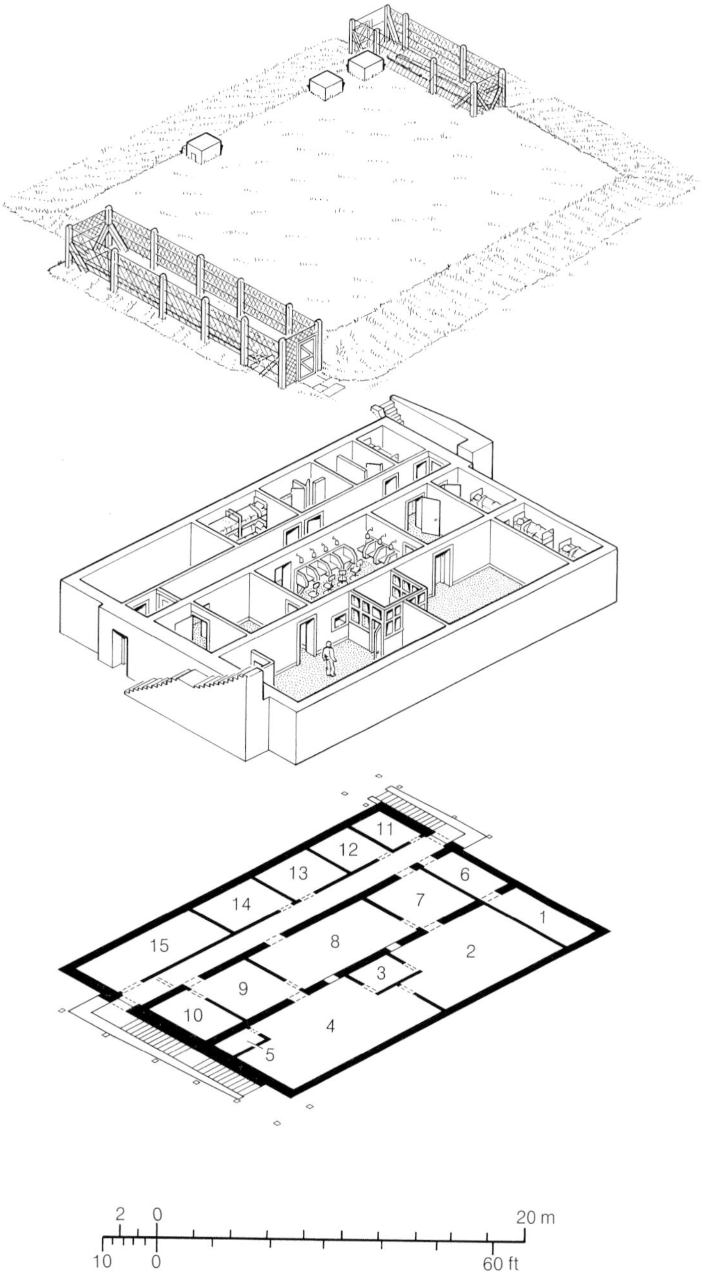

Figure 9.30
Plan of Civil Defence Sub-
Divisional Control Centre,
Gravesend, Kent, 1954.
[Original material courtesy
of Gravesham Borough
Council]

1   Male dormitory
2   District control room
3   Controller's office
4   Sub-divisional control room
5   Office
6   Male dormitory
7   Liaison officer
8   Message room
9   Messenger's room
10 Unidentified
11 Male dormitory
12 Men's toilets
13 Ladies' toilets
14 Women's dormitory
15 Power and ventilation plant

is a simple single-level bunker, with an off-centre corridor running the length of the building and three functional areas – domestic, communications, and control. The level of safety it offered was rudimentary, lacking even protection against poison gas.

In 1952 civil defence was split into two tiers – the local organisation, and mobile fire and civil defence columns. Difficulties in recruitment meant that most of the mobile columns were manned by the armed forces, and in 1955 the Mobile Defence Corps was established, though it only lasted four years. Vehicles for the mobile columns were held at

Home Office stores some distance from likely target areas, but garages for local civil defence vehicles were often built next to training centres or in council yards. The garages in local authority depots were usually taken over by the local council after the Corps was disbanded in 1968, making identification without documentary evidence extremely difficult.

The close association of the emergency services with civil defence is clearly reflected in a number of new building projects. At the fire station built in 1953 at Chatham, Kent, a reinforced-concrete storeroom was incorpo-

Figure 9.31
Main corridor of the Civil
Defence Sub-Divisional
Control Centre, Gravesend,
Kent, 1954 [AA98/07969]

rated into the otherwise brick structure, so that it could double as an emergency watch room. At Kidderminster, Worcestershire, a large room in the police divisional headquarters was set aside for civil defence, and large police stations housed receivers for the emergency warning system while many had warning sirens on their roofs. Opportunities were also taken to incorporate civil defence services into other local authority developments. In London, the former St Marylebone Borough Council included a civil defence conference room, store, records room and toilet, all below a doctor's surgery which was itself part of a multi-storey car park development. The Ministry of Works also issued suggestions on how shelters could be built into new houses (though no examples have been identified by fieldwork) and local authorities were required to identify buildings such as church halls and schools (with large communal kitchens)

which could be used for civil defence use – as air-raid shelters, rest centres for displaced people, or feeding centres.

In January 1968 civil defence was scaled down to a 'care and maintenance' basis, and the CDC and associated organisations were disbanded on 1 April. Some civil defence centres and stores continued to be maintained by local authorities, but most were closed and sold. During the 1970s little practical effort was made to maintain credible civil defence. Revised Home Office regulations, issued in 1974, merely required local authorities to draw up plans, and the stress was now laid on survival and recovery rather than rescue. Design work continued on the adaptation of some former Rotor bunkers into RGHQs, but little actual construction took place. Civil defence planning was revived in the early the 1980s, this time with an emphasis on community volunteers working on their own and largely without equipment or purpose-built facilities. This was in contrast to the Continent, and especially to eastern Europe, where civil defence was maintained at a consistently high level of preparedness throughout the Cold War. Renewed interest is being shown in civil defence by many governments as rogue states or terrorist groups develop the potential to threaten large centres of population.

You're on your own

During the Second World War government policy for protecting the civil population was a mixture of evacuation and stay-put. Children and the mothers of babies were encouraged to leave the cities, but mass evacuation from the urban areas was deemed undesirable as it would have left the war industries understaffed and would have created fresh problems of accommodation and food supply.

Throughout the 1950s government committees regularly discussed evacuation plans. Planning assumptions focused at first on a bombing campaign against London and other major conurbations, mounted by aircraft with relatively low yield atomic weapons. An official civil defence training film of the period, *Operation Exodus*, naively suggested evacuation could be undertaken, in an orderly manner, a few days after the initial strike. Moving, and finding accommodation for, large bodies of people in the relatively small area of the United Kingdom was, however, an intractable problem, compounded by a potential influx of refugees from the Continent. Some planning even foresaw the possibility of evacuating the population by sea, on ships supplied with stockpiled ration packs. With the prospect of the H-bomb, however, it was realised that nowhere in the country would be safe from a radioactive cloud which would cover the whole nation, though evacuation continued to crop up in government thinking until the early 1980s.

If the population could not be safeguarded by evacuation, could it be protected by shelters? In the years following the war much of the civil defence resource had been directed towards removing wartime shelters. By the 1950s this policy was reversed, to keep them unless there was a pressing development need or they cost too much to maintain. After high level discussions the Chiefs of Staff Joint Global War Committee even asserted, following the lead of the United States and the Soviet Union, that where large public shelters had been built, 'full shelter protection for the civil population' could be achieved by 1969–70. In reality such a scheme was financially impossible, and no shelter could offer complete protection.

Accordingly, by the early 1960s official policy began to emphasise the home as the unit of survival. This was not taken to its logical conclusion, as it was in Switzerland where every new house had to include a shelter. Instead the civil defence booklet of the time gave basic advice about creating shelters in different types of houses and staying put until advised to move – advice that was reissued virtually unaltered in the 1980s.

In the 1980s, however, more detailed advice was also issued about the construction of domestic shelters ranging from crude earth and timber refuges (which could be erected in a few days preceding an attack) to elaborate purpose-built or off-the-shelf designs (Fig 9.32). It is hard to assess how many such shelters were built, though advertising leaflets and newspaper cuttings suggest that the 'doom boom' of the early 1980s prompted a growth in construction. At that time a variety of firms offered to build shelters ranging from high specification concrete capsules to more modest prefabricated steel chambers which could be buried in a garden, often using components from Swedish and Swiss civil protection companies. At best they might offer a family protection against the worst effects of radiation for a couple of weeks but eventually people would have had to emerge; and into a very different world from the one they had left.

Figure 9.32
An example of a domestic nuclear shelter being installed at the Home Office training centre, Easingwold, North Yorkshire, in the early 1980s. [Job 07292 film B frame 15]

10
The 'white heat' of defence technology

In the closing years of the Second World War, jet aircraft, guided weapons, rockets, radar, and the atomic bomb had ushered in the technological advances that were to drive the Cold War. In the ensuing stand-off demonstrating scientific domination was an important way of asserting superiority short of actual war, and made it possible for the West to exert constant pressure on the Soviet Union's economy and scientific manpower.

The need to keep one step ahead led to an increase in the number and size of research establishments (Fig 10.1), which absorbed a growing proportion of the budgets for defence and for government science and research, and fuelled the growth of industries supplying new generations of weapons. Both research and manufacturing centres were often sited away from what had been the traditional areas of armament production.

The drive for research

In the 19th century there were few purpose-built research and development sites, and it was only from about 1900 that the State became increasingly involved in scientific research. In the early 20th century new technological advances revolutionised the conduct of war by introducing aviation, mechanised transport, radio and the development of the electrical and electronics industry.

In 1902 the government established the National Physical Laboratory at Teddington, Middlesex. Although it was not primarily a military institution, its work, including pioneering research on aeronautics, benefited the services. During the First World War the number of research establishments concerned with military technology grew rapidly. Most were closed after 1918 but some survived, notably the Royal Aircraft Establishment at Farnborough, Hampshire.

The Second World War witnessed a similar proliferation of scientific research, and as Germany was overrun its research institutes became major prizes; the Allies often competing with each other to capture them, their scientists and equipment. They not only provided Britain with scientific equipment, which was scarce after the war, but also with an envious glimpse of what a properly funded institution might aspire to.

The wide range of post-war research establishments in Britain, many of which are unique in Europe, are a legacy of national aspirations to retain 'superpower' status, with Britain keeping the capacity to develop

and manufacture high-tech weaponry independently. After a slight dip in defence research and development (R and D) spending in the late 1940s, expenditure rose again in the 1950s to absorb more than half of total government spending on R and D, and by 1961 it represented over 15 per cent of the defence budget. It may have been the achievements of this decade of spectacular spending that influenced Labour leader Harold Wilson to envisage, in 1963, an ultra-modern Britain that would be 'forged in the white heat' of a 'scientific revolution'.

Many of the decisions which led to the forging of defence technology in the 'white heat' of the 1950s, such as development of the atomic bomb and of aircraft, which would later evolve into the V-force, as well as plans to modernise the naval research establishments, were taken soon after the end of the war. The urgent need for this work was further reinforced by deteriorating relations with the Soviet Union, and the realisation that it too was developing an advanced military capability. This was revealed not only by its detonation of an atomic bomb in 1949 but also when western forces were confronted by Soviet MIG-15 jet fighters in the early stages of the Korean War. From 1950 rearmament began, and the physical fabric of the research stations shows that investment in their infrastructure peaked during the following decade, as Government realised that the Cold War confrontation would be a long haul.

Aviation research and development sites

The most important aviation research centre was Farnborough in Hampshire. Before the First World War it was the site of His Majesty's Balloon Factory, later the Royal Aircraft Factory and finally, in 1918, the Royal Aircraft Establishment (RAE). Specialised structures for the investigation of flight and testing aircraft components began to appear. They included small wind tunnels and the 'whirling arm' – a steel lattice arm that revolved around a central bearing and was used to test propellers – the base of which still survives. As at other research establishments the inter-war years were characterised by structures erected to test particular questions, such as catapults for launching aircraft from ships, which were dismantled when no longer required.

More enduring has been the 24ft (7.3m) wind tunnel, which was operational by 1936

and was large enough to take a complete single-seater fighter of the day; it is still in use and has been listed for its architectural and historic importance. In 1942 two further wind tunnels were built: a high-speed tunnel which could test 6ft (1.83m) wide models in air speeds of 600mph (965.4kph), and a low-speed tunnel for air speeds up to 270mph (434.43kph).

Soon after this, the advent of the jet engine led to the need for supersonic testing. Although existing tunnels had been run at supersonic speeds, simulating the effects of flying at or near the speed of sound was more difficult, but it was found that the necessary airflow could be achieved by using a perforated or slotted wall (Fig 10.2) in the working area of the tunnel, where the model was suspended. In 1950, however, the English Electric Aircraft Co Ltd, at Warton, Lancashire, built the first transonic tunnel. At Farnborough, work to convert the wartime high-speed tunnel to transonic running took place between 1954 and 1956 and the redesigned tunnel was used to test the designs of most British military aircraft. At the same time, the analysis of data was improved by the use of computers; in the early days these were huge and the largest occupied a whole room.

At the end of the Second World War the RAE was housed in a variety of buildings, many dating from before 1914. One of the few new buildings was for the investigation

Figure 10.2
RAE Farnborough, Hampshire. Working section of the transonic wind tunnel showing slotted walls; the working area is 8ft × 6ft (2.44m × 1.83m). [BB98/26804]

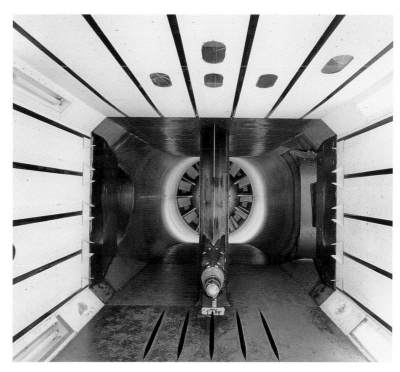

of new procedures for aircraft control and reporting – a subject outside the usual remit of the RAE – perhaps built in response to the 1945 Cherry Report, which proposed the development of new sector control and reporting centres. The front is a standard three-storey office block (Fig 10.3a), but at the rear are two identical open rooms, surrounded on three sides by galleries (Fig 10.3b) and separated from one another by a central spine of corridors. The layout of these rooms, and the data handling procedures devised in them, may have influenced the design of the later Rotor-period sector operations centres (*see* Figs 5.15a and b).

On the opposite side of the Farnborough airfield, remote from prying eyes and cordoned off with corrugated-iron fencing, a secure area described as the Airfield Research Laboratory was established in

Figure 10.4
RAE Farnborough,
Hampshire.
a: (above) Airfield
Research Laboratory
[BB98/26745]

b: (far left)
Still from a 1950s cine film
showing loading trials with
the atomic bomb 'Blue
Danube' beneath a Valiant
bomber. [© Crown
copyright. Photo courtesy of
AWE]

c: (above left)
1990s radio-frequency
shielded chambers inserted
inside a 1950s hangar
[BB98/26743]

1952 (Fig 10.4a). In order to restrict knowledge about particular projects exclusively to the teams involved, each section of the laboratory was partitioned off to keep its work from the gaze of other teams; a typical layout of research establishments and their buildings. Despite its ramshackle appearance – it looked like a collection of sheds – many important projects were carried out inside, including trials for fitting nuclear weapons to the V-bombers (Fig 10.4b) and the top secret Project 'E' concerned with adapting United States nuclear weapons for British aircraft. Many buildings which had outlived their original purpose were repeatedly reused to house sophisticated scientific equipment (Fig 10.4c).

As aviation technology became more complex the research establishments set up specialised 'outstations'. In 1946 the

Figure 10.5
RAE Bedford.
a: A supersonic wind
tunnel, 8ft × 8ft (2.4m ×
2.4m), nearing completion
in June 1955. The vertical
spinning tunnel is on the
left. [G05717/3]

b: Low speed wind tunnel,
13ft × 9ft (4m × 2.75m), in
May 1955. Attached to
each tunnel are buildings
with offices and laboratories
as well as plant to blow,
compress, evacuate, cool
and dry the air in the
tunnel. [G5650/27]

National Gas Turbine Establishment, on the area to the north-west of the main airfield at Pyestock, Hampshire, became the main centre for research into jet engines. A wartime outstation at Whetstone in Leicestershire was closed and from 1948 activity was concentrated at Pyestock, which was expanded: its new buildings included complex test cells to simulate flight at high altitudes. A year earlier the Guided Weapons Department was formed at Farnborough, and the formerly independent Guided Projectile Establishment at Westcott, Buckinghamshire, became the Rocket Propulsion Department of the RAE. Remote ranges for testing guided weapons were maintained at Larkhill, Wiltshire, at Aberporth and Llanbeder, Ceredigion, and at West Freugh, Dumfries and Galloway.

Between 1951 and 1957 the RAE saw its largest post-war development – the creation of a new centre for aerodynamics research – construction of which involved 700 companies and cost £30 million. It was spread across three wartime airfields in Bedfordshire – Little Saughton, Thurleigh and Twinwood. Work included laying a new main runway 10,500ft (3,200m) long, and a shorter cross runway. The associated buildings have a simple functional style, and the use of a limited range of materials and colours (white, blue and yellow) contributed to the architectural cohesion of the scheme (Figs 10.5a and b). Other design considerations involved speed of erection and flexibility of building design to allow for expansion or changes of use. Most of the larger buildings have prefabricated steel or reinforced-concrete frames and are clad in brick, asbestos or aluminium sheets, though the new four-storey control tower, completed in 1956, has load-bearing brickwork. The most expensive buildings were five wind tunnels, one of which used equipment salvaged from the German establishment at Volkenrode. Other structures included an aluminium-framed and clad maintenance hangar with an internal span of 200ft (61m), a fire station and canteen. Also based at Bedford were the Blind Landing Experimental Unit and the Naval Air Department, which used specialised equipment (including catapults and arrestor gear) to simulate landings on the deck of a ship.

Closely associated with the RAE is the Aeroplane and Armament Experimental Establishment at Boscombe Down, Wiltshire, which undertakes testing of military aircraft and associated equipment and has several specialised structures, such as a powerful blower tunnel for testing the jettison of cockpit canopies from jet fighters.

Naval research and development sites

In 1939, at the start of the Second World War, there were twelve experimental stations for the Royal Navy, mostly in the Portsmouth area but a few in west London, as well as a metallurgical laboratory in Sheffield and an explosives inspection laboratory at the Royal Naval Cordite Factory (RNCF), Holton Heath, Dorset. Ten years later there were twice as many sites, reaching as far as the west of Scotland where there was a new torpedo facility at Greenock, Renfrewshire.

Many of the pre-war establishments had been placed in existing buildings, a pattern reinforced by the wartime need to make the best use of any available structure. This, as a post-war survey showed, meant that many organisations were in places or buildings for which they were ill-suited. The Admiralty Materials Laboratory, for example, occupied a section of the First World War explosives

Figure 10.6
ARL Teddington.
a: Annular test. The rotating beam was 120ft (36m) long and weighed 60 tons (60.96 tonnes).
[BB98/02883]

Figure 10.6
b: In the foreground is the
building which housed the
high speed tunnel. This is
joined to the annular tank
(to the rear) by a range of
offices. Also note the
concern for the
establishment's environment
shown by the planting of
ornamental trees.
[BB98/02897]

factory at Holton Heath, though there was little outward alteration to the buildings. A committee set up in 1947 to investigate the structure of naval experimental sites recommended the creation of five or six large purpose-built facilities. As this was too expensive in the years of post-war 'austerity' a more pragmatic solution was adopted, with the creation of two groups of establishments: one between Edinburgh and the Clyde and the other in a triangle bounded by London, Portsmouth in Hampshire and Portland in Dorset. Few centres were in fact moved, most surviving until the 1990s rationalisation programme.

Although old sites were retained, new extensions were added, though usually not until the re-armament programme of the early 1950s. At that time new facilities were created for the Radar and Radio Establishment at Portsdown, Hampshire, the Gunnery Establishment at Portland, Dorset and for the Naval Construction Research Establishment at Rosyth, Fife. The Underwater Detection Establishment at Portland was extended. Soon after the war the Admiralty Research Laboratory (ARL), sited since 1921 next to the National Physical Laboratory at Teddington, Middlesex, acquired a second site in Bushey Park (also Middlesex), with an 18th-century house and other

buildings dating from both World Wars. On these sites researchers investigated two main problems – underwater noise reduction and the design of high-speed underwater weapons (which included work by a small team of German scientists on guidance systems). In the late 1940s a water tunnel (obtained from Kiel in Germany) was installed, which operated much like a wind tunnel, forcing water past a fixed model at high speed. In the mid-1950s a more ambitious scheme saw the construction of an annular (ring-shaped) tank 136ft (41.5m) in diameter and 15ft (4.6m) deep, which held 1,000,000 gallons (4,546,000 litres) of clear water and was covered by a domed roof (Fig 10.6a). At its centre was a massive rotating arm operated from a control chamber set high on the dome, used to drag models through the tank at high speed. The behaviour of the models under test was observed from behind thick armoured glass windows set into the walls of the tank. The annular tank was linked by an office block to the fluid dynamics laboratory which housed a water tunnel similar to the German one, but which was capable of obtaining better measurements (Fig 10.6b). The cost of this scheme was just over £1 million, almost equally split between the buildings and the equipment (Fig 10.6c).

c: The boiler house, executed in contemporary 1950s style [BB98/02831]

Conventional explosives research and development sites

After the war the centre of conventional explosives research was the former Royal Gunpowder Factory at Waltham Abbey, which covered about 150 hectares (370 acres) and was served by 5 miles (8km) of navigable waterways. Although production there had stopped in 1943 the site was opened again in 1945 as an experimental station of the Armament Research Department (ARD). In 1948, it became home to the subsidiary Chemical Research and Development Department (CRDD), changing its name later that year to the Explosives Research and Development Establishment (ERDE). Early research priorities included the development of rocket propellants, non-erosive propellants for guns, investigations into the chemistry of high explosives and initiators (which start the detonation process),

the storage of explosives under tropical conditions, and new manufacturing techniques for the high explosive RDX.

The new department inherited a site where some buildings were more than 150 years old and materials were moved around the site and taken in and out mainly by barge. Gradually, new roadways were laid and the canals were used as dumping grounds for waste. Building activity involved not only adapting former factory buildings but also building new structures tailored for modern purposes. The bayed form of many buildings was ideally suited to containing the risks posed by the hazardous experiments carried out in the new laboratories, but the open verandahs at the front of the buildings were enclosed to create continuous corridors (Fig 10.7a). As in all explosives laboratories, the amount of explosive which could be kept was carefully regulated, with stocks being stored in distinctive locker magazines (Fig

Figure 10.7
Explosives Research and
Development Establishment
(ERDE) Waltham Abbey,
Essex.
a: 19th-century gunpowder
mills. After the war they
were converted into
laboratories. [BB92/26175]

b: (below)

H66 locker magazine,
1950. This building
displays many features
common to all explosives
handling buildings,
including lightning
conductors, copper earthing
straps, electrical fittings
attached to the exterior, and
outward opening doors to
make it easier to escape.
[BB92/26044]
c: L189 firing point, 1953,

10.7b). In the remote northern area of the site the boiler houses of the gunpowder drying stoves were lined internally with steel plates and converted into firing points, and in the early 1950s new purpose-built firing points were added, mainly to aid investigation of the sensitivity of explosives (Figs 10.7c and d). The new structures consist of a central, armour-plated firing chamber surrounded by an earthen mound and with a steel-plated roof supported by relatively insubstantial steel columns covered by a thick layer of earth, designed to collapse and smother an over-powerful explosion. Firing was controlled from a room next door, from which experiments could be viewed through an armoured glass window. On the opposite side of the chamber was another strengthened window, behind which was a high-speed camera. A similar firing point was placed in an unused section of the Second World War nitroglycerine factory, and specialised climatic cubicles were built to test explosives under varying storage temperatures (Fig 10.7e).

Chemical and biological weapons research and development sites

Since the First World War, Porton Down in Wiltshire has been the centre for research into chemical and, later, biological weapons. At the end of the Second World War, in common with other establishments, it occupied a disorderly collection of structures, thrown up to meet wartime needs with little thought to the efficient functioning of a peacetime organisation. In 1947 a plan was drawn up to remodel the site, but it resulted only in a new engineering section and a housing estate in nearby Salisbury. The importance attached to the development of biological weapons was, however, demonstrated by the construction between 1948 and 1951 of a large campus to house the Microbiological Research Department. The new buildings cost £2.25 million, spent at a time when the nuclear programme was also absorbing vast amounts of research resources. In the same period, in 1949, an outstation was established on a wartime

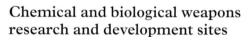

showing the detached monitoring room to the left, and the mound surrounding the firing chamber to the right [BB92/26131]

d: L189 firing point, 1953.

Steel-lined firing chamber [BB92/26132]

e: L190 climatic test cubicles, 1951 [BB92/26203]

airfield at Nancekuke, Cornwall, for the manufacture of CS gas (tear gas) and anti-dotes to nerve agents; it was regularly refurbished through the 1960s and was closed in 1979.

Developing Britain's atomic bomb

In 1947 the Labour Government, led by Clement Attlee, resolved that Britain should proceed with her own atomic bomb, and created a remarkable scientific and industrial programme to develop and manufacture the weapon. Development was at first closely associated with the conventional explosives research establishments, both to share facilities and hide its true purpose (as did its cover name – 'Basic High Explosive Research', later abbreviated to HER). The project was overseen by physicist William Penney, a for-

mer member of the wartime Los Alamos team which had engineered the atomic bombs dropped on Japan. In contrast to the Los Alamos group of internationally acknowledged scientists, Penney's team was largely composed of government specialists from the Armament Research Department of the Ministry of Supply.

Despite the importance of the project, it was initially housed in modest facilities. The headquarters was in a fenced-off enclosure of existing buildings at Fort Halstead near Sevenoaks, Kent, and a new range was established on Foulness Island, Essex, where the facilities, while of higher standard than temporary wartime ones, were still utilitarian (Fig 10.8).

A new base was only sought in autumn 1948, when it was decided that the team should manufacture the radioactive components of the bomb, and not until the following year was Aldermaston, Berkshire, selected as the site for what was then known as the Atomic Weapons Research Establishment (AWRE). Slightly later another range, at Orfordness, Suffolk, was developed for testing assembled weapons. (Later still, in 1987, AWRE became AWE – Atomic Weapons Establishment – controlling a number of factories and research sites.)

Atomic Weapons Research Establishment Foulness

From 1947, Foulness Island in Essex was developed as an extension of the Shoeburyness range, specifically to study the fragmentation of munitions. In the late 1940s it also assumed significance as the main centre for researching the use of conventional explosives in nuclear weapons. The research fell into two main areas: investigating the physics of explosives, and simulating the effects of nuclear explosions. The work was carried out by a highly skilled team of engineers, mathematicians, computer scientists, and electronics and instrumentation specialists who, with their support staff, were housed at the north end of the range, in an area initially developed at the end of the 1940s and later expanded to include a canteen, workshops and laboratories.

As on other ranges designed for handling explosives, the structures are widely spaced, but at Foulness this also reflects a security regime in which knowledge was tightly compartmentalised. Many of the structures are unique, as at other research stations, having been designed to meet precise experimental needs: some were specific to the needs of the

Figure 10.8
Atomic Weapons
Establishment (AWE)
Foulness, Essex. Building
A2 ARE 1949. Entrance to
the main administrative
building where William
Penney, director of the
British atomic bomb
programme, had his office
[BB99/15966]

AWRE, though others (such as the sensitivity, climatic and hazard assessment facilities) are similar to those on other explosives research sites.

In the 1950s many of the atmospheric nuclear tests carried out in the United States, the Soviet Union and the Pacific were designed to see how equipment and structures would withstand a nuclear explosion. Opposition resulted in a moratorium in 1958 on this kind of testing, which lasted until 1961 when it was broken by the Soviet Union, though in 1963 the Limited Test Ban Treaty prohibited tests in the atmosphere, outer space or underwater. Thereafter there were two options: underground testing, and simulation of the effects of nuclear explosions.

There is no completely accurate way of simultaneously mimicking all the consequences of a nuclear explosion, though the four main effects (blast, heat, radiation and electromagnetic pulse – see Chapter 9) can be simulated individually. The main concern at Foulness was with replicating blast and heat effects.

The blast simulator is a 676ft (206m) long, tapering steel tube, with a firing chamber 6ft (1.8m) in diameter at its narrow end, inside which explosive charges were detonated to create a blast wave (Fig 10.9a). Objects up to the size of a tank or single seat aircraft (including scale models of buildings) could be tested by being placed either on a central sliding section of the tube or at its far end, which is 35ft (10.7m) in diameter. Tests were primarily assessed using high-speed photography and strain gauges. A distinctive feature of the wide end of the tunnel is a semi-permeable barrier created by horizontal scaffold poles, intended to prevent a return wave travelling down the tube.

Tests investigating the effects of thermal radiation (heat) on small and medium-sized objects were carried out in laboratories, but those on larger equipment, such as a truck or helicopter, required an open-air facility. The facility amounted to not much more than a shed, which housed control equipment and gas bottles, and a platform on which the test object was placed (Fig 10.9b). A short burst of intense heat was generated by burners fuelled with liquid oxygen and powdered aluminium. Experiments to simulate the effects of electromagnetic pulses were carried out at Aldermaston (Fig 10.9c), where the reaction of bomb components to radiation was conducted in a small reactor (see Fig 10.11b).

In addition to the experimental work, Foulness was used to prepare explosives manufactured in the Royal Ordnance Factories (ROFs) for use in nuclear weapons or

Figure 10.9
AWE Foulness, Essex.
a: Blast tunnel showing permeable barrier of scaffold poles at the end of the tunnel and also external lights and camera positions. On the left is the movable section on which a test object could be placed. [BB99/15988]

b: (below)
Thermal test facility. Equipment to be tested was lifted onto a platform – behind the shed – which was reached by the steps. In the foreground is a block of earth that could be raised onto the roof of the shed and was used to hold a manikin dressed in combat equipment. [BB99/15986]

Figure 10.9

c: (above) Electromagnetic pulse simulator (at AWE Aldermaston, Berkshire); mock-up of frigate's bridge under test [107786 © Crown copyright. Photo courtesy of AWE]

d: (right) Building X34 vessels. These steam-jacketed vessels were used to melt high explosives for casting into intricate shapes to form the explosive lenses surrounding the fissile material. [BB99/15980]

for research. This was undertaken in a distinct explosives area, which has many features in common with large explosives factories, including a changing room and a 'clean way' for moving explosives between the buildings. The buildings where the work was carried out are, however, small – a reflection of the low, but carefully crafted, output of this section, which included high explosives cast into intricate shapes (Fig 10.9d) and machined with exceptional precision, as well as assembled explosive devices (Fig 10.9e).

Atomic Weapons Research Establishment Orfordness

The second range, at Orfordness, is on a remote area of the Suffolk coast. Its associa-

tion with armament experiments dated back to the First World War, and during the 1930s it was briefly connected with the development of radar. The AWRE occupied the site from 1953, at first working on the ballistics of 'Blue Danube' (*see* Chapter 3) and later on the physical stresses the bomb experienced before detonation. To support this work a series of concrete and shingle test chambers were erected (Fig 10.10a): some had rigs for testing resistance to vibration, while in others the extremes of temperature encountered during flight were simulated. Although the tests involved no nuclear material, these massive structures were designed to absorb accidental detonation of the conventional explosive elements of the

e: Building X6. In this building in 1952 the non-fissile components of the first British atomic bomb were assembled, before it was dispatched on board HMS Plym to the Monte Bello Islands, Australia, for detonation. [AA99/09781]

Figure 10.10
AWRE Orfordness, Suffolk.
a: Building E2, used for
vibration testing. This type
of structure was known as a
'Pagoda'. [AA021750]

bomb, and the test chambers are similar to those at Waltham Abbey (*see* Figs 10.7b and c).

Other specialised structures included camera booths for recording weapons in flight, centrifuges for studying 'G' forces on bomb components (Fig 10.10b), a rocket sled track, and control rooms where the results of experiments were remotely recorded. After work on Blue Danube was completed, research continued on new warhead and bomb casing designs, some of which required further development of the site, such as the new centrifuge building E1 erected during the early 1960s to support the Polaris programme. By the end of that decade most of the work was transferred to Aldermaston, which was also equipped with Pagoda-like structures. Atomic weapons research at Orfordness ended in 1971, shortly before the short-lived 'Cobra Mist' radar on the northern part of the site was

erected (*see* Chapter 6). (The National Trust now owns the former AWRE area.)

The manufacture of nuclear weapons

The geography of nuclear weapons manufacture reflected the availability of tracts of land that were controlled, or had been recently relinquished, by the Government. Former ROFs at Windscale (now Sellafield), Cumbria, at Capenhurst and Risley, Cheshire, and at Burghfield, Berkshire, were rebuilt for production, as was a poison gas factory at Springfields, Lancashire. Aldermaston was itself built on a wartime airfield, as was the research laboratory at Harwell, Oxfordshire. Some components were made at the Royal Arsenal Woolwich, Chatham dockyard and ROF Chorley, Lancashire; an explosives filling factory which manufactured specialist production machines.

b: F1 centrifuge chamber viewed from the control room [AA021772]

At Sellafield (which was known as Windscale until the 1970s) work began in September 1947 to build two air-cooled nuclear reactors, the 'Windscale Piles', the first of which went critical in October 1950. The primary purpose of the Windscale Piles was to produce plutonium for the core of the bomb, and smaller quantities of polonium for the initiators (*see* Chapter 3). The piles were dominated by two 360ft (108m) ventilation shafts, each supporting 2,000 ton (2,032 tonne) filters (both are now being partially dismantled as part of the decontamination programme). The two original reactors were shut down on 10 October 1957 after a serious fire, and were replaced by four gas-cooled (later called 'Magnox') reactors, which came into operation between 1956 and 1959 at two new power stations on the site: Calder Hall A and B. There is a similar group of reactors at Chapel Cross, Dumfriesshire.

Aldermaston (Figs 10.11a and b) was developed both for nuclear weapons research and for manufacturing radioactive components. For the first tests disc-shaped pieces of plutonium were received from Sellafield and taken to a special 'hot' laboratory (designed to handle radioactive materials). Here they were cast into blanks before being machined into the two interlocking hemispheres which formed the core of a bomb (*see* Fig 3.12b), and gold plated to prevent corrosion. The uranium tamper, or casing, and its polonium initiator, also encased in uranium, were also made at Aldermaston; as was the first operational British atomic bomb, 'Blue Danube', which was built in a three-bay shed, with overhead gantry cranes in each bay to lift the heavy assemblies. Today, Aldermaston covers 880 acres (356ha), and has around 1,000 densely packed buildings, split into at least eleven functional areas: some are standard office accommodation, but others are special

Figure 10.11
AWE Aldermaston,
Berkshire.
a: Building A1.1,
constructed in 1952 to
manufacture the plutonium
core for use in the first
British atomic bomb
[G3469/3 © Crown
copyright. Photo courtesy
of AWE]

b: Building R61, which
contained a small research
reactor, constructed to test
the effect of radiation on
bomb components
[G7268/2 © Crown
copyright. Photo courtesy
of AWE]

research and manufacturing structures.

From about 1954 the nearby Royal Ordnance Factory at Burghfield was redeveloped for warhead manufacture, assembly and inspection. At about the same time that the British H-bomb was introduced, around 1960, two new warhead assembly buildings were built (Fig 10.12), linked to other structures by closed corridors. They were specially designed to contain the risk from an explosion during assembly: their concrete domed roofs, made of steel mesh covered by sprayed concrete, would minimise the risk from flying debris. Around the outside is loose gravel which would fall in to smother an explosion (hence the domes' colloquial name, the 'Gravel Gerties'). Architecturally they are almost identical to the United

States' nuclear weapons final assembly plant at Pantex, Carson County, Texas.

Industrial archaeology of the Cold War defence industry

At the end of the First World War there had been a rush to dispose of newly constructed munitions factories. At the end of the Second World War, however, the Government either found new uses for them or retained the factories on a 'care and maintenance' regime. Most of them were in the traditional engineering areas of the North and the Midlands, and many had been deliberately placed in areas to the west of Britain, at the extreme range of bombers from the Conti-

Figure 10.12
AWE Burghfield, Berkshire. A view of the warhead assembly facilities in 1963; construction was completed in 1961 [4593 © Crown copyright. Photo courtesy of AWE]

Figure 10.13
Former de Havilland,
factory, Stevenage,
Hertfordshire.
a: Front offices 1954, with
later extension to the right
and large production shops
to the rear. This factory
covered 36,111 sq m
(388,714 sq ft) and
employed more than 2,000
people (see also Fig
10.20). [BB98/27541]

nent. Heavy engineering factories in Leeds, Newcastle upon Tyne and Nottingham continued to produce armoured vehicles, and naval shipbuilding yards (also used for nuclear submarines) remained the major employers in Barrow in Furness and Birkenhead. The war had, however, revealed the crucial importance that aerospace, communications and electronics, the 'ACE industries', would play in any future conflict. They were new enterprises, the development of which was to become one of the significant features of the Cold War. Many were, and still are, world leaders in their field and are amongst Britain's most successful exporters.

The war had left the country with a legacy of newly-built aircraft and engine factories, and no fewer than thirty-five manufacturers – many more than required in peacetime. Military aircraft production continued, and by about 1950 the RAF had been substantially re-equipped by eight major manufacturers. A number of wartime aircraft factories were reactivated, such as at Squires Gate Blackpool, Lancashire, and other smaller factories were taken over for component production. Elsewhere extensions were made to production areas, as at Glosters, Gloucester (to produce the Javelin), but the most noticeable new structures were administrative and design offices. They reflected the company pride of individual manufacturers and their confidence in the future; more practically they provided space for ever larger design sections because, by 1962, up to 39.5 per cent of the industry's workforce was managerial, administrative, technical or clerical.

In keeping with their technologically advanced products, most firms chose contemporary architectural designs, such as de Havilland at Hatfield and Stevenage, Hertfordshire (Figs 10.13a and b). Exceptionally, Hawkers opted for a plain, neo-classical style

for their Kingston upon Thames factory (Fig 10.14); which contrasts with the clean modern lines of the Hunter aircraft produced there (*see* Fig 7.3a).

By the early 1960s, following government pressure, two major groups of manufacturers had emerged – the British Aircraft Corporation and Hawker Siddeley Aviation – while the aero-engine manufacturers joined Rolls-Royce. Not only have famous company names been lost but the number of sites where aircraft are manufactured has been reduced, so that today military aircraft production is now concentrated at the BAE Systems factory in Warton, Lancashire.

The increasing complexity of aircraft led to ever more extended, and thus costly, research and development, with the design of a new aeroplane taking five to ten years. To maintain their technological edge manufacturers needed to keep investing in increasingly complex research apparatus, including

wind tunnels, previously only normally found in government facilities. During the 1950s, engine test cells and running-up areas (with detuners to protect those working in them and their neighbours from noise) became common features of aero-engine and aircraft factories (Fig 10.15). Some facilities grew organically as they were squeezed into existing complexes (Fig 10.16). Others were on greenfield developments, such as the high altitude test facility built by Rolls-Royce near its Derby works in 1958, at a cost of £5.8 million.

The development and manufacture of guided weapons and rockets had very close links with the business of researching and building military aircraft: in most instances the companies involved in aircraft manufacture supplied their airframes and engines. In the mid-1950s one of the largest research projects was the development of intermediate range ballistic missile (IRBM)

b: Rear extension erected during the late 1950s, in preparation for the assembly of 'Blue Streak'. The offices were specially raised on V-shaped piers to allow launch vehicles on their road trailers to pass beneath. [BB98/27547]

*Figure 10.14
Kingston upon Thames.
The 1957 administrative
and design offices of
Hawker Aircraft Ltd. The
executive architects were
Norman and Dawburn,
and consultant architect for
the facade was Sir Hubert
Worthington. In this
building the revolutionary
Harrier jump jet was
designed. [BB93/07562]*

*Figure 10.15 (below)
Gloster Aircraft Factory,
Gloucester. Early 1950s
detuners sited at the back of
the engine test cells
[BB94/17588]*

'Blue Streak' (Fig 10.17). This involved both government and private contractors, and dedicated facilities were built at the Government's Rocket Propulsion Department at Westcott, Buckinghamshire (Fig 3.36), by Rolls-Royce at Ansty, Warwickshire, and by de Havilland at Hatfield. The most ambitious facilities, on Spadeadam Moor, Cumbria, were completed in under three years at a cost of around £20 million (Figs 10.18a and b). A large range was built, covering 8,006 acres (3,240ha), with a separate administrative area and liquid oxygen plant, and component, engine and missile testing areas for static firing tests which took place before the missiles were sent to Woomera, Australia, for launch. To support the programme, Saunders Roe (of Cowes on the Isle of Wight) developed the 'Black Knight' rocket for testing the re-entry heads for Blue Streak's warhead, on a test site on West High Down near The Needles (Fig 10.19).

The ACE industries required a workforce that included a high proportion of specialist engineers and skilled blue-collar workers – and in contrast to wartime production it was predominantly male. Products were generally few in number and high in value, freeing the industries from many of the geographical constraints posed in traditional areas of munitions manufacture, but the Government exerted considerable influence on the location of the industry. The increasing range of intercontinental bombers and the advent of the atomic bomb also created new strategic considerations for the siting of manufacture.

At first attempts were made to spread it evenly across the country but, with the realisation of the destructive power of the H-bomb, it became apparent that nowhere was safe and that the potential to replenish armaments after an initial attack was slight (unlike the position in the much larger United States and Soviet Union). Nevertheless, the

Figure 10.16 (above) Hatfield, Hertfordshire. De Havilland's research area, 1969 [69 362 22 July 1969. Reproduced from Ordnance Survey air photos on behalf of the Controller of Her Majesty's Stationery Office © Crown copyright Licence No. GD 03085G/02/01]

Figure 10.17 This contemporary diagram illustrates the complexity of the 'Blue Streak' project, the close relationship between government and private establishments and the massive infrastructure building programme to support the enterprise. [© de Havilland]

Figure 10.18
a: (above)
Spadeadam, Cumbria.
Missile test stand C3.
During testing a rocket was
set on top of the stand and
the stream of hot efflux
gases from its engine were
directed into a mild-steel
deflector mounted on the
angled support visible
beneath the stand. During
firing this would be cooled
by water discharged at
20,000 gallons (90,920
litres) per minute. [Picture
Charles H Martin]

b: (right)
The surviving remains of
missile test stand C2
[AA94/02968]

post-war settlement pattern of Britain was influenced by the threat posed by nuclear weapons, and in 1948 the Minister for Town and Country Planning stated that some of the new towns 'were being built for mainly strategic reasons and would be about 25 miles [40km] from the great centres of population'. Elsewhere, new settlement resulting from defence manufacturing was restricted to housing estates, for example Seascale which was built for Sellafield, and most research establishments had housing attached, as at Aldermaston, or nearby, such as Brampton, built for Spadeadam. In rationed post-war Britain this often formed an attractive incentive for staff recruitment.

A crude indication of the geographical concentration of the defence communications and electronics industry can be obtained from a 1960s defence equipment catalogue. Of the fifty-two major firms listed, forty-five were in the South East, with a noticeable concentration in the Greater London area. A broader survey of defence industry sites in the late 1980s revealed a similar pattern, but with other marked concentrations in the Bristol region, Birmingham, Coventry, Lancashire, and west Scotland.

The new industries were the kind of enterprise the new towns were keen to attract, and nearly all the new towns in south-east England were associated with at least one ACE firm. Stevenage was closely linked to the Cold War aerospace industry, which is reflected in the town plan, with the industry firmly zoned between the main north-to-south railway line and the A1(M) (Fig 10.20). Companies usually had the option of leasing land on which to build a factory of their own design, as de Havilland did in 1954 (*see* Figs 10.13a and b) or, as in the case of English Electric, the development corporation could design and build an appropriate factory (Fig 10.21). By the end of the 1950s both these factories had expanded and were involved in prestigious projects, de Havilland in Blue Streak and English Electric in a surface-to-surface missile, 'Blue Water', and in 1960 they

Figure 10.19
West High Down test facility, Isle of Wight, used to test the 'Black Knight' and 'Black Arrow' rockets. At either end were test stands, and in the centre a blockhouse and pump room. The site is owned by the National Trust and is open to the public.
[18516/33]

Figure 10.20
Gunnels Wood Road
industrial estate,
Stevenage, Hertfordshire,
1969. From the 1960s to
the 1980s nearly a third of
this area was occupied by
aerospace factories.
[MAL/69031 LN8992
Frame137]

1 *Hawker Siddeley*
   Dynamics (formerly de
   Havilland)
2 *British Aircraft Corp-*
   oration Ltd (formerly
   English Electric)
3 *Marconi Instruments*
   Ltd
4 *British Aircraft*
   Corporation Ltd

Figure 10.21
English Electric, Stevenage,
Hertfordshire. This factory
was designed and built by
Stevenage Development
Corporation to the firm's
design in the late 1950s.
[BB98/30552]

employed between them 63 per cent of the workforce of the Gunnels Wood Industrial Area.

The design of the new defence factories erected during the 1950s followed contemporary patterns, with the use of steel or ferro-concrete frames with brick or prefabricated glazed panels. As with the aircraft factories, the plans of the buildings reveal the increasing importance of large in-house design teams of engineers, supported by rows of draughtsmen, in what has been called the 'mental assembly line': at each stage of the manufacturing process they could attend to any minor modifications. This is reflected in the high proportion of space devoted to offices and in the provision of large well-lit areas for design activities, while production areas were relatively smaller than in earlier munitions factories, usually consisting of large, adaptable open

areas. Sizeable car parks around the factories indicate the growing prosperity of their workforces with increasing numbers of employees preferring private to public transport.

Heavy dependence on the defence industry rendered Stevenage particularly vulnerable to shifts in defence policy. In 1960, the IRBM Blue Streak was cancelled, but the de Havilland factory survived with the promise of future orders for a space launch vehicle. More serious was the abandonment of Blue Water in 1963, which led to the loss of 1,500 jobs at Stevenage and the closure of English Electric's Luton factory, though the more modern plant at Stevenage was retained. It produced many of Britain's successful guided missiles, including Swingfire, Thunderbird, Vigilant and, later, Rapier.

Most of the well known electrical manufacturers in post-war Britain (Associated

Figure 10.22
Chelmsford, Essex.
a: Marconi, Waterhouse Lane. The trees planted in front of the factory illustrate the greater care taken during the 1960s to make the environment of industrial estates more pleasant. [AA99/01820]

b: Marconi Radar Systems, Writtle Road. A now redundant factory – one of the consequences of reduced defence expenditure [AA99/01812]

261

Electrical Industries, Cossor, Decca, English Electric, EMI, Ferranti, Marconi, Plessey, Pye and Racal) were suppliers of components to the military. There were also many specialist component suppliers, including Dowty, Lucas Aerospace and Smiths Industries. Established firms were at first able to use existing premises, but new sites were developed as demand for all forms of electronic equipment increased. Marconi, with its headquarters at Chelmsford, Essex, pioneered the manufacture of radio equipment at the end of the 19th century, and was one of the leading developers and suppliers of radar equipment in the Second Word War. It subsequently retained its position and, in the late 1940s, was the prime contractor for the supply of radar equipment for the Rotor programme (*see* Chapter 5), and the application of radio and radar to different types of defence equipment enabled the company to boom. Not only did it supply the British and foreign governments, but it also successfully transferred defence technology to civil uses, particularly air traffic control, marine radar and communication equipment. Expansion to meet the new opportunities is evident on existing sites, and as Chelmsford expanded new factories were built on greenfield sites next to the eastern by-pass, reflecting the rise of road transport (Fig 10.22a). Marconi also acquired Crompton's Second Arc Works (Fig 10.22b), a well-established site for electrical equipment manufacture which became the headquarters for the supply of radar systems, and by the late 1980s it occupied six major sites in and around Chelmsford and six elsewhere in Essex.

The military electronics division of EMI was also an important supplier of radar and electronics systems. Its main wartime research and production site was at Hayes, Middlesex, but after the war other factories were acquired. In 1950 it took over the General Aircraft works at Feltham, Middlesex, and the Baird Television Company's Penleigh Works at Wells, Somerset, followed three years later by the acquisition of a former loudspeaker factory in Wembley, Middlesex.

In addition to the new industries of the Cold War, many other manufacturers profited from increased defence spending. The General Electric Company, with large factories at Manchester and Stafford, was a major supplier of generators and electrical equipment. Specialist instrument suppliers across the country also benefited from orders, while other firms grew to meet specific needs, such as the General Radiological Company, London, which supplied radiation monitoring equipment.

Post Cold War cutbacks

In the 1990s disposal programmes the research sites were particularly vulnerable to closure. Many were obsolete, having been expediently placed in existing and often unsuitable establishments, and often had buildings that could not be adapted. Also, past methods of physically replicating the effect to be studied were being superseded by computer modelling. During the 1990s the Defence Research and Evaluation Agency (DERA) progressively concentrated its activities at Farnborough, often for the first time providing programmes with a purpose-built research environment and bringing together specialists from diverse fields. To support its work a supercomputing centre has been established – probably the largest and best equipped of its kind in Europe; it is operated by a consortium including British Aerospace and GEC Marconi, and illustrates the continued blurring of the distinction between the government and private research sectors. International collaboration, particularly with European partners (as in the £165 million European Transonic Wind Tunnel at Cologne-Porz, Germany) has also reduced the need for facilities in the United Kingdom. Britain's defence policy will, nevertheless, probably remain committed to high technology products, as a means of enabling it to 'punch above its weight'.

Cuts in defence expenditure have also resulted in the closure of factories supplying the armed services (Fig 10.22b). Other factors have also been at work: the privatisation in 1985 of the armaments manufacturers Royal Ordnance, and the purchase of ammunition (sometimes from abroad) in the open market, have led to factory closures and around 15,000 job losses. In common with defence research, most new large projects are collaborative, as in the case of the European fighter aircraft, Typhoon. In the United Kingdom, the trend towards consolidation is continuing as companies seek to operate at a global level, often in partnership with foreign firms; the result is the concentration of manufacturing activity on fewer sites. Despite this, at the end of the 1990s Britain was the world's second largest arms exporter, taking 25 per cent of this lucrative market.

11
The legacy of the Cold War – an international perspective

The beginnings

The first atomic explosions and the devastation they caused soon made people realise that the development of the atomic bomb had been a profound turning point in history. The idea of registering monuments and erecting memorials to the opening of the nuclear age soon emerged. Some in the United States wished to commemorate the use of 'the bomb' as a military and technological triumph. As early as 1946 Senator Carl Hatch, a keen supporter of the atomic bomb project, wanted to have Trinity Site in New Mexico, where the first atomic bomb was detonated, listed as a National Historic Landmark – a designation it received only in 1975. The infrastructure of the first hostile use of atomic bombs, in the form of the pits over which the B-29 bombers that went to Hiroshima and Nagasaki were rolled to be loaded, are preserved at North Field on Tinian Island, Commonwealth of the Northern Marianas

(Fig 11.1). However, the nearby bomb assembly buildings have been reduced to footings.

In Hiroshima and Nagasaki, by contrast, the desire was to bury and clear the reminders of destruction, although beneath the streets the soil bears witness to the advent of the nuclear age with the layer of ash resulting from the inferno that followed the nuclear attack of August 1945. One of the few surviving pre-war structures in Hiroshima is the twisted remnant of the dome of the former Industrial Exhibition Hall, which has been retained as a memorial to those who died and today forms part of a museum and peace park.

The only other sites that bear witness to the awesome power of atomic weapons are the early test sites. One of the earliest, and the first to be archaeologically investigated, was the site of the detonation of two nuclear devices in 'Operation Crossroads', carried out at Bikini Atoll in the Marshall Islands in1946. The bombs, 'Able' and 'Baker', were

Figure 11.1
North Field, Tinian Island, Commonwealth of Northern Marianas. Atomic bomb loading pit used for the attack on Japan in August 1945 [© Bill K Harris]

tested on a small fleet of redundant United States' Navy and captured enemy vessels in the island's lagoon. The Bikinians were removed from the atoll in 1946, before the tests, and taken 125 miles (200km) to the island of Rongerik. In the early 1970s Bikini Atoll was declared to be safe and some people returned, but in 1978 further tests showed that the land was still contaminated and the residents were once again evacuated. In 1990 the United States National Parks Service rediscovered the unique assemblage of sunken ships, many of which are historically important in their own right as well as on account of their association with the nuclear tests, and archaeological evidence has dispelled many myths and misunderstandings surrounding the fate of certain vessels. The wrecks now offer the potential for the development of an underwater park and the generation of income from sport divers to assist the displaced Bikinians. In Nevada (USA) an identification survey has been carried out at the site at which atmospheric tests into the effects of nuclear weapons were conducted, from 1951 onwards. Features recorded include range infrastructure (Figs 11.2 a–c), mock-ups of buildings to test their resistance to nuclear explosions, structures from an abandoned experiment into nuclear propulsion for space travel, and the Sedan Crater, created in 1962 to explore potentially peaceful uses of nuclear explosions. The site is listed on the National Register of Historic Places.

c: A 1957 bank vault specially constructed to allow assessment of the effects of a nuclear explosion on its structure. It was manufactured by the Mosler Bank Vault company, and survived the detonation of a nuclear device equivalent to 37,000 tons of TNT. [NF 12895. Provided by the National Nuclear Security Administration]

Recording Cold War cultural resources

It was not until the end of the Cold War that the historic significance of its recently redundant sites was recognised. The most comprehensive approach to assessing the material cultural resources of the Cold War was set up in 1991 under the Legacy Resource Management Program of the United States Department of Defense. One of the main sections of this was the Cold War Project, which was 'to inventory, protect, and conserve the physical and literary property and relics of the Department of Defense, in the United States and overseas, connected with the origins and development of the Cold War'. This has produced site-specific and national studies. Also active in the recording of Cold War sites is the Historic American Engineering Record (HAER). The HAER surveys have included missile silos as well as Nike anti-aircraft missile batteries, which are spread across North America, Europe and Japan. The global distribution of some kinds of sites, such as the Nike batteries, shows just how widely the Cold War has left its traces. Elsewhere in North America, when the BAR-1 radar station (part of the Arctic Distant Early Warning Line) in the Ivvavik National Park was due to be decommissioned, Parks

Canada emphasised the importance of gathering oral testimonies before it finally closed, as well as collecting artefacts and documentary material.

In Europe, the study of Cold War remains has been sporadic. Modern defensive lines along the Swedish coast, and the post-war refurbishment of the sections of the French Maginot line, have both been studied. In The Netherlands, the Rijksdienst voor de Monumentenzorg has surveyed the Ijssellinie, a barrier of water and fixed defences (including Sherman tanks set in concrete), which was in operation between 1950 and 1968. Dutch post-war aircraft observation towers have also attracted attention, and it has been shown that the way in which they were run was remarkably similar to that of the Royal Observer Corps in Britain.

The reduction in defence expenditure has had a particularly marked effect on the landscape of Germany which, in both its former east and west entities, was one of the most heavily militarised countries during the Cold War. Many problems surround former military areas, including contamination from materials such as asbestos and unexploded ordnance, and local unemployment. The only readily accessible sources of information on the historic infrastructure of the sites themselves are reports by enthusiasts.

Information is even scarcer in areas formerly occupied by the Warsaw Pact. Mirroring experiences in the West, many structures from before the Second World War such as administrative buildings and barracks, often near city centres, have found ready reuse by local authorities or have been turned into civilian housing. More problematical are the remote, abandoned, post-war Soviet bases which were often shoddily built, poorly maintained, and have caused serious environmental contamination, especially where leaking or discarded fuel has penetrated the ground water. Many such sites bear a superficial resemblance to their western counterparts, with underground command bunkers and hardened aircraft shelters. Specific cataloguing of their components and analysis of their layout helps in comparing how different military doctrines, and bureaucratic and political systems, influenced the development of technology, which was in turn reflected in the organisation of military installations. In eastern Europe not all communist regimes were loyal supporters of the Soviet Union, and the political divisions which existed in the Balkans are illustrated by the proliferation of small mushroom-shaped pillboxes across Albania, erected for fear of attack from the former Yugoslavia.

Figure 11.3
Nike Missile Site SF-88L restored for public display. Golden Gate National Recreation Area, San Francisco. [© David Clarke, FSG]

Cold War museums

The military draw down at the end of the Cold War is a phenomenon that has affected the built environment around the globe. During the 1990s many recent military bases have moved rapidly from active use to sites of historic interest, and a few have been opened as museums. In the United Kingdom, preservation and display have so far largely been through private initiative, as at Anstruther (in Fife, Scotland), Hack Green (Cheshire), Kelvedon Hatch and Mistley (both in Essex). A number of Royal Observer Corps underground monitoring posts have also been acquired by individuals for preservation. At RAF Neatishead, Norfolk, the Cold War operations room (*see* Fig 5.25) has been preserved as it was on closure in 1993, and forms the centrepiece of an air defence museum. Responsibility for the former regional seat of government beneath Dover Castle has been acquired by English Heritage and sections of it, including its canteen, may be visited. English Heritage also owns the former Royal Observer Corps Group Headquarters at York (*see* Figs 8.17a–d), which is now a scheduled monument, and there are plans to restore it for public display. Although all these projects are prompted by the desire to preserve a particular building, many have also been active in saving important collections of artefacts.

There is a similar picture abroad. In Canada the Diefenbunker near Ottawa, built between 1959 and 1961 for the Canadian government, has been acquired by a development group that wishes to turn it into a Cold War museum. In the United States preservation has also focused on saving and interpreting a number of monuments, including a Nike missile site near the Golden Gate Bridge, San Francisco (Fig 11.3), and a Titan II missile silo, south of Tucson, Arizona (Fig 11.4). Both sites display their original missiles.

The deactivation and destruction of some installations is controlled by international treaty. Nevertheless, within the Strategic Arms Reduction Treaty, protocols did allow for the preservation of a limited number of sites, and in South Dakota a Minuteman II missile launch facility, close to Ellsworth Air Force Base, and an associated remote silo (complete with a missile) have passed to the National Parks Service. Elsewhere many other sites survive as derelict structures or have been adapted to new uses.

In Germany a number of Cold War

Figure 11.4
Tucson, Arizona, Titan II
missile silo museum
[© Audrey Trotti-Corbett]

Figure 11.5
Treptower, Berlin,
September 2002. One of the
few remaining towers from
the Berlin Wall, it con-
tained electronic
surveillance and
communication equipment,
a detention cell, sleeping
quarters and a control room
on the top floor.
[© W D Cocroft]

bunkers, while remaining the property of the Federal or provincial governments, have also been opened to the public by individuals or small groups. At Söllichau, Sachsen-Anhalt, the former East German 1980s army bunker complex is officially recognised as a monument by the provincial authorities. Elsewhere, along the former Inner-German Border, no fewer than twenty-six museums and monuments have been established commemorating the post-war division of the country. In Berlin, where the cityscape has been transformed since the end of the Cold War, only short sections of the emblematic fortification of the post-war divide, the Berlin Wall, remain (Fig 11.5). But other buildings, such as the former state security (Stasi) headquarters and prison, have been preserved as memorials and as documentation centres, to acknowledge such sensitive issues as the legacy of a regime which had, for almost fifty years, pressured its citizens to put loyalty to the State before personal relationships.

Controversy will continue to surround the preservation and interpretation of the artefacts and monuments of the nuclear age; none more so than the display of *Enola Gay* – the B-29 bomber which dropped the atomic bomb on Hiroshima – at the Smithsonian Institution, Washington. After criticism in the 1990s of a new narrative, challenging hitherto accepted views that justified dropping the atomic bombs on Japan, *Enola Gay* was exhibited with a simplified story line concerning only the heroism of the crew and the restoration of the aircraft for exhibition. In contrast, at the National Atomic Museum in Albuquerque, New Mexico, American prowess in designing nuclear weapons is displayed openly and unapologetically. Similarly, at Sarov in Russia, 249 miles (400km) east of Moscow, nuclear weapons are displayed alongside portraits of the scientists who designed them, as a matter of national pride in technological achievement.

Although many of the technological artefacts of the Cold War (aircraft, missiles, radars, rockets, and bomb casings) were saved as they left service, and have been preserved by various museums of the armed forces in Britian, are they rarely displayed in a wider context. One exception is the Imperial War Museum, London, which seeks to use its collections to explain the nature of conflict. In its 'Conflicts since 1945' gallery, planned in the mid-1980s (but not opened until 1996), the main display focuses on the clash between the superpowers. In 2000 the National Museum of American History in Washington opened a new gallery entitled 'Fast Attack and Boomers', which presents the evolution of post-war submarine and missile design against the backdrop of Cold War strategy of nuclear deterrence.

Statutory protection of Cold War remains

Recognition of the historical and social importance of buildings, sites and monuments of associated with the Cold War – a consideration which was still very new when our fieldwork began ten years ago – is leading to measures to protect the most significant and best-preserved examples. In Europe, English Heritage is at the forefront of assessing and developing strategies for the conservation of important Cold War sites. As part of wider assessment of England's 20th-century defence sites, the Monuments Protection Programme has drawn up criteria (based partly on the work behind this book) that enable sites and their components to be assessed and national importance or historic interest to be determined for each. This assessment has taken place within a typological framework that includes thirty-one separate monument classes or groups of related classes. The selection of sites and structures has emphasised those that reflect the primary mission of the Cold War forces, and their relevance to British or NATO defence policy at a given time. As a result of this survey more than one hundred sites have been identified as being of national importance and are being considered for protection as either scheduled monuments or listed buildings. These vary in scale from individual Royal Observer Corps monitoring posts to sections of airfields.

In the United States the designation and protection of monuments is devolved to a local Federal land agent or to the National Parks Service in each state. Some of the most important sites have been designated National Historic Landmarks, which represent just 3 per cent of Historic Landmarks. Amongst them are the sites of historic atomic 'firsts', such as Trinity Site, New Mexico, and North Field, Tinian Island, discussed earlier (*see* Fig 11.1), as well as sites at which missile and rocket technology was perfected during the 1950s. Many sites, such as Space Launch Complex 10 at Vandenberg Air Force Base, California, are also relics of the space exploration programme. Vandenberg Air Force Base was where the RAF

Thor crew carried out live test launches (*see* Chapter 3), and is another example of a monument type with a global distribution.

Epilogue

This book was written in what has been called the 'disarmament decade', in which the uses of defence land after the Cold War were still emerging. Trends that began in the final phase of the Cold War are continuing – especially the move away from vulnerable fixed installations to fully mobile equipment. This trend is particularly strong among radar, air defence and missile launch systems. That policy has been reinforced by the lessons learnt from conflicts during the 1990s, such as the 1991 Gulf War and NATO's air attacks on Serbia in 1999, which have shown that precision-guided munitions are able to seek out the weak points in even the most hardened structures. Cold War, and earlier, defence structures continue to be occupied and adapted for new uses, often simply in order to contain costs. With less demand on budgets for the protection of

bases against nuclear, chemical and biological attack, it was possible to spend more on improving the living and working environment (Fig 11.6) – an important consideration at a time when all those western armies that rely on volunteers rather than conscription have found it more difficult to recruit and retain personnel. The increased numbers of short-term overseas postings exacerbates the problem, as they are far more disruptive to personal lives than the longer-term deployments of the Cold War. Operations in the 1990s have required the rapid mobilisation of forces and, partly in response to that, 'superbases' that combine several operational roles are being developed at places such as Brize Norton in Oxfordshire, Lakenheath and Mildenhall, both in Suffolk, and Waddington in Lincolnshire. The pattern which is emerging is moving away from the heavily militarised landscape of the 20th century, towards a model more akin to that of the 19th century, but in which bases for air armadas have replaced the great dockyards as the springboards for overseas expeditions.

Figure 11.6
RAF Neatishead, Norfolk. Building for combined ranks' mess – an example of one of the many architecturally more imaginative buildings erected on the defence estate during the 1990s. The design expressed the military desire to distinguish between rank: at its centre a kitchen serves three separate dining areas or messes for the ordinary ranks, sergeants and officers. [AA98/05763]

Sources

The information used in the writing of this book was largely gathered by a field-based study of the sites described, and there is a vast array of primary and secondary historical sources which could be drawn on to provide their historical and technological context. The sources have been arranged according to the chapter to which they principally relate, but will often contain information used elsewhere in the book. Within each section they are divided into published books and articles, and primary sources; the latter are available at the Public Record Office, Kew, unless otherwise stated. Most of the published works contain detailed bibliographies that will enable readers to explore the individual topics in more detail.

The most important repository of information on Cold War sites and their wider historical context is the Public Record Office at Kew. Colin Dobinson (1998, *The Cold War*) has catalogued material relating to Rotor radar stations, Bloodhound and Thor missiles sites and the Royal Observer Corps, but there is a wealth of other material, and more will be released over the coming years. Architectural drawings of Cold War sites, and individual structures within them, are less easy to locate. Some are held by the Public Record Office, the Royal Air Force Museum, Hendon, and by the National Monuments Record (NMR), Swindon. Others passed into private ownership when sites were sold. In the absence of easily available plans, air photographs are an invaluable source of information. The most readily accessible collection is the National Library of Air Photographs held by the NMR, which also holds the large photographic archive of the former Property Services Agency, which has images of many post-war defence sites. In addition, the NMR holds the archive supporting this book, which includes detailed site reports, ground photography, specially commissioned air photographs and entries on the national archaeological database, NewHIS. County and city record offices will usually hold information on civil defence organisations, and plans for local emergency government. The internet is also becoming a significant source of information on the Cold War, including websites maintained by official organisations, Cold War museums and research groups.

1 Introduction

Bold, J 2000 *Greenwich: An Architectural History of the Royal Hospital for Seamen and the Queen's House*. Newhaven and London: Yale

Dobinson, C S, Lake, J and Schofield, A J 1997 'Monuments of war: Defining England's 20th-century defence heritage'. *Antiquity* **71**, 288-99

Douet, J 1998 *British Barracks 1600–1914*. London: The Stationery Office

RCHME 1994 *Historic Buildings Report: The Royal Arsenal, Woolwich*. London: RCHME (unpublished typescript)

2 The Cold War: military and political background

Ball, S J 1998 *The Cold War: An International History 1947–1991*. London: Arnold

Bown, C and Mooney, P J 1986 *Cold War to Détente 1945–85*. London: Heinemann Educational Books

Campbell, D 1983 *War Plan UK*. London: Paladin

Dobinson, C 1998 *The Cold War* (Twentieth Century Fortifications in England, Volumes XI, 1 and 2). York: Council for British Archaeology

Dockrill, M 1989 *British Defence Since 1945*. London: Blackwell

Gaddis, J L 1997 *We Now Know: Rethinking Cold War History*. Oxford: Clarendon Press

Halliday, F 1983 *The Making of the Second Cold War*. London: Verso

Isaacs, J and Downing, T 1998 *Cold War: For 45 Years the World Held its Breath*. London: Bantam Press

MacDonald, C 1990 *Britain and the Korean War*. Oxford: Blackwell

McCauley, M 1995 *The Krushchev Era 1953–1964*. London: Longman

Miller, D 1998 *The Cold War: A Military History*. London: John Murray

Roberts, P 2000 *The Cold War*. Stroud: Sutton

Walker, M 1993 *The Cold War*. London: Fourth Estate

Young, J W 1996 *Cold War, Europe 1945–1991: A Political History*, 2 edn. London: Arnold

The intelligence war

Andrew, C and Gordievsky, O 1993 *Instructions from the Centre*. London: Sceptre

Berkeley, R 1994 *A Spy's London*. London: Leo Cooper

Kennedy, V 1983 *The Intelligence War*. London: Salamander Books

Lashmar, P 1996 *Spy Flights of the Cold War*. Stroud: Sutton

Melton, H K 1996 *The Ultimate Spy Book*. London: Dorling Kindersley

Peebles, C 1987 *Guardians Strategic Reconnaissance Satellites*. Shepperton: Ian Allan

3 MAD – 'Mutually Assured Destruction'

Anon 1994 'The V-force in the 1950s'. *Airfield Review* **66**, 26–8

Brookes, A 1982 *V-force: The History of Britain's Airborne Deterrent*. London: Jane's

Campbell, D 1981 'The British bomb: part 2. The wings of the green parrot'. *New Statesman*, 17 April 1981, 10–11

Gibson, J N 1996 *Nuclear Weapons of the United States*. Altglen: Schiffer Publishing Ltd

Hill, C N 2001 *A Vertical Empire: The History of the UK Rocket and Space Programme, 1950–1971*. London: Imperial College Press

HMSO 1956 *Statement on Defence 1956* (Cmnd 9691). London: HMSO

HMSO 1957 *Defence: Outline of Future Policy, 1957* (Cmnd 124). London: HMSO

HMSO 1958 *Supply of Ballistic Missiles by the United States to the United Kingdom* (Cmnd 366). London: HMSO

Jackson, P 1999 'Bin the bomb'. *The Royal Air Force Yearbook 1999*, 22–4

Jackson, R 1981 *Modern Combat Aircraft 11: V-bombers*. Shepperton: Ian Allan

Lonnquest, J C and Winkler, D F 1996 *To Defend and Deter: The Legacy of the United States' Cold War Missile Program* (USACERL Special report 97/01). Washington DC: USACERL

Menaul, S 1980 *Countdown: Britain's Strategic Nuclear Forces*. London: Hale

Nash, P 1997 *The Other Missiles of October. Eisenhower, Kennedy, and the Jupiters 1957–1963*. Chapel Hill: University of North Carolina Press

Norris, R S, Burrows, A S and Fieldhouse, R W 1994 *Nuclear Weapons Databook, Vol V: British, French, and Chinese Nuclear Weapons*. Boulder: Westview Press

Rawlings, J D R 1984 *The History of the Royal Air Force*. Feltham: Temple

Scott, S 1994 *Scampton* (Airfield Focus No. 15). Peterborough: GMS Enterprises

Stumpf, D K 2000 *Titan II: A History of a Cold War Missile Program*. Fayetteville: University of Arkansas Press

Virilio, P 1994 *Bunker Archeology*. Paris: Les éditions du semi-cercle

W T G 1958 'Thor: A study of a great weapon system'. *Flight*, 5 December 1958, 862–72

Wynn, H 1994 *RAF Nuclear Deterrent Forces*. London: HMSO

Public Record Office sources

AIR 2/13675 Blue Streak: Underground Launching Site 1956–1958

AIR 2/13676 Blue Streak: Underground Launching Site 1956–1958

AIR 2/13677 Blue Streak: Underground Launching Site 1956–1958

AIR 2/13683 Tactical Atomic Bomb (Red Beard): Operational Requirements 1957

AIR 2/13689 Fuzing Systems for Atomic Bombs 1947–1955

AIR 2/14947 USAF Feltwell Works Project: Thor IRBM 1958–1959

AIR 2/14975 Blue Streak: Works Project 1958–1960

AIR 2/15246 Blue Streak: Selection of Sites 1959–1966

AIR 2/17377 Blue Streak: Works Services 1959–1960

AIR 19/1014 Blue Steel Development 1961–1964

AIR 25/1592 Operations Record Book No. 40 Group, Jan–Oct 1959–July 1961; No. 41 Group Jan 1956–Dec 1960

AIR 27/2952 Operations Record Book Jan 1961–Jul 1963, No. 77 Sqn Feltwell

AIR 28/1501 RAF Feltwell, Norfolk, June 1958–August 1963

AIR 28/1571 RAF Driffield, Jan 1961–Dec 1963

DEFE 4/224 Chiefs of Staff Meetings (68). Meetings 1–9, Jan 2–30 1968

DEFE 7/1339 RAF Production Programmes for Guided Weapons: Blue Steel 1962–1963

DEFE 7/1340 RAF Production Programmes for Guided Weapons: Blue Steel 1962–1963

DEFE 13/121 Siting of Thor Missiles in UK 1958–1959

4 The United States 'umbrella'

Bowyer, M J F 1994 *Force for Freedom: The USAF in the UK Since 1948*. Sparkford: Patrick Stephens Ltd

Campbell, C 1984 *Nuclear Facts*. London: Hamlyn

Campbell, D 1986 *The Unsinkable Aircraft Carrier: American Military Power in Britain*. London: Paladin

Francis, P 1996 *RAF Upper Heyford*. Airfield Research Publishing (typescript report for Cherwell District Council)

Hewish, M 1983 'Countdown to cruise'. *New Sci*, March, 878–885

Jackson, R S 1986 *Strike Force – The USAF in Britain since 1948*. London: Robson Books

Lindsay, P 1980 'Britain's Americans'. *Air International*, May, 223–46

Moody, W S 1995 *Building a Strategic Air Force*. Washington, DC: Air Force History and Museums Program

Peacock, L T 1988 *Strategic Air Command*. London: Arms & Armour Press

Snyder, T S and Harrington, D F 1997 *Historical Highlights of the United States Air Force in Europe 1947–1997*. Ramstein Air Base (Germany): USAFE Office of History

Steijger, C 1991 *A History of USAFE*. Shrewsbury: Airlife

Tsipis, K 1977 'Cruise missiles'. *Scientific American* **236**(2), 20–29

Public Record Office sources

AIR 2/10759 Aerodromes (Code B.3): Provision of airfields in the United Kingdom for B29s December 1949–April 1950

AIR 2/10760 Aerodromes (Code B.3): Provision of airfields in the United Kingdom for B29s April 1950–August 1956

The peace movement

Minnion, J and Bolsover, P 1983 *The CND Story*. London: Allison & Busby

Ruddock, J 1987 *CND Scrapbook*. London: Macdonald Optima

Schofield, J and Anderton, M 2000 'The queer archaeology of Green Gate: Interpreting contested space at Greenham Common Airbase'. *World Archaeol* **32**(2), 236–251

5 Early warning and detection

Anon 1969 *Royal Air Force Manual Control and Reporting 1*, 2 edn. London: MoD

Buderi, R 1997 *The Invention that Changed the World*. London: Abacus

Bullers, R F 1991 *We Guard the Skies. RAF Neatishead: A History*. Tri Services Magazines

Gough, J 1993 *Watching the Skies. A History of Ground Radar for the Air Defence of the United Kingdom by the Royal Air Force 1946 to 1975*. London: HMSO

Fowle, E N, Key, E I, Millar, R I and Sear, R H 1979 *The Enigma of the AN/FPS-95 OTH Radar*. Bedford MA

Jackson, P A 1993 'Horizons'. *Fighter Command Yearbook*, 11–14

Kampe, H G 1996 *The Underground Command Bunkers of Zossen, Germany*. Altglen: Schiffer Publishing Ltd

Latham, C and Stobbs, A 1996 *Radar: A Wartime Miracle*. Stroud: Sutton

Mason, R A 1990 *To Inherit the Skies. From Spitfire to Tornado: Britain's Air Defence Today*. London: Brassey's

Ministry of Defence, 1969 *British Defence Equipment*, 2 edn. London: Combined Services Publication Unit

Pretty, R T 1982 *Jane's Weapons Systems 1981–82*. London: Jane's

Public Record Office sources

AIR 8/1630 Restoration of the UK control and reporting system (Operation 'Rotor') May 1950–Oct 1953

6 Warning of ballistic missile attack

Dong, Y H 1971 'World's largest log-periodic antenna'. *Journal of the Structural Division. Proceedings of the American Society of Civil Engineers*, September, 2371–89

Kinsey, G 1981 *Orfordness, Secret Site. A History of the Establishment 1915–1980*. Lavenham: Terence Dalton Ltd

Klass, P J 1971 'HF radar detects Soviet ICBMs'. *Aviation Week & Space Technology*, December 6, 38–40

Public Record Office sources

AIR 2/16262 BMEWS Progress Committee Meeting 1962–1964

AIR 2/18399 USAF BMEWS in the UK 1961–1962

AIR 2/18764 Cobra Mist – Over the Horizon Radar 1970–1976

AIR 2/16022 Defence Against Ballistic Missiles: BMEWS 1960

AIR 19/1137 RAF Fylingdales: BMEWS 1962–1966

AIR 20/10077 BMEWS: Air Defence Against Ballistic Missiles 1959

AIR 20/10078 BMEWS: Air Defence Against Ballistic Missiles 1959–1963
AIR 20/10594 BMEWS: USAF Special Facilities in UK 1957–1959
AIR 20/10715 BMEWS at Fylingdales 1959–1960

7 The response – air defence

Abraham, B and Reid, I 1998 'Royal Air Force Binbrook: An examination'. *Airfield Review*, October, 9–18
Bowyer, M J F 2000 *Action Stations Revisited: The Complete History of Britain's Military Airfields, No. 1 Eastern England*. Manchester: Crécy Publishing Ltd
Dobinson, C 1996 *Twentieth Century Fortifications in England, Vol 1: Anti-Aircraft Artillery, 1914–46*. York: Council for British Archaeology (typescript report)
Francis, P 1993 *Control Towers: The Development of the Control Tower on RAF Stations in the United Kingdom*. Ware: Airfield Research Publishing
Gething, M J 1993 *Sky Guardians: Britain's Air Defences 1918–1993*. London: Arms & Armour Press
Jackson, P A 1990 'Life in the old dog'. *Royal Air Force Yearbook 1990*, 78–80
Nash, F C 1998 *World War Two Heavy Anti-Aircraft Gun Sites in Essex*. Chelmsford: Essex County Council (typescript report)
Routledge, N W 1994 *History of the Royal Regiment of Artillery: Anti-Aircraft Artillery 1914–55*. London: Brassey's
Taylor, M J H and Taylor, J W R 1972 *Missiles of the World*. Shepperton: Ian Allan
Taylor, W J 1989 *Raynham Reflections*. Corby: Services Publishing Services
Taylor, W J 1990 'Bloodhound Force'. *Air Forces Monthly*, January, 10–13
Taylor, W 1994 *North Coates* (Airfield Focus No. 12). Peterborough: GMS Enterprises
Twigge, S R 1999 'Ground-based air defence ABM systems' *in* Bud, R and Gummett, P 1999 *Cold War, Hot Science: Applied Research in Britain's Defence Laboratories, 1945–1990*. Amsterdam: Harwood Academic Publishers, 85–115
Twigge, S R & Scott, C 2000 *Planning Armageddon: Britain, The United States and the Command of Western Nuclear Forces 1945–64*. Amsterdam: Harwood Academic Publishers

Public Record Office sources

AIR 10/8309 Bloodhound MK2 SAM Systems: Radar Type 86, Amendments 1–9, 1963–1966
DEFE 7/1338 RAF Production Programmes for Guided Weapons: Bloodhound 1958–1963
DEFE 7/1846 War Office Production, Guided Weapons: Thunderbird Red Shoes 1962–1963

8 Observation and monitoring

Buckton, H 1993 *Forewarned is Forearmed: An Official Tribute and History of the Royal Observer Corps*. Leatherhead: Ashford, Buchan & Enright
Catford, N 1999 'The Royal Observer Corps underground in Norfolk'. *J Norfolk Ind Archaeol Soc* **6**(4), 51–70
Home Office 1974 *United Kingdom Warning and Monitoring Organisation*. London: HMSO
Wood, D 1976 *Attack Warning Red: The Royal Observer Corps and the Defence of Britain 1925 to 1992*, 2 edn. Portsmouth: Carmichael & Sweet

9 The home front

Anon 1954 'Medway Fire Station, Chatham, for Kent County Council'. *Official Architecture & Planning* **17**, January 1954, 21–3
Anon 1955 'Police development at Kidderminster for Worcestershire County Council'. *Official Architecture & Planning* **18**, August 1955, 406–7
Anon 1957 *To Put You in the Picture*. Chester: City of Chester Civil Defence Corps
Anon 1958 'Wood Green civic centre'. *The Architect & Building News*, 2 July, 11–16
Anon 1958 'Civic centre for the Borough of Wood Green'. *Official Architecture & Planning* **21**, June 1958, 259–63
Anon 1967 'GPO microwave relay station'. *Tubular Structures* 7, February 1967, 22
Anon 1968 'Parking in Westminster'. *Building*, 5 January, 80–3
Anon 1998 'Cohen plea for civil defence'. *The Times*, 26 September 1998, 16
Aqumen Services Ltd 1998 'Former Home Office 4.2 Station, Days Lane, Biddenham, Bedfordshire'. Sale brochure
Central Office of Information 1981 *Civil Defence: Why We Need It*. London: HMSO
Dewar, M 1989 *Defence of the Nation*. London: Arms & Armour Press
Fox, S P 1999 *Control Chain: Civil Defence 1948–1968*. Privately printed pamphlet
Fox, S P 2000 *Plan for Survival: Civil Defence 1971–1993*. Privately printed pamphlet
Gimson, A 1998 'Germans to sell Cold War bunker'. *Daily Telegraph*, 3 November 1998, 3
Goodwin, P 1981 *Nuclear War: The Facts on our Survival*. London: Ash & Grant
Grace, C S 1994 *Nuclear Weapons: Principles, Effects and Survivability*. London: Brassey's
Hansard 1948 Vol 448 (1947–48), Mar 1 to Mar 25
Hansard 1948 Vol 457 (1948–49), Oct 26 to Nov 12
Hansard 1954 Vol 529, 5 Jul
Hansard 1963 Vol 672, 1 Mar
Hansard 1963 Vol 679, 27 Jun
Hennessy, P 2002 *The Secret State. Whitehall and the Cold War*. London: Penguin
HMSO 1963 *Advising the Householder on Protection Against Nuclear Attack*. (Civil Defence Handbook 10). London: HMSO
Home Office, Scottish Home Department 1951 *Preliminary Memorandum on the Organisation of Civil Defence in Industrial and Commercial Premises*. (Civil Defence Industrial Bulletin 1) (1953 report). London: HMSO
Home Office, Scottish Home Department 1953 *The Industrial Civil Defence Service*. (Civil Defence Industrial Bulletin 2). London: HMSO
Home Office, Scottish Home and Health Departments 1983 *Civil Defence, the Basic Facts*. Ring-bound report
Home Office 1976 *Protect and Survive* (1980 reprint). London: HMSO
Home Office, Scottish Home and Health Departments 1980 *Nuclear Weapons* (3rd impression). London: HMSO
Home Office 1981 *Domestic Nuclear Shelters*. London: HMSO
Home Office 1982 *Domestic Nuclear Shelters: Technical Guidance*. London: HMSO
Home Office 1985 *Final Working Party on Civil Defence Communications*. Home Office internal report
Home Office 1985 *Communal Shelters*. (Emergency Planning Guidance to Local Authorities (EPG) Handbook 2). Home Office (ring-bound handbook)
Home Office 1988 *Civil Protection*. London: HMSO

Home Office 1989 *Civil Defence Community Volunteers* (A discussion paper by the Co-ordinator of voluntary effort). Easingwold: Home Office (ring-bound handbook)

Home Office 1989 *Communications*. (Emergency Planning Guidance to Local Authorities (EPG) Handbook 4). Home Office (ring-bound handbook)

Holliss, B R and Thompson, J C 1995 *The Green Machine: Vehicles of the Auxiliary Fire Service and Mobile Columns*. Newport Pagnell: Enthusiasts Publications

Jack, T G 1972 'The electricity supply industry in war, Part 2'. *Royal Observer Corps Journal* **14**(6), 93–5

Jones, T 1998 'Living with the bomb: Civil defence in Denbighshire, 1948–68'. *Denbighshire Hist Soc Trans* **74**, 137–75

Kohan, C M 1952 *Works and Buildings*. London: HMSO

Lamb, W H 1967 'The London Cable Tube Systems'. Lecture notes for Institution of Post Office Engineers (original held by BT Museum)

Lamb, W H 1971 'London's telephone cable tunnels'. *Electrical Review*, 2 July, 18–9

Laurie, P 1970 *Beneath the City Streets*. Harmondsworth: Penguin

MAFF 1985 *Civil Defence and the Farmer*. London: HMSO

McCamley, N J 1998 *Secret Underground Cities*. London: Leo Cooper

O'Brien, T H 1955 *Civil Defence*. London: HMSO

Omerod, R 1983 *Nuclear Shelters: A Guide to Design*. London: The Architectural Press

Public General Acts and Measures 1939 *Regional Commissioners Act, 1939*. 2 & 3 George 6, c76

Public General Acts and Measures 1945 *Civil Defence (Suspension of Powers) Act, 1945*. 9 & 10 George 6, c5

Public General Acts and Measures 1948 *Civil Defence Act, 1948*. 12 & 13 George 6, c5

Public General Acts and Measures 1951 *Home Guard Act, 1951*. 15 George 6, c8

Public General Acts and Measures 1954 *Civil Defence (Electricity Undertakings) Act, 1954*. 2 & 3 Elizabeth 2, c19

Public General Acts and Measures 1959 *Post Office Works Act, 1959*. 7 & 8 Elizabeth 2, c43

Public General Acts and Measures 1986 *Civil Protection in Peacetime Act, 1986*. Elizabeth 2, c22

Purdie, H 1969 'A telephone city under London'. *Courier*, November, 6–7

Sauter, U 1999 'Underground culture'. *Time*, 1 March, 63

Searle, A 1999 'Absolutely bunkers'. *The Guardian Saturday Review*, 20 February, 5

Smith, M 1999 'Dr Strangelove bunker under Wiltshire quarry'. *The Daily Telegraph*, 6 January, 11

Stokes, P 1996 *Drakelow Unearthed: The Secret History of an Underground Complex*. Privately published

Tandy, E 1940 'Regional organisation during and after the war'. *J Roy Soc Arts* **88**, 368–81

Townroe, B S 1951 'Civil defence and the official architect'. *Official Architecture & Planning* **14**, April 1951, 196–7

Vale, L J 1987 *The Limits of Civil Defence in the USA, Switzerland, Britain and the Soviet Union*. Basingstoke: Macmillian Press

Virilio, P 1994 *Bunker Archeology*. Paris: Les éditions du semi-cercle

Public Record Office sources

AN 97/24 Civil Defence (Railways) Committee: Minutes 1–79 1956–1959

DEFE 7/719 Civil Defence: Policy 1947–1949

DEFE 7/722 Official Committee on Civil Defence: Evacuation and Care of the Homeless 1949–1953

DEFE 7/750 Review of Civil Stockpiling Policy 1954

DEFE 7/751 Review of Civil Stockpiling Policy 1954–1955

DEFE 7/752 Review of Civil Stockpiling Policy 1955–1961

HO 186/89 Regional Organisation: Formation of Regional Organisation 1939

HO 186/940 Air Raids: Manchester Region War Rooms Procedure 1942

HO 186/2899 Regional Organisation: Power of Regional Commissioners 1939–1946

HO 223/44 Regional Organisation: Regional Directors of Civil Defence. Miscellaneous conference papers (CD training grounds); conference of regional directors of civil defence, minutes and paper 1956–1963

HO 225/78 Some Long-Term Shelter Possibilities 1956

HO 338/17 Effects of Air Attack on Building Structures. Use of Reinforced Brickwork: Design of Control Centres to Withstand Attack 1949–1957

HO 338/34 Operation of Scientific Teams at Regional Civil Defence Headquarters 1959–1961

HO 338/66 Shelters: Channel Islands' Protected Accommodation 1961–1967

HO 338/105 Shelter and Protected Accommodation: Standards of Fallout Protection to be Provided at Regional, Sub-Regional, Group and Area Controls 1960–1965

HO 338/116 Communications: Effects of a Nuclear Attack on GPO Communications 1956–1964

MAF 99/1912 Government Cold Stores: Application of Government Pledges after Decontrol of Cold Stores 1954–1956

MAF 99/1922 Buffer Depot Management Contracts 1950–1957

MAF 250/94 Food Packs: Post Nuclear Attack Period 1955–1959

WORK 28/36 Provision of Emergency Central War Room in Government Buildings, Whitehall. ARP works carried out in various Whitehall offices, etc, 1938–1941

WORK 28/42 Acquisition of Deep Tube Shelters Bill. Miscellaneous papers 1956–1957

Cambridge Central Library

C35.2 1953 Cambridgeshire County Council Agenda and Reports

Cheshire Record Office

CCC1/9/2/1 Cheshire Civil Defence Committee 1950–56

10 The 'white heat' of defence technology

Anon 1952 'Dousing the decibels'. *Flight*, 5 September, 337–8

Anon 1954 'Silencing the swift'. *Flight*, 8 October, 542

Anon 1957 'Buildings for the Royal Aircraft Establishment, Bedford'. *Official Architecture & Planning* **20**, 385–87

Anon 1957 'Opening day at Bedford'. *Flight*, 5 July, 4–5

Anon 1957 'RAE Bedford and its facilities: (1) the wind-tunnel site'. *Flight*, 5 July, 18–20

Anon 1957 'RAE Bedford and its facilities: (2) the airfield'. *Flight*, 12 July, 54–56

Anon 1957 'After Woomera, the tomb'. *The Architect's Journal*, September 12, 378

Arnold, L 2001 *Britain and the H-Bomb*. Basingstoke: Palgrave

Anon 1956 'Hydrodynamic laboratory for the Admiralty'. *Official Architecture & Planning* **19**, January 1956, 28–9

Anon 1958 'Altitude plant'. *Flight*, 3 October, 551–4 & 558

Balchin, J 1980 *First New Town: An Autobiography of the Stevenage Development Corporation 1946–1980*. Stevenage: Stevenage Development Corporation

Becklake, J 1998 'German engineers: Their contribution to British rocket technology after World War II', *in* Jung, P (ed) 1998 *History of Rocketry and Astronautics* (American Astronautical Society History series **22**), 157–172

Carter, G B 1992 *Porton Down: 75 Years of Chemical and Biological Research*. London: HMSO

Cathcart, B 1994 *Test of Greatness: Britain's Struggle for the Atom Bomb*. London: John Murray

Cheeseman, R 1994 'Introducing a computer revolution'. *DRA News* **32**, September, 13

Cocroft, W D 2000 *Dangerous Energy. The Archaeology of Gunpowder and Military Explosives Manufacture*. London: English Heritage

Cookson, J and Nottingham, J 1969 *A Survey of Chemical and Biological Weapons*. London: Sheed & Ward

Cooper, P J 1996 *Forever Farnborough: Flying the Limits 1904–1996*. Aldershot: Hikoki Publications

Edgerton, D E H 1991 *England and the Aeroplane: An Essay on a Militant and Technological Nation*. Basingstoke: Macmillan

Edgerton, D E H 1991 'Liberal militarism and the British state'. *New Left Review* **185**, 138–69

Gardner, C 1981 *British Aircraft Corporation: A History*. London: Batsford

Hartcup, G 1988 *The War of Invention: Scientific Developments, 1914–18*. London: Brassey's

Hartcup, G 1993 *The Silent Revolution: The Development of Conventional Weapons 1945–8*. London: Brassey's

Hawkings, D J 2000 *Keeping the Peace: The Aldermaston Story*. Barnsley: Leo Cooper/Pen & Sword

Kinsey, G 1981 *Orfordness, Secret Site: A History of the Establishment 1915–1980*. Lavenham: Terence Dalton Ltd

Markusen, A and Yudken, J 1992 *Dismantling the Cold War Economy*. New York: Basic Books

Martin, D nd (?1987) *Thorn EMI: 50 Years of Radar*. Radar Division, Thorn EMI

Quigley, P 1989 *Tanks and turbines: Jobs in Coventry's Defence Industry*. Coventry: Coventry Alternative Employment Research

RCHME 1994 *The Royal Gunpowder Factory, Waltham Abbey, Essex. An RCHME Survey 1993*. London: RCHME

RCHME 1999 *Buildings of the Radio Electronics Industry, Chelmsford, Essex*. Typescript report

Schroeer, D 1984 *Science, Technology and the Nuclear Arms Race*. New York: John Wiley & Sons

Sherwood, R 1989 *Superpower Britain*. Cambridge: Willingham Press

Simons, R W and Sutherland, J W 1998 'Forty years of Marconi radar, from 1946 to 1986'. *GEC Review* **13**(3), 172–189

Tredici, R D 1987 *At Work in the Fields of the Bomb*. London: Harrap

Twigge, S R 1993 *The Early Development of Guided Weapons in the United Kingdom, 1940–1960*. Chur: Harwood Academic Publishers

Wilkinson, A 2002 *Enough has been bulldozed! Save Farnborough, the Cradle of British Aviation*. SAVE Britain's Heritage

Public Record Office sources

DEFE 7/295 Research and Development, Further Works: Building Sites, 1948–1949

DEFE 7/296 Research and Development, Further Works: Building Sites, 1949–1951

11 The legacy of the Cold War – an international perspective

Baker, F 1993 'The Berlin Wall: Production, preservation and consumption of a 20th-century monument'. *Antiquity* **67**, 709–33

Beck, C M, Goldenberg, N, Johnson, W G and Sellers, C 1996 *Nevada Test Site Historic Structures Survey*. Las Vegas: Desert Research Institute

Bergener, P 2000 *Befehl 'Filigran' die bunker der DDR – führung für den ernstfall*. Berlin: Drucherei Lippert

Carlson, C M and Lyon, R 1996 *Last Line of Defense: Nike Missile Sites in Illinois*. Denver: National Park Service

Cocroft, W D 2001 *Cold War Monuments: An Assessment by the Monuments Protection Programme*. London: English Heritage (typescript report)

Day, D A 2000 'Relics of the space age: Space archaeology at Vandenberg Air Force Base, part 1'. *Spaceflight* **42**, 59–62

Department of Defense 1994 *Coming in from the Cold: Military Heritage in the Cold War*. Washington DC: Department of Defense

Delgado, J P, Lenihan, D J and Murphy, L E 1991 *The Archeology of the Atomic Bomb: A Submerged Cultural Resource Assessment of the Sunken Fleet of Operation Crossroads at Bikini and Kwajalein Atoll Lagoons*. Santa Fe: United States National Parks Service

Delgado, J P 1996 *Ghost Fleet: The Sunken Ships of Bikini Atoll*. Honolulu: University of Hawaii Press

Feversham, P and Schmidt, L 1999 *The Berlin Wall Today: Cultural Significance and Conservation Issues*. Berlin: Verlag Bauwesen

Gander, T 1991 'Coastal defence in the nuclear age: The Swedish approach'. *Fortress* **10**, 54–9

Hoffecker, J F and Whorton, M 1996 *Historic Properties of the Cold War Era: 21st Space Wing*. Colorado: Petersen Air Force Base

Neufeld, D 1997 'Trigger for atomic holocaust: Aircraft detection on the DEW line'. *Cultural Resource Management* **20**(14), 10–11

Post, R C and Mollella, A P 1997 'The call of stories at the Smithsonian Institution: History of technology in crisis'. *Icon* **3**, 44–82

De Reijer, E C 1997 *De Ijssellinie 1950 1968*. Zeist: Rijksdienst voor de Monumentenzorg

Sakkers, H and den Hollander, J nd *Luchtwachttorens in Nederland*. Middelburg: Stichting Natuur – en Recreatieinformatie

von Pfeiffer, I 1997 'Stahltüren im ex DDR – Regierungsbunker 'Filigran' bei Berlin für immer verschlossen'. *IBA – Informationen* **30**, 44–50

Wahl, J-B 1998 'Le bloc 8 du Schoenenbourg. Évolution d'un bloc-entrée d'ouvrage'. *Fortifications and Patrimoine* **5**, 36–46

Index

Illustrations are denoted by page numbers in **bold** or by *illus* where figures are scattered throughout the text.